Increasing Returns and Economic Efficiency

Increasing Returns and Economic Efficiency

Yew-Kwang Ng

First published 2009 by
PALGRAVE MACMILLAN

Palgrave Macmillan in the UK is an imprint of Macmillan Publishers Limited, registered in England, company number 785998, of Houndmills, Basingstoke, Hampshire RG21 6XS.

Palgrave Macmillan in the US is a division of St Martin's Press LLC, 175 Fifth Avenue, New York, NY 10010.

Palgrave Macmillan is the global academic imprint of the above companies and has companies and representatives throughout the world.

Palgrave® and Macmillan® are registered trademarks in the United States, the United Kingdom, Europe and other countries.

ISBN-13: 978-0-230-20209-2 hardback
ISBN-10: 0-230-20209-8 hardback

This book is printed on paper suitable for recycling and made from fully managed and sustained forest sources. Logging, pulping and manufacturing processes are expected to conform to the environmental regulations of the country of origin.

A catalogue record for this book is available from the British Library.

A catalog record for this book is available from the Library of Congress.

10 9 8 7 6 5 4 3 2 1
18 17 16 15 14 13 12 11 10 09

Printed and bound in Great Britain by
CPI Antony Rowe, Chippenham and Eastbourne

Dedicated to my beloved wife
Siang
[which, in Chinese, means fragrance (Xiang in Pinyin), but in Malay, means dawning or 'having light/brightness', which is the Chinese meaning of Yew Kwang (or You Guang in Pinyin), the personal name of the author.]

Contents

List of Illustrations   x

Acknowledgement   xi

Preface   xii

1   Introduction   1

2   Devastating Implications of Increasing Returns on Some
Traditional Conclusions   9
   2.1   Possible non-neutrality of money   9
   2.2   Pecuniary external effects may have real
efficiency implications   16
   2.3   Market equilibrium no longer Pareto optimal   18

3   Equity and Efficiency versus Freedom and Fairness:
An Inherent Conflict   22
   3.1   Introduction   22
   3.2   The *E-F Conflict*   25
   3.3   A specific model   34
   3.4   Concluding remarks   38
   Appendix 3A   39

4   Existence of Average-Cost Pricing Equilibria with
Increasing Returns   40

5   The Efficiency of Encouraging Goods with
High Degrees of Increasing Returns   46
   5.1   The general case   46
   5.2   A specific case illustrated   52

6   Division of Labour: Increasing Returns at the Economy Level   55
   6.1   Introduction: Marginal versus inframarginal analysis   55
   6.2   Basic inframarginal analysis of division of labour   57
   6.3   Pareto optimality of general equilibrium in
the new framework – the higher role of entrepreneurship   59
   6.4   Some welfare economic issues of division of labour   62
   6.5   Some implications   66

Appendix 6A: A simple model of the Yang–Ng framework of
division of labour   70
Appendix 6B: Division of labour, coordination, and
entrepreneurship   72

7   The Smith Dilemma and Its Resolution   76
    7.1   Towards a resolution of the Smith dilemma   77
    7.2   The efficiency of the market: A simulation using
          the Dixit–Stiglitz model   80
    7.3   Concluding remarks   86

8   Why Should Governments Encourage Improvements on
    Infrastructure? Indirect Network Externality of
    Transaction Efficiency   88
    8.1   Why should governments encourage improvements in
          transaction efficiency?   88
    8.2   A perspective from the Yang–Ng framework   91
    8.3   Introducing the role of the government   98
    8.4   Concluding remarks   100

9   Average-Cost Pricing, Increasing Returns, and
    Optimal Output: Comparing Home and
    Market Production   101
    9.1   A model with home and market production   104
    9.2   A model with home and differentiated market
          production   112
    9.3   Concluding remarks   120

10 Do the Economies of Specialization Justify
    the Work Ethics? An Examination of
    Buchanan's Hypothesis   122
    10.1   Introduction   122
    10.2   Specialization and consumption constraints   124
    10.3   Does the economy of specialization make
           work ethics welfare-improving? A terms-of-trade
           approach   129
    10.4   Does the economy of specialization make work
           ethics welfare-improving? Further investigations   134
    10.5   Concluding remarks   147
    Appendix 10A   150

11 Specialization, Trade, and Growth   154
    11.1   Introduction   154
    11.2   The new classical trade theory   156

11.3   The enrichment of a sector benefits others:
       The case of trade for specialization   164

12   Conceptual and Policy Implications:
     Concluding Discussion   169

Notes   177

References   182

Author Index   195

Subject Index   199

Illustrations

Figures

2.1	Neutrality of money under perfect competition	11
2.2	Non-neutrality of money under imperfect competition	12
2.3	The labour market	14
2.4	The long run	15
2.5	Pecuniary externality: no efficiency implication in the absence of increasing returns	17
2.6	Pecuniary externality: possible efficiency implications in the presence of increasing returns	18
3.1	The conflict between efficiency and equity	26
3.2	The *E-F conflict* in terms of marginal utility curves	28
3.3	The *E-F conflict* in terms of utility possibility curves	30
4.1	Illustrating the continuous transformation	43
4.2	Productively efficient general equilibrium under average-cost pricing	44
6.1	Evolution of division of labour	58
8.1	The effect of transaction efficiency on the optimal number of traded goods	98
10.1	Production possibility	125
10.2	Consumption possibility – many individuals	126
10.3	Consumption possibility – two individuals	128
10.4	Leisure choice – many individuals	129
10.5	Trade opportunity	131
10.6	Leisure choice	133
12.1	The price increases more than the increase in costs/taxes	172
12.2	The big incentive for demand promotion	174

Tables

7.1	Simulation results for three equilibria	82
7.2	Comparative statics for fixed cost a	83
7.3	Comparative statics for income I	84
7.4	Comparative statics for marginal cost c	84
7.5	Comparative statics for sub-utility parameter α	85
7.6	Comparative statics for utility parameter γ	85

Acknowledgement

I am grateful to the Australian Research Council for a research grant bearing the same title as that of this book during 2005–2007. While most of the research was done at Monash University, the final stage of the completion of the monograph was undertaken at the Division of Economics, Nanyang Technological University in the second half of 2008. I also wish to thank my co-authors Siang Ng and Dingsheng Zhang for allowing me to use the content of some of our joint papers in this book, and to Siang for her contribution of Chapter 11. I also wish to thank Palgrave/Macmillan and the publishers/editors of the following journals for having no objection to the use of parts of my previous publications in this book: *Journal of Economic Behavior and Organization, Journal of Economics, Kyklos, Public Finance and Management, Singapore Economic Review.*

Preface

Much of economic analysis (especially on the optimality of market equilibrium) is based on the absence of increasing returns. However, due to indivisibilities, knowledge needed for production, learning by doing, external economies, and the economies of specialization, increasing returns are ubiquitous. Recognizing increasing returns plays havoc to much of the established wisdom in economic analysis, such as the efficiency irrelevancy of pecuniary external effects, the neutrality of money, and the Pareto optimality of general equilibrium. This book discusses these problems and ways in which they can be handled. The analysis can also explain many phenomena in the real world with implications different from the traditional analysis.

The presence of a significant degree of increasing returns (such as in the training of soldiers, especially if learning by doing is included as generalized increasing returns) may make freedom and fairness inherently in conflict with equity and efficiency. Productively efficient general equilibrium may exist in a market equilibrium with average-cost pricing imperfectly competitive firms. However, ignoring administrative costs and side effects like rent-seeking, encouraging the expansion of a sector with a higher degree of increasing returns is efficiency-improving. Using the Yang–Ng framework to analyse increasing returns at the economy level through the economies of specialization made possible by the division of labour, the importance of entrepreneurship and organizational efficiency are underlined.

Organizational efficiency refers to the choices between different economic structures, including different numbers of goods produced/marketed, different degrees of the division of labour, different numbers/layers of intermediate inputs, and the organization of firms. While allocative efficiency is important, organizational efficiency may be even more important in the long run. The analysis of organizational efficiency at the economy level could help answer question such as 'Why should governments encourage investment in infrastructure?' While this may partly be explained by the public goods nature, the presence of indirect network externalities of a higher degree of transaction efficiency (from the improved infrastructure) that results in a higher degree in the division of labour, may also be important. Other organizational efficiency issues involving the network of division of labour, such as home versus market production, the desirability of encouraging work, and international trade are also discussed.

1
Introduction

One clear conclusion is that there are many important areas of economics in which the recognition of increasing returns makes a big difference, and changes the established wisdom significantly. ... we have not yet reached the point of diminishing returns in the study of increasing returns: there is a long way to go, and the results of the work yet to be completed will be interesting

Geoffrey Heal 1999, p. xxvi

Factors (including indivisibility, fixed costs, learning) leading to the existence and importance of increasing returns both at the firm level and at the economy level are discussed. The focus and conclusions of the monograph are outlined.

Instances of increasing returns are omnipresent. Two examples may be used to illustrate the existence of increasing returns. First, there is the Chinese saying 'Practicing for ten years, the reward would be sharing the same ferry (with someone you love, presumably); practicing for a hundred years, the reward would be sharing the same bed.' Surely, sharing the same bed is much more than ten times a reward than that of sharing the same ferry! One may say that this is just a saying; whether it is valid may be questionable. So, let us look at history. The second example is the famous three visits to the hut of a recluse by the first emperor of Shu (one of the Three Kingdoms in ancient China) before he became the emperor to invite the recluse to help him unite the nation. The returns to the first and second visits were nothing. But the returns to the three visits is the dedicated assistance of the wise recluse, producing everything from zero (the empty castle plot) to nine (the nine

1

expeditions to conquer the North). (A full list of these ten accomplishments of ZHUGE Liang is available with the author.)

Although both examples are meant to be jokes, at least the second one is related to a most common cause of increasing returns, the existence of sizable fixed costs before any output may be expected. This is true for all types of production for at least two reasons. First, one has to learn how to produce a good before actually producing it. So there are some fixed learning costs. (Arrow 1995 explains how the relevance of information and knowledge in production makes increasing returns prevalent. See also Wilson 1975; Radner & Stiglitz 1984; Arthur 1994.)[1] Second, there are usually some minimum amounts of certain inputs required before production is possible, e.g. machines, shops, etc. If your display room is so small that no one can enter, you have to sell your products to frogs and ants, but unfortunately they have no cash!

It has been believed that we must have indivisibility in some inputs for increasing returns to arise; in the absence of indivisibility, constant returns to scale must rule. A doubling of all inputs must at least double the output since two identical units of the original production arrangement could be used to produce twice the output. A doubling of all inputs cannot more than double the output since this implies that the original production arrangement is inefficient. This is so since, in the absence of indivisibility, half of the new production arrangement that produces more than twice the original output could be used to produce more than the original output, or so the argument goes.

A counter-example against the implication of constant returns of the absence of indivisibility has been given. Consider the transportation of oil (or other liquids) from point A to point B through a pipeline. Within a certain range (where the thickness of the pipe may be unchanged), the output (flow of oil) varies directly with the area of the cross-sectional cycle of the pipe while the costs of constructing the pipeline varies directly with the circumference of the pipe. The circumference of a cycle equals $2\pi r$ (r = radius; $\pi \approx 3.1415926535898$ is the ratio of the circumference to the diameter of a cycle) while the area of the cycle equals to πr^2. Thus, a doubling of the radius of the pipe doubles the cost but quadruples the output, giving rise to a very high degree of increasing returns. This is true despite the radius of the pipe and all inputs in the building of the pipe may be perfectly divisible. The defender of the proposition of constant returns then suggested that the location and distance between A and B are indivisible. This seems to be a rather contrived interpretation of indivisibility!

Apart from the existence of fixed costs, learning by doing (producing) also gives rise to increasing returns. The more one produces, the more one learns and hence the lower the unit cost of production due to the higher productivity through learning. If the learning is from other producers, the concept of external economies (external to the firm but usually internal to the industry) is involved. This has been used by Marshall to reconcile perfect competition with increasing returns at the industry but not at the firm level. (See Chipman 1970.)

Another source of increasing returns neglected by orthodox analysis based on atemporal models applies to most retailing businesses and relates to the time element of keeping stock. Items of high demand have lower average lengths of staying in stock. This does not only reduce the storage costs but also reduces the period of capital turnover. If the firm needs 10% annual return on its capital to be in the black, it has to make 21% profit on items that remain in stock for two years. On the other hand, it has only to make less than 1% profit on items that can be sold in one month. Higher demand thus contributes to a substantial reduction of unit costs. It may, however, be argued that this source of increasing returns is ultimately related to the existence of some indivisibility or some fixed costs (such as in ordering stock replacement).

The existence of fixed costs does not rule out perfect competition and the possibility of (local) constant returns. If both the marginal and average cost curves are upward sloping (typically after an initial horizontal or downward-sloping ranges), this may offset the downward-sloping average fixed-cost curve to produce a horizontal and even upward-sloping (overall U-shaped) average-cost curve. However, there is another important factor that makes increasing returns prevail over the relevant range for most cases. The products of different producers of the same good are not perfect substitutes in the view of consumers. Products are differentiated in quality, in location, and in numerous other aspects. You are not going to spend an extra hour driving to have lunch at a far-away restaurant simply because its prices are half a dollar cheaper. This makes the demand curve for the product of each firm downward sloping, making its tangency with the average-cost curve (to ensure that the amount of profits equals zero for a long-run equilibrium) at a point of increasing returns. The prevalence of this can be confirmed by asking a random sample of firms whether they want to sell more at the same price. I bet that more than 99% of them would say 'yes'. A perfect competitor does not want to sell more at the same price, as his marginal cost exceeds the price (= marginal revenue) for units after the equilibrium output. Perfect competition applies to no more than a few percentage of firms, if any.

It may be emphasized that increasing returns and non-perfect competition (including monopolistic competition, oligopoly, monopoly and their mixtures) play havoc with many important results of the traditional economic analysis. It is well known that general equilibrium may not exist and may not be Pareto optimal. (See, e.g., Arrow 1987, 2000; Arthur 1994; Guesnerie 1975; Quinzii 1992a; Villar 1996. See also chapters collected in Buchanan & Yoon 1994b and Heal 1999.) It is less well known that pecuniary externalities may then have efficiency implications (see Section 2.2). It is also not well known that money may no longer be neutral even ignoring such complications as time lags, money illusion, menu costs and similar frictions, as shown in Ng (1980, 1986a, 1998) and discussed in Section 2.1. Other economists have concluded that 'Imperfect competition by itself does not create monetary non-neutrality. ... It is the combination of imperfect competition with some other distortion which generates the potential for real effects' (Dixon & Rankin 1994, p. 178). In fact, they have only shown that a real equilibrium under imperfect competition can still be an equilibrium even if the money supply changes. However, they have not shown that a change in the money supply (or any other factor causing a change in nominal aggregate demand) may not trigger a shift from one real equilibrium to another. Such a shift may not be relevant if the equilibrium is unique. However, the presence of increasing returns and non-perfect competition may make a model with a unique equilibrium into one with multiple or even a continuum of equilibria and hence make the above-mentioned shift relevant, making money possibly non-neutral even without any friction.

The proofs of the existence of general equilibrium usually assume perfect competition and the absence of increasing returns. Chapter 4 provides a proof of the existence and productive efficiency of general equilibrium under monopolistic competition with average-cost pricing and increasing returns. Chapter 5 shows that, at an average-cost pricing market equilibrium, higher efficiency (Pareto-superior) could be achieved by increasing the output of a good with a higher degree of increasing returns and decreasing the output of another good with a lower degree of increasing returns.

Increasing returns prevails not only at the firm level but also at the economy (and even the global) level through at least two channels. First, there is the public-goods effect in many areas including research and development, provision of legal, social and economic infrastructures.

Up to the relevant capacity levels where serious congestion sets in, many facilities such as airports, ports, and railways, can be utilized at fairly low marginal costs (in comparison to the usually high fixed costs of providing such facilities). Also, there is no congestion for the additional use of knowledge. Thus, with the increasing importance of the knowledge components of the modern economy, increasing returns will also become more and more important.

Second, there is what Buchanan calls 'generalized increasing returns' through the economies of specialization facilitated by the division of labour. A larger economy in terms of both the population size and per-capita production may increase the extent of the market and facilitate (rather than 'limit') the division of labour. This second source of increasing returns at the economy level[2] was of course emphasized much by the classical economists including Adam Smith (1776). (See Sun 2005 for a selection of readings in the economics of the division of labour.) However, after the neoclassical revolution, the focus shifted to the marginal analysis of resource allocation between different inputs, different goods and different sectors. The equally important problems of division of labour and economic organization at the economy level have been left largely unanalysed. The need to assume perfect competition and the absence of increasing returns for the existence and efficiency proofs of general equilibrium also contributed to the neglect of increasing returns. Despite the emphasis on the importance of division of labour by Young (1928) and Houthakker (1956),[3] modern analysis did not emerge until the recent decades. (See Cheng & Yang 2004 for a survey of the relevant literature and Tombazos & Yang 2006 for selected chapters on development issues.)

While there are other ways of modelling generalized increasing returns through the division of labour (e.g. Locay 1990), the approach pioneered by Yang (main monographs are Yang & Ng 1993 and Yang 2001, 2003) tackles the division of labour at the most basic level of individual choices of consumption, production/occupation and the general-equilibrium interaction between individuals (discussed in Chapter 6). It reflects the spirit of economies of specialization of classical economists most.[4] It is no wonder that it rapidly attracts a large team of followers and the strong endorsement of James Buchanan who organized a workshop on it in June 2002. (See the website http://mba.ntu.edu.tw/~jiren/mirror/e-index.htm for details.) Banking on this strength, a centre on Increasing Returns and Economic Organization has been established in the Department of Economics, Monash University. A book series 'Increasing Returns and Inframarginal Economics' (edited by Buchanan,

Ng, and Yang) and a new journal *Division of Labour and Transaction Costs* have also been published. The reason the term 'inframarginal economics' is used needs explanation. Since the neoclassical revolution, economists have focused on the marginal analysis of resource allocation, examining the benefits and costs of making a marginal adjustment in input and output levels. While this is no doubt important, the presence of increasing returns and economies of specialization suggest that it is not sufficient. No less important problems are as follows: Whether to self-produce or buy from the market? Whether to set up a business or to work as an employee? Specializing in the production of which good? Whether to become an economist, a philosopher, or an engineer? Due to increasing returns, the relevant choice is typically all or nothing. A farmer does not work in the factory; a factory worker does not grow rice. An economist does not teach or do research in physics or chemistry. Since optimal choices typically occur at corners (with the values of many variables equal to zero), we have to compare different disconnected corner solutions. Marginal analysis is insufficient for such comparisons.

The need for considering total costs and benefits was recognized rather early, e.g. Hicks (1939, p. 707) mentioned the need of 'total conditions' for Pareto optimality concerning the introduction of new goods or method of production. However, a framework that allows the general-equilibrium analysis of the marginal and inframarginal economic choices of individuals and their interaction through the social division of labour that allows the taping of economies of specialization giving rise to generalized increasing returns was provided by Yang. Moreover, Yang's framework also analyses how the evolution of the division of labour affects not only productivity but also economic organizations. Issues including trade, growth, development, industrialization, urbanization, the emergence of firms are analysed with interesting and important results.

An essential tradeoff analysed in the new framework is that between economies of specialization and transaction costs. Due to increasing returns, specialization increases productivity. Due to the preference (if not the necessity) for diverse consumption, specialization requires the purchase of other goods from others, incurring transaction costs. Thus, the optimal choice of the degree of specialization (how many goods to self-provide) involves the tradeoff between the gain of specialization on the one hand and the costs of additional transactions on the other.

One implication thrown into focus by the new framework is the need to take account of the indirect effects on the structure of economic organization or the network of division of labour. Any changes that affect the organizational structure of the economy may have indirect effects that may be neglected if we only have the traditional framework as our model of the economy. In particular, this may be seen clearly with respect to the effects of infrastructure investment. Improvements in transportation, telecommunications, law and order, and other areas do not only contribute directly to the users of these facilities, but also indirectly since the resulting improvement in transaction efficiency (lowering of transaction costs) leads to a higher degree of division of labour which increases productivity of the whole economy. This results in a second-level public-goods nature ignored both by the private market economy (hence possibly making government encouragement of infrastructure investment desirable) and in traditional analysis, as discussed in Chapter 8.

As increasing returns are prevalent and economic analysis involving the presence of increasing returns has been spotty and inconclusive, increasing attention to increasing returns is warranted. This is so particularly with the increasing importance of the knowledge economy since the importance of knowledge increases the importance of increasing returns. While not ruling out the relevance of the more traditional methods of economic analysis, for the generalized increasing returns through the social division of labour at the economy level, the new framework does offer significant advantages. It has already been applied and extended in many directions with very substantive results, as surveyed by Cheng and Yang (2004).

First, an important strength of the framework is that it is a general-equilibrium analysis of the social division of labour right at the basic level of individual optimization choices of self-production or trade, what or how many goods to produce and consume, be an employer or an employee, etc., capturing the insights of classical economists on the economies of specialization. Second, the framework can examine the evolution of economic organization especially in the network of division of labour and includes the emergence of firms, developments of urbanization, industrialization, vertical structure (roundaboutness) in production, etc. Third, the framework is flexible enough to allow many modifications, extensions, and applications to analyse different problems, as has been done already. It can also be combined with some more traditional methods of analysis. For example, Ng and Zhang (2007) combine it with the Dixit–Stiglitz (1977) analysis of monopolistic competitive firms to have a model combining home and firm production (Chapter 9).

Partly due to our focus on issues of economic efficiency and partly because I am in favour of dealing with problems of equality or income distribution through the general tax/transfer policy, allowing the use of purely efficiency approach ('A dollar is a dollar') in specific issues (Ng 1979, appendix 9A, 1984), the distributional implications of increasing returns are not dealt with. It may just be noted here that the increasing income inequality in the past few decades may well be related to increasing returns. The past few decades witnessed the increasing importance of knowledge-driven growth instead of capital-driven growth (though the two are related and they are interrelated with division of labour and productivity; see Ng 2005). On one hand, capital accumulation tends to reduce inequality by increasing the marginal productivity of labour; on the other hand, higher demand for skilled labour under skill-biased growth and the winner-takes-all effect associated with mass production under increasing returns tend to increase inequality. (See, e.g., Borghans & Groot 1998; Frank & Cook 1995; Epifani & Gancia 2006; Pomini & Tondini 2006. On the role of increasing returns for the persistence of inequality and for the skill-biasedness of scale, see, respectively, Semmler & Marvin 2007 and Epifani & Gancia 2006.)

This book does not deal with some issues such as that of economic geography raised by the presence of increasing returns (except the issue of *E-F conflict* discussed in Chapter 3) as analysed by Krugman (1991b), Fujita et al. (1999), Baldwin et al. (2003), Henderson (2005), Mossay (2006) and others.

2
Devastating Implications of Increasing Returns on Some Traditional Conclusions

The presence of increasing returns with the related imperfection in competition plays havoc with many traditional results. Money may no longer be neutral; changes in nominal aggregate demand may affect either the real output or the price level. Pecuniary external effects may have efficiency implications. Market equilibria may be Pareto inefficient. All these may be true in the absence of other causation factors such as real external effects.

The presence of increasing returns also plays havoc with many conclusions of orthodox economics. Some of these repercussions are discussed below. (Others could be added, e.g. the costs of protection may be much higher in the presence of increasing returns; see Panagariya 2002.)

2.1 Possible non-neutrality of money

The problems caused by increasing returns may be seen by using concepts familiar even to first-year undergraduates. If the producer is a perfect competitor in the factor market, he takes input prices as given. Increasing returns thus makes his average-cost curve downward sloping. With a horizontal demand curve for his product, he will increase output indefinitely, at least either until increasing returns no longer apply or until he is no longer a perfect competitor. The assumption of perfect competition thus does not allow the continued existence of increasing returns.

With firms not perfectly competitive, it can be shown that many traditional results have to be drastically revised. For example, the neutrality of money (changes in money supply, or other changes in nominal aggregate demand, affect only the price level but do not affect real variables) may no longer hold. Even in the absence of time lags, money illusion, and other frictions, just the relaxation of perfect competition may make a change in nominal aggregate demand affect either the price level (the monetarist case) or the real output (the Keynesian case).[1] Let us see the crux of the difference briefly. It is two sided. On the demand side, with a horizontal demand curve under perfect competition, the curve cannot shift left or right. It can only shift upward or downward. But an upward shift means an increase in price. In the absence of money illusion, time lags, etc., an increase in prices (for the whole economy) proportionately increases costs, leading to the absence of any real changes. (This is the crux for the neutrality of money result under perfect competition.) In contrast, under non-perfect competition, with a downward-sloping demand curve consistent with a downward-sloping average-cost curve due to increasing returns, the demand curve may shift either upward/downward or rightward/leftward, allowing for possible real effects of a change in nominal aggregate demand.

On the supply side, a profit-maximization equilibrium with a horizontal demand curve implies an upward-sloping MC (marginal cost) curve. This allows [use 'makes'] an expansion in output to be associated with a higher MC which calls for a higher price. But a higher price is contractionary as it decreases real aggregate demand at a given level of nominal aggregate demand. In contrast, in non-perfect competition, the MC curve may be horizontal or even downward sloping. The decrease in MC with a higher output, if not more than offset by an upward shift in the MC curve as aggregate output expands, may make higher output levels possible equilibria. (The full analysis takes into account consistency with the general-equilibrium effects of infinite rounds of feedback between a firm and the rest of the economy, including the effects on its cost and demand functions.) In fact, cases of expectation wonderland (where the outcome depends on the expectation of firms which will then be self-fulfilling) and cumulative expansion/contraction are also possible, partly explaining some real-world phenomena such as the business cycles, the importance of confidence, and the difficulties of economic prediction (Ng 1980, 1986a, 1992c, 1998, 1999).[2] In such non-traditional cases, there exists *an inter-firm macroeconomic externality* where the expansion of each firm benefits other firms *apart from* the familiar income multiplier effects. This is an area where welfare economics, macroeconomics and its micro-foundation intersect; an area that is yet to be adequately studied. My analysis is based on a representative firm but it takes into account the influence of macro variables and the interaction with the rest of the economy, using a simplified general-equilibrium method. Moreover, a fully general-equilibrium analysis is used to show that (1) for any (exogenous) change in cost or demand, there exists, in a hypothetical sense, a representative firm whose response to the change *accurately* (no approximation needed) represents the response of the whole economy in aggregate output and average price, and (2) a representative firm defined by a simple method of a weighted average can be used as a good approximation of the response of the whole economy to any economywide change in demand and/or costs that do not result in drastic interfirm changes. (See Ng 1986a, appendix 3I.)[3] I started the analysis from the demand function for the product of a representative firm by consumers (Ng 1977, 1980, 1982). In fact, this demand function may be derived from the budget-constrained utility maximization of consumers, as shown in the mathematical appendix of Ng (1999).

To elaborate the points given above, let us use some simple graphs first-year microeconomics students are familiar with. In the case of a perfect competition, a firm faces a horizontal demand curve for its product. Given output determinacy at the firm level, the short-run marginal cost curve of the firm must be upward sloping, as illustrated in Figure 2.1. The equilibrium output is at q where the MC curve cuts the demand curve. Given the production or cost function, the equilibrium output can change only if the price changes. However, with the full response of costs to prices (absence of money illusions, time lags, etc.), the MC curve responds by the full extent as the price line, leaving the equilibrium output unchanged. A change in money supply in such a model can thus

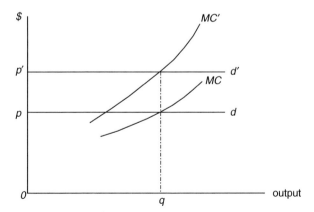

Figure 2.1 Neutrality of money under perfect competition

only change the price level without affecting the output. For example, an increase in nominal aggregate demand shifts the demand curve from d to d'. However, since this means that the price level increases from p to p', the MC curve also moves up from MC to MC', leaving the equilibrium output unchanged at q.[4] We thus have the neutrality of money and the classical dichotomy between money and the real sectors.[5] (Figure. 2.1 provides the essential microeconomic foundation of the celebrated neutrality of money in virtually all macro models as they are based implicitly or explicitly on the assumption of perfectly competitive firms.) However, this classical dichotomy can be broken simply by the introduction of non-perfect competition.

With non-perfect competition (compelling under increasing returns and/or product differentiation), the firm faces a downward-sloping demand curve, as illustrated in Figure 2.2. (Linearity in the demand and cost curves is not necessary for our argument.) The initial equilibrium is at A where the MC curve cuts the MR curve. An increase in nominal aggregate demand may shift the demand curve to d' and hence the MR curve to MR'. (This is a proportional shift with no change in the price elasticity of demand at any given price, e.g. elasticity at B is the same as that at A.) If the MC curve is horizontal over the relevant range and does not shift, as illustrated in Figure 2.2, the new equilibrium is at B, with an increase in output and no change in price. (The absence of a price change is important since a change in the price of the representative firm means

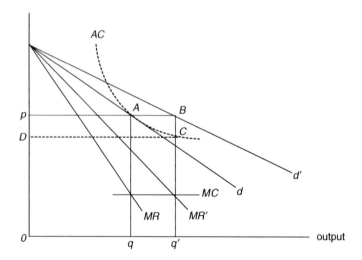

Figure 2.2 Non-neutrality of money under imperfect competition

a change in the general price level which will shift the demand curve, making *B* no longer the final equilibrium point.) Alternatively (not illustrated), if the upward shift in the *MC* curve as aggregate output expands is offset by the downward-sloping *MC* curve and/or the increase in the (absolute) demand elasticity (which lift *MR* at given price), we may still have an increase in real output with no change in price.

It may be thought that it is unlikely for the slope of the *MC* curve, the shift in the *MC* curve, and the change in *MR* (through a change in demand elasticity) to be at such a precise combination that the profit-maximizing price remains exactly unchanged. However, for our non-traditional result to hold, we need only the resulting profit-maximizing price not to increase. If it remains unchanged, we have the case of a continuum of equilibria as illustrated in Figure 2.2 for a specific case. If the profit-maximization price decreases (due to either the *MC* curve being downward sloping or the demand curve becoming more elastic), both the demand curve *d′* and the *MC* curve (which are drawn given the price level being equal to *p*) will shift. The *MC* curve will shift vertically downward and the demand curve will shift vertically downward (with the lower price level) and proportionately rightward (with a higher real aggregate demand, as the price level falls relative to the nominal aggregate demand). The combined shifts lead to further output expansions and price falls. Thus, if the responses of costs and demand elasticities lead to a fall in the price level, we have a *cumulative expansion* as aggregate demand increases, a case even more radical than a continuum of equilibria. We may refer to both cases as non-traditional.

For non-perfectly competitive firms, non-upward-sloping *MC* curves are quite prevalent, especially when increasing returns are important. Also, for an economy with union power, it is also quite likely that the *MC* curves of firms may not shift up as aggregate output and employment expand over certain ranges. For example, if a representative union chooses wage-rate to maximize the expected utility of an average worker which depends on the real wage-rate and the probability of employment, it can then be shown (Ng 1986a, chapter 13) that, before full employment, unions maximize by leaving their wage demand unchanged as aggregate demand changes, shifting the demand-for-labour curve horizontally in or out. This is illustrated in Figure 2.3 where *I* and *II* are the indifference curves of the union. An increase in aggregate demand shifts the demand-for-labour curve from d_L to d'_L, with an increase in employment but with the optimal wage-rate W^* unchanged. This would also be the result if the unions have the Dunlop (1944) objective function of maximizing the wage bill (wage-rate times employment), making their

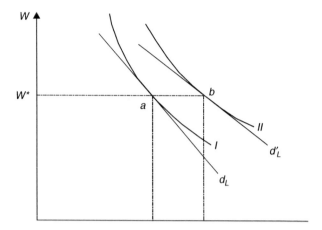

Figure 2.3 The labour market

indifference curves a rectangular hyperbola as in Figure 2.3. Then, each indifference curve has (absolute) unit elasticity throughout the whole curve. At the point *a* where the demand-for-labour curve d_L is tangent to the indifference curve *I*, the elasticity of the curve d_L must also be unitary. Then, as it shifts rightward proportionately (hence isoelastically at given *W*) as aggregate demand increases, the new demand-for-labour curve d'_L must also be of unitary elasticity at the point *b* on the same horizontal level as *a*. Hence, this new demand-for-labour curve d'_L must also be tangent to the higher indifference curve *II* (which is also of unit elasticity throughout the whole range) at point *b*.

It is true that, for the case where a change in nominal aggregate demand may increase real output without affecting the price level (with Figure 2.2 illustrating a specific sub-case of this case), we really have multiple or even a continuum of equilibria over the relevant range. However, this continuum of equilibria may precisely be the result of non-perfect competition (with the related increasing returns) in the following sense. With perfect competition, we must have a unique equilibrium under certain traditional assumptions such as no money illusion, no time lags, and the absence of indeterminacy at the firm level. Under the same traditional set of assumptions, the introduction of non-perfect competition alone (in the sense of not introducing menu costs or other transaction costs or distortions) may make a continuum of equilibria to prevail. It is true that this possibility depends on certain appropriate conditions regarding how costs respond to output (both the output at the firm level, referring to whether *MC* is upward or downward sloping, and the aggregate output at the economy level, referring to how *MC* shift, e.g. through changes in wage-rates, as aggregate output and employment change). However, the introduction of non-perfect competition also makes such conditions more likely to be fulfilled as horizontal or even downward-sloping *MC* curves and an increase in absolute demand elasticity becomes possible.

The demonstration of the possible continuum of equilibria and non-neutrality of money in a non-perfectly competitive economy is within a model with a given number of firms. It may thus be thought that if the long-run variation in the number of firms is taken into account, the possibility will no longer exist. However, allowing for free entry and exit of firms, I have shown (Ng 1986a, chapter 4) that the possibility of a continuum of equilibria and non-neutrality of money still exists without considering any friction. Certain (more complicated than above) appropriate conditions regarding costs and demand elasticity are sufficient. In fact, since the entry of new firms, as aggregate demand increases, makes the absolute demand elasticity higher by increasing the degree of competition, the appropriate conditions for a continuum of equilibria are easier to satisfy in this respect. This is illustrated in Figure 2.4. The representative firm is initially at equilibrium at *A* where *MR* = *MC* and *p* = *AC*. An increase in aggregate demand shifts the demand curve to the right and makes it more elastic (competition effect), making it possible for the firm to reach a higher equilibrium point at *B* with no

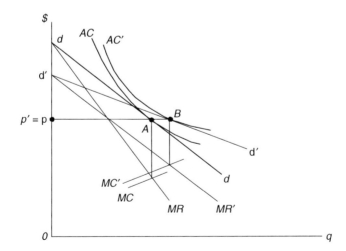

Figure 2.4 The long run

change in price, even if the cost curves shift upward as the aggregate output of the economy expands.

Our result on the possibility of a continuum of equilibria and cumulative expansion/contraction has important implications for the real-world issues of unemployment, business cycles, sluggish adjustments, relevance of business confidence, etc. It is surprising that it has not attracted the attention it deserves.

2.2 Pecuniary external effects may have real efficiency implications

While external effects such as pollution may cause serious problems, it is well known that market relationships (where the supply/demand decisions of some participants may affect others) are not real external effects. They are pecuniary external effects, which do not affect the efficiency of a perfectly competitive economy. This may be shown using the simple supply–demand analysis. The usefulness of this simple method has been underrated as a partial-equilibrium analysis. However, it can really be used as a general-equilibrium analysis because of the following consideration. This consideration is so important that I am surprised not to have seen it mentioned anywhere at all. The Hicks composite commodity theorem says that if the relative prices between all goods in a given set of commodities remain unchanged, the set may be lumped into a single composite commodity, with the quantity of this composite commodity being the total expenditure on all commodities in this set divided by one of the prices in the set and with the price of the composite commodity being the price used as the divisor. On the other hand, Walras's law says that, in an economy with G commodities, equilibrium in any $G-1$ markets implies equilibrium in all markets (as the net demand for any good by any trader has to be financed by some net supply). Thus, for the numerous situations where we may lump all the commodities into two composite commodities, we may use the supply–demand analysis on any one of the two commodities and the analysis is also one of general equilibrium. It may be true empirically that relative prices do not usually remain unchanged. However, for most economic analysis (excluding computable general-equilibrium analysis), we seldom consider changes in the relative prices of more than two sets of goods simultaneously.[6] Thus, at least for such analytical purposes, such as the one being discussed here, the supply–demand method may be used as a general-equilibrium analysis.

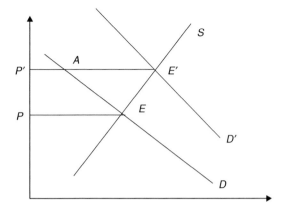

Figure 2.5 Pecuniary externality: no efficiency implication in the absence of increasing returns

First consider the 'normal' case of an upward-sloping supply and downward-sloping demand curves. Let the demand curve shift outward, causing the price of the goods in question to increase from P to P' as shown in Figure 2.5. This increase in demand could be from new consumers (including foreign demand) or from some of the existing consumers. The increase in price makes the original consumers worse off by the area $P'PEA$. (See Ng 2004, chapter 4 on the general acceptability of using the Marshallian measure of consumer surplus.) However, it is easy to see that no inefficiency is involved as the loss in consumer surplus is fully offset by the gain in producer surplus of $P'PEE'$ (with an additional surplus of $\Delta AEE'$ due to the increase in net surplus by catering to the additional demand).

Next, consider the case of a downward-sloping supply curve as may be caused by increasing returns. The increase in demand then causes the price to fall (from P to P' as shown in Figure 2.6) instead of an increase. Original consumers in fact gain in having higher surplus. However, there is no corresponding decrease in real producer surplus, as producers are still breaking even at the now lower average costs of production. For the previous case of upward-sloping supply curve, the competitive firms also just break even at the higher price and higher average cost. However, the suppliers of inputs to these firms gain in having higher surplus or rents, through the higher prices for these inputs. In the case of a downward-sloping supply curve, there is no corresponding decrease in surplus for input suppliers as the decrease in the costs of production is due to real factors that cause the increasing returns (e.g. economies of

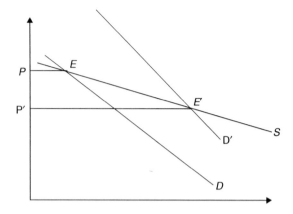

Figure 2.6   Pecuniary externality: possible efficiency implications in the presence of increasing returns

bulk purchase/usage, specialization, scale) rather than to decreases in input prices. Thus, for the present case of a downward-sloping supply curve from increasing returns, pecuniary external effects may have real efficiency implications.

2.3   Market equilibrium no longer Pareto optimal

In the traditional framework, the existence and Pareto optimality of a competitive equilibrium depend on the absence of increasing returns. It is well known that increasing returns may give rise to certain efficiency problems in a market economy (e.g. Arrow 1987, 2000; Guesnerie 1975; Heal 1999; Quinzii 1992a; Villar 1996).

The problems caused by increasing returns may be explained in a simple way. The existence of increasing returns causes the average-cost curve of a firm to be downward sloping and the marginal cost to be less than the average cost. This makes marginal-cost pricing for efficiency unlikely to be feasible as losses will be involved. Moreover, this means that an increase in demand that causes the average cost of production to fall may benefit others, as will be the case with average-cost pricing, thus explaining the efficiency implication of pecuniary externalities discussed in the previous Section 2.2.

Nearly a century ago, some economists (in particular, Pigou 1912) advocated the taxation/subsidization of goods with increasing/ decreasing costs of production or with upward/downward-sloping supply curves to increase overall surplus. However, Pigou referred to competitive industries, where in the absence of real external effects, efficiency should rule. As Young (1913) pointed out in his review of Pigou's book, the upward-sloping supply curve involves higher rents for the relevant factors of production, involving the transfer of purchasing power. Further discussion (on costs and returns reprinted in AEA 1952) revealed some problems in Pigou's analysis. Pigou used an example of a non-congested, wide but uneven road and a congested, narrow but well-surfaced road to illustrate the overuse of the narrow road with increasing costs. Knight (1924) correctly pointed out that this is due to the failure of pricing the congested road. With optimal pricing (in the absence of pricing costs, optimal both for the private owner of the road and for social efficiency), no overuse will be involved. This is not surprising to modern economists taught with the Pareto optimal nature of a competitive equilibrium in the absence of unaccounted external effects. More than half a century ago when environmental consciousness was not high, economists could confidently conclude that the 'departure of the economist's *free* competition from the ideal of social costs is in fact negligible for external economies' (Ellis and Fellner 1943, p. 511). However, even if we ignore external costs such as environmental disruption, the undisputed widespread existence of increasing returns still makes a competitive equilibrium non-existent (in the sense NOT that the economy remains competitive but equilibrium does not exist but that the economy cannot remain perfectly competitive), not to mention the issue of its Pareto optimality. Thus, if we apply Pigou's argument not for the case of perfect competition, the verdict is different.

In the presence of increasing returns, since a firm finds its average cost to be downward sloping over the whole relevant range, it will expand output indefinitely as long as it is a price taker. The expansion will eventually make price-taking behaviour no longer relevant. We may then have the monopolistic restriction of output, with price above marginal cost (which equals marginal revenue). This will lead to under-production if all other sectors are perfectly competitive. What is the situation if monopolistic competition is prevalent? Dixit and Stiglitz's (1977) pioneering analysis show that no general conclusion can be made.[7] The more specific models of Heal (1980, 1999) show that the combination of imperfect competition and increasing returns leads to the over-serving of large markets and under-serving of small markets. (See also Spence 1976 and Lancaster 1979 on optimal product variety. For a survey of the earlier literature on the economics of product variety which is related to monopolistic competition and increasing returns, see Lancaster 1990.) This is consistent with the simple partial-equilibrium intuition that may be illustrated with a downward-sloping average-cost curve. To abstract away from the problems arising from monopolistic power, assume free entry/exit such that the price of each good equals average cost in long-run equilibria.

Even so, it can be shown (Chapter 5) that, from the viewpoint of Pareto optimality, the industries with increasing returns are under-expanded relative to those without increasing returns and those with higher degrees of increasing returns are under-expanded relative to those with lower degrees (thus going beyond Pigou, even if we reinterpret or re-apply Pigou's case to non-perfect competition), at least if we start from a position of average-cost pricing equilibrium as is likely to be the case for long-run equilibrium under free entry. Subsidies on goods produced under conditions of (high degrees of) increasing returns financed by taxes on goods produced under non-increasing and lower degrees of increasing returns may increase efficiency (ignoring other effects like second-best and externalities that may offset increasing returns as well as ignoring administrative and indirect costs such as rent-seeking activities).[8]

The intuition why the basic point is valid is not difficult to see. With a falling average-cost curve, even pricing at average cost (in contrast to a possibly much more restrictive policy of pricing at marginal revenue = marginal cost) involves pricing at above marginal cost (as MC is below AC when AC is decreasing), hence implying under-production. (In contrast to Pigou's case of perfect competition, the higher/lower costs here refer to actual resource costs rather than changes in the prices/rents of inputs.) This partial-equilibrium intuition remains true in a general-equilibrium framework unless offset by other considerations such as the second-best interrelationship of being very complementary/substitutable to another good of opposite/similar efficiency considerations that cannot be dealt with directly. That this is true can be seen by taking all other goods as a composite good, making the partial equilibrium analysis also a general equilibrium one. On the other hand, apart from applications to certain areas like international trade (e.g. Helpman and Krugman 1985; Kemp 1964), the more sophisticated analysis of increasing returns in the recent decades (e.g. chapters collected in Heal 1999) focuses more on the existence of general equilibria and in particular, the existence and Pareto optimality of marginal-cost pricing equilibria.

Nevertheless, the inclination of economists against intervention need not be mistaken. First, while increasing returns are prevalent, we or the government may not know which industries are subject to higher degrees of increasing returns than others. Thus, if we consider a model where all goods have the same degree of increasing returns, then the market equilibrium cannot be improved upon by taxes and subsidies, given the infeasibility of taxing leisure. Second, imposing taxes/subsidies on goods with high degrees of increasing/decreasing returns would open up a floodgate of rent-seeking activities that are likely to consume an enormous amount of resources many times the gain of the optimal taxes/subsidies. Perhaps it is optimal to continue to pretend that increasing returns do not exist.

3
Equity and Efficiency versus Freedom and Fairness: An Inherent Conflict

In the presence of very substantial increasing returns, freedom (such as in the choice of jobs or the place of residency) and fairness (horizontal equity) may be inconsistent with the attainment of (vertical) equity (interpersonal equalization of marginal welfare of income) and/or efficiency, even abstracting from familiar factors (incentive effects, administrative costs) accounting for the equity-efficiency trade-off. The imposition of congestion taxes on urban residency or the offer of high salaries to attract volunteer soldiers may achieve an efficient division of the population consistent with freedom and fairness but is unlikely to coincide with the equalization of the marginal welfare of income. This conflict may partly explain the urban–rural segregation in China and the prevalence of conscription in many countries. Needless to say, it does not justify most illiberal policies.

3.1 Introduction

Economists are well acquainted with the conflict between efficiency and equity. The outright pursuit of Pareto efficiency may result in an unacceptably unequal distribution of income. The society may be willing to achieve a more equal distribution at the cost of imposing such inefficiencies as the excess burden of taxation.[1] The conflict between (vertical) equity and efficiency on the one hand, and freedom and fairness (horizontal equity) on the other (which we may call the *E-F conflict* for brevity) has not been adequately discussed.

As far as I know, Atkinson and Stiglitz (1976, 1980) first pointed out that an optimal system of indirect taxes may involve different rates, if feasible, on individuals of identical tastes and endowments (horizontal inequity of unfairness). Balcer and Sadka (1982) derived sufficient conditions to rule out unfairness. While the conditions are strong for a model with labour-incentive, they are quite reasonable for a model with only education-incentive.

In this chapter, by considering the problem of allocating the population into urban and rural residents, or to military and civilian services, or some other similar problems, in the presence of significant degrees of increasing returns, we see that unfairness may be optimal under very general conditions even if both labour and education incentives are assumed absent. Moreover, in addition to fairness, freedom may also be violated, i.e. it may be optimal to have selective conscription and not to allow freedom of choice of residency. The elucidation of the *E-F conflict* may thus partly explain the prevalence of certain social policies such as conscription despite their violation of equity, efficiency, freedom, and fairness. (See Ng 2008 for more detailed analysis of the possible desirability of conscription in the presence of significant increasing returns due to the *E-F conflict*.)

The conflict between optimality and fairness originally pointed out by Atkinson and Stiglitz may appear to many people as mainly of academic interest, as the administrative costs and the costs of violating fairness are likely to be overwhelming in comparison to the slight gain in efficiency in the tax system. However, the issue of rural–urban division for countries like China and India, the issue of conscription for most countries, etc. are important practical problems. Moreover, the introduction of such 'either-or' choices made relevant by the existence of strong increasing returns increases the extent of the *E-F conflict*. (Pedagogically, this allows our elucidation of the conflict to be put in the very simple terms of Section II below, accessible to all economists.) The *E-F conflict* (which extends the Atkinson–Stiglitz conflict to freedom) we discuss here is thus of important and direct policy significance. This exemplifies the general rule that many intellectual contributions may appear practically useless at first but may be shown otherwise with further development and application.

I was drawn to the concept of *E-F conflict* whilst reflecting on my argument against the unfair and illiberal Chinese policy of segregating rural and urban residents. Those born to families of farmers are not allowed to move into towns and be registered as urban residents. (This restriction has been weakened after the economic reforms in the recent decades.) I raised the issue of this objectionable practice during a discussion with a number of students from China. A party member, who is rather liberal on many other issues, defended the policy on the ground that, without segregation, rural residents would flood into the cities, creating an impossible situation. I replied that this is so only because of the inequitable policy of widening the gap between the living standards of rural and urban areas by wages and prices policies as well as the provision (or the lack) of social services. (One may add the lack of economic development that would provide a healthy absorption of the expanding labour force.)

The next day, as I reflected, trying to reassure myself that my reply was correct, I became less confident. While it captures part of the truth, it may not be the whole truth. Even with the operation of the ideal policies with respect to prices, incomes, and social services, including achieving the equity condition of the equality of marginal social welfare significance of income between rural and urban residents, we cannot be sure that the free movement between urban and rural residents will not result in an undesirable degree of crowding or congestion in the urban area. It may be thought that the congestion can be reduced to any desired level by an appropriate taxation/subsidy scheme. However, such a scheme may lead to a level of urban income considered too low to satisfy the equity condition.

The condition for freedom and fairness is in terms of individual indifference (or the equality of *total* utilities) between urban and rural residency, while the condition for equity is in terms of the equality of *marginal* social welfare significance of income. The two conditions can be achieved simultaneously only by sheer coincidence. In fact, there is a presumption that the two will always conflict as most people prefer to live in the urban area even with the same income, and the opportunity of useful consumption is higher in cities, unless the urban area is allowed to be so overcrowded as to balance its advantages.

In a more developed economy, the distinction between urban and rural living is not so high, so the conflict is negligible. The best policy may then be to opt for freedom and fairness. However, the conflict may be more acute for other problems. For example, the division between military and civilian services especially during wars. Compulsory military service for persons of specified ages is required in many countries. While economists are naturally inclined towards paying the soldier his hire (Parish and Weisser 1970), a soldier's pay might have to be many times higher than the civilian average to attract a sufficient number of volunteers. While other factors are involved in opting for a conscript army, intuitive awareness of the *E-F conflict* may be a possible explanation.

The elucidation of the *E-F conflict* allows us to realize that social choices that are inconsistent with equity, efficiency, freedom, and fairness need not necessarily be sub-optimal. Since the four objectives cannot be achieved simultaneously, sacrificing a little of each may yet be the optimal policy. Needless to say, the *E-F conflict* does not justify all departures from equity, efficiency, freedom, and fairness.

The source of the *E-F conflict* may be the presence of strong increasing returns. In the absence of increasing returns, everyone may choose to serve as a soldier for a short period, earning enough incomes to maintain the easier civilian life. However, due to strong increasing returns, if the military forces consist mainly of such short-term soldiers, the efficiency will definitely be very low. Due to the high costs of training and the importance of learning by doing and the accumulation of experience, the productivities of soldiers have very high degrees of increasing returns. If we need 1% of the working population to serve in the military forces, we cannot have each person serving about one month every nine years. Rather, we need a small fraction of people to serve for many years, even decades. If it costs too much to attract sufficient number of people to volunteer for military services, conscription especially at times of emergency/wars, need not be undesirable. For the case of the rural–urban problem, the very existence of cities is due to increasing returns in the provision of infrastructures and facilities in cities. As economists largely ignore the existence of increasing returns, most of them are not aware of the potential *E-F conflict.* I became aware of this conflict only after my debate with Chinese students regarding the rural–urban segregation policy in China, as mentioned above.

3.2 The *E-F Conflict*

The familiar conflict between equity and Pareto efficiency may be illustrated in Figure 3.1. If all the conditions for Pareto efficiency are satisfied, the economy is at a point on the utility possibility curve *(UPC).* Depending on the initial endowment, it may be at a point such as A. According to the specific welfare contours depicted, the (social) welfare maximum point is at B where the slope of the welfare contour $(-W_i/W_j,$ where $W_i \equiv \partial W/\partial u^i)$ equals the slope of the UPC $(-u_x^j/u_x^i,$ where u_x^i is the marginal utility of income for person i). At the maximal welfare point, we thus have

$$\frac{W_i}{W_j} = \frac{u_x^j}{u_x^i}, \text{ or } W_i u_x^i = W_j u_x^j$$

or the interpersonal equality of the marginal welfare of income (through personal marginal utility). This condition is the same as Condition (3.4) in the formal model of Section 3.3.

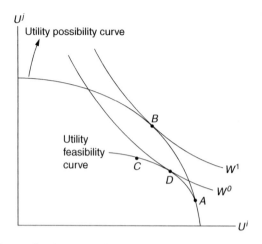

Figure 3.1 The conflict between efficiency and equity

It is normally infeasible to move from *A* to *B*. Due to disincentive effects, administrative costs, etc., the attempt to move to *B* will lead us to *C* instead. Rather than accepting this substantial loss in efficiency, the society may settle on a compromise (between equity and efficiency) at point *D*.

It is, however, not our objective to discuss this familiar conflict between equity and efficiency. We will thus highlight our central issue and simplify our discussion by abstracting from this familiar conflict. That is, we assume the absence of disincentive effects and administrative costs such that the welfare-maximal point *B* is attainable. In a model of many individuals, the feasibility of attaining *B* also depends on the feasibility of person-specific lump-sum taxes/subsidies, which will be assumed. This last feasibility is not required if we assume that the marginal welfare of income ($W_i u_x^i$) is the same for all persons of the same income. An appropriate system of (anonymous) income taxes would then be sufficient to attain the welfare-maximal point.

Another innocuous simplifying assumption is that of identical individual taste. Conceivably, differences in taste might be such that some of the individuals in the population prefer to serve in the military and the rest prefer to be in the civilian sector in such a way that the division is efficient, with income levels satisfying the equality of the marginal welfare of income. Such a happy situation may approximately be the case in peace time but is unlikely to be so in war time when more soldiers are required unless patriotism dramatically lowers the supply curve. Since the introduction of differences in taste does not resolve the conflict, at least not generally, we will simplify the argument by ignoring taste differences.

Now let us discuss our concepts more precisely. An *allocation* specifies the amounts of all goods (including jobs and places of residence where relevant) consumed by each individual, and the amount of public goods in each locality. An (perfectly *efficient)* allocation (or *efficiency)*, requires the non-existence of an alternative allocation that makes some individual better off without making any individual worse off. An (perfectly) *equitable* allocation (or *equity)* requires the equalization across all individuals of the marginal welfares of income (marginal utilities weighted by social welfare weights), continuity being assumed. (The relaxation of continuity does not in general alter our conclusion.) *Fairness* of an allocation requires that similar individuals (of the same utility function) enjoy the same amount of total utility in the same situation. *Freedom* requires, among others, letting people choose their jobs and their places of residence at their own free will.

Note that the above are *necessary* conditions for *perfect* efficiency, equity, fairness, and freedom respectively. Thus, the violation of a necessary condition for say (perfect) efficiency does not necessarily mean complete inefficiency. But since our aim is only to establish the existence of *some* conflict, it does not matter. However, the necessity (not sufficiency) nature of our conditions leaves open for anyone who may wish to add additional conditions to the concepts. For example, one may wish to require *fairness to* involve treating all individuals (whether having the same utility function) in the same situation similarly. But since this implies the same total utility for similar individuals, our condition allows for more generality. Similarly, while different people may have somewhat different ideas of what freedom exactly means, most will agree that full freedom at least requires free choice of jobs and the place of residence.

We are now ready to state and prove our proposition.

Proposition 3.1: The achievement of efficiency and equity is in general inconsistent with freedom and fairness even if disincentive effects and administrative costs are absent (i.e. lump-sum taxes/subsidies are feasible).

Proof: The existence of the *E-F conflict* in one example satisfying the required conditions (absence of disincentive effects, administrative costs) is sufficient to establish the proposition. This (quite general) example is illustrated in Figure 3.2. Suppose that, at the optimal division of the population between urban and rural areas (taking account of all costs

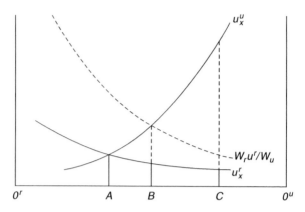

Figure 3.2   The *E-F conflict* in terms of marginal utility curves

and benefits), the amount of income available to be allocated between a rural and an urban resident is represented by the distance O^rO^u in Figure 3.2. The income allotted to the rural resident is measured from O^r and that to the urban resident[2] is measured *leftward* from O^u. The curves u^r_x, u^u_x are the marginal utility of income curves for the rural and the urban residents respectively.[3] Despite our assumption of identical taste, the two curves are not symmetrical since urban living is different from rural living. Typically, both the total and the marginal utilities are much lower for the rural resident due to the poor facilities there and the lack of useful opportunities to spend money.

The poor facilities may be but need not be due to a neglect of the rural area. Since the rural area is less densely populated, we expect fewer public facilities there even if the Samuelsonian optimality condition for the supply of public goods is satisfied both for the urban and the rural areas.

Given the situation depicted in Figure 3.2, *a* pure utilitarian SWF would divide income at the point A where the marginal utilities are equalized. But consider even an egalitarian (in terms of income) SWF dictating the division at the mid-point B or a SWF so much sympathetic to the low utility rural resident (W_r/W_u much larger than one, where $W_r \equiv \partial W/\partial u^r$ is the marginal social welfare weight for the rural resident, and W^u that for the urban resident) as to dictate an approximately equal division (say at the point *B*).

Suppose, as is likely, that urban living offers so many more opportunities that, with equality between urban and rural incomes, people much prefer to be urban residents. To make people indifferent between urban and rural livings, the per capita income of rural residents may have to be much higher than that of urban residents (a point like C). This may grossly violate the optimality condition for the equality of the marginal welfare in income. If society does not want this to happen, freedom of choice of residence may have to be restricted.

Alternatively, if the incomes of urban and rural residents are equalized or determined at levels to satisfy the equality of marginal welfare, and if there is also freedom of choice of residence, too many people may flood to the cities. While an urban resident may still enjoy the same utility level as a rural resident, the marginal contribution to social welfare of an urban resident may well be negative, taking account of the external diseconomies imposed on others in the form of congestion and reduced job opportunities. In other words, the efficient division of the population between urban and rural residents may have to be sacrificed. In general, freedom and fairness are thus inconsistent with the achievement of either equity of efficiency or both, QED.

It may be mistakenly thought that equity and efficiency can be achieved without sacrificing freedom by the imposition of a congestion tax on urban residents. At an appropriate level, a congestion tax can achieve the Pareto optimal division of the population between urban and rural residency. However, except by coincidence, the net of tax incomes need not be consistent with the equality of marginal welfare of income unless the social welfare function (SWF) is Rawlsian, giving an infinitely large weight to the individual with the lowest utility.

If we go along with the maximization of ex-ante expected utility, the choice in Figure 3.2 would be the utilitarian one of dividing income at the point A (cf. Harsanyi 1953, 1955). A person who does not know whether he will be a rural or an urban resident would maximize his expected utility by agreeing in advance that, if his lot is to be a rural resident, he will receive $O'A$ and $O''A$ if urban. Thus, the choice even at B involves losses in terms of ex-ante expected utility, not to mention the choice at C.

An alternative to the marginal utility approach of Figure 3.2 is the utility possibility curves of Figure 3.3, where UPC_u^1, is the utility possibility curve if individual 1 is in the urban area, and individual 2 is in the rural area, and UPC_u^2 is that for the reverse situation. The points for equal income levels might be at E^1 and E^2 respectively. But a moderately concave *SWF* as represented by the welfare contour W^1 is indifferent between A^1 and A^2, both involving a higher income level to the urban residents. A Rawlsian *SWF* as represented by the angular welfare contour W^2 chooses, however, a point of equal utility E^u.

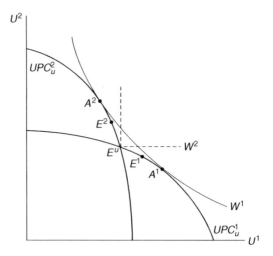

Figure 3.3 The *E-F conflict* in terms of utility possibility curves

An explanation why the urban-rural or the military-civilian choice tends to create *E-F conflict* is that the 'either-or' choice due to increasing returns creates in general non-convexity, a condition conducive to unfairness. That an indivisible 'either-or' choice creates non-convexity was first discussed in Ng (1965). But the discussion of Hillman and Swan (1979, 1983) is closer in its presentation to Figure 3.3.

While the example of rural–urban residency given above refers to the externality of congestion, etc. to increase the magnitude of the *E-F conflict*, the existence of external effects is not essential. Unless the distribution of personal income in accordance to the marginal productivities of factors owned happens to correspond to the interpersonal equalization of the marginal welfare of income, the *E-F conflict* is still present in the absence of external effects. This can be best seen in the soldiers versus civilians example. During war, the productivity (in the wide sense of safeguarding properties and lives) of defence may be so high and the life of a soldier so risky that, if a soldier is paid his marginal product, his income may have to be many times that of a civilian before voluntary recruitment will result in the efficient number of soldiers. But this may grossly deviate from the interpersonal equality of the marginal welfare of income. However, if a soldier is paid less than his marginal product, voluntary recruitment may not yield sufficient soldiers to satisfy efficiency.

In our simple analysis, while people prefer urban to rural residency, their preference (including their adaptation to the living conditions, capacity to enjoy, etc.) itself is not affected by their place of residence. With such a simple assumption, the *E-F conflict* can easily be resolved if it is not too costly to rotate urban and rural residents. Thus, if it is optimal to have m (a fraction) of the population living in the urban and $(1 - m)$ in the rural area, each individual can spend m of their life in the urban and $(1 - m)$ in the rural area. While in the urban area, he/she receives an income equal to O^uA in Figure 3.2 and while in the rural area, he/she receives O^rA. Then the total life-time utility is maximized and equalized across individuals.

However, apart from the physical costs (transportation, change of accommodation, etc.) of the rotation, there are the more important considerations of preference formation such as adaptation, accustomization, learning, etc. A person born and brought up in the city (countryside) is more accustomed to urban (rural) living and working conditions. Due to the better facilities and opportunities in the urban area, a farmer's son or daughter may yet prefer to move to a city. But the gain in utility of such a transfer may be much smaller than the loss in utility and productivity suffered by the reverse transfer. A person accustomed to the facilities of urban living may suffer a tremendous loss if posted to a rural area. This was overwhelmingly witnessed by the 'sent-down' youths in China in the 1950s and 1960s. Despite strong indoctrination and years of hardship in the countryside, most of these 'sent-down' youths could not accustom themselves to rural living. Virtually all of them had been allowed to return to the cities.

A further consideration is that the relatives and friends one has are usually related to one's place of residence. It would be quite impracticable to transfer all friends and relatives to the same village since the relationships of friends and relatives are interconnected rather than in the form of distinct unconnected groups. This consideration increases the cost of rotation.

For the division between military and civilian services, there is of course the significant cost of training, both to the government and to the trainees discussed above. Unless it is deemed desirable to have the whole population trained (as in a very threatened country like Israel), it may be too costly to have a system of rotation in military services. It may thus be better (in terms of maximizing expected utility) to have a system of selective conscription. Typically, young men between the ages of 18 and 30 are the principal target. But economists may be in favour of making the probabilities of being drafted subject to purchase and sale. A person hating military service very much can then have his probability reduced at the cost of paying someone else whose probability correspondingly increases. (See Bergstrom 1986 for the argument that an army recruited by a draft lottery with probabilities of being drafted subject to purchase and sale is ex-ante Pareto-superior to an all-volunteer army.)

Most people regard discrimination by sex and age with respect to military service not necessarily unfair. Since women would probably suffer more hardship and contribute less to the defence of the nation if drafted, it makes sense to draft young men who have fewer family responsibilities. However, most people regard the possibility of reducing one's probability of being drafted by paying someone else unfair, since the rich could then afford to be free from military services. This belief ignores the fact that, by widening the sphere open to monetary transaction, the utility of having more money is increased and hence the rich can be taxed more without increasing the disincentive effect. Thus, provided that the widening of the sphere open to monetary transaction is accompanied (at least in the long run) by increasing the progressivity of the income taxation system, both the rich and the poor can be made better off (Ng 1984). Nevertheless, before people are persuaded by this argument, making the draft probabilities subject to sale may weaken the morale of the soldiers. Typically, one is prone to think, 'since the rich do not have to sacrifice to defend the country, why should I fight?' This reasoning is wrong because those who pay to reduce their draft probabilities contribute to defense by reducing resources at their command (both through paying and through a higher tax). Moreover, it is Pareto optimal for them to make their contribution this way. However, before people accept this argument, the morale weakening effect will persist. Taking account of this morale effect, it may then **NOT** be desirable to make the draft probabilities subject to sale.

While the conflict between equity/efficiency and fairness (but not freedom) with respect to military services may be partially solved by a selective draft (at a considerable cost to efficiency if the system of sale in draft probabilities is not acceptable to the population), that with respect to the rural/urban residency is more difficult to solve by a similar method. This is so for the following reason. The children of soldiers do not lead the life of soldiers before they themselves become soldiers. But the children of rural (urban) residents are themselves rural (urban) residents by the fact of living with their parents. They are thus accustomed to their respective places of residence and interwoven into their respective groups of friends and relatives. As discussed above, it may then be very costly to transfer them.

From the above considerations, if it is desirable to restrict the number of urban residents, the most efficient and equitable (but not fair) method may be to disallow the movements of rural residents into the urban area except for those who distinguish themselves through the education process as capable of contributing significantly in the urban area. This was (and to some extent still is) the policy practiced by the Chinese government. Such a policy is of course not without significant costs. The inefficiency created by the almost complete immobility must be very substantial. More importantly, there are the issues of freedom and fairness. Is the gain in restricting an excess influx into cities worth the costs involved? The Chinese policy was of course also partly if not mainly a matter of administrative and political control of the population. We shall however ignore such factors.

Consider the following two situations: (A) If a person, by accident of birth, happens to be a boy, he is destined to serve in the armed forces on the reasoning that a boy makes a better soldier than a girl; (B) If a person, by accident of birth, happens to be a farmer's child, he or she is destined to live in the rural area on the reasoning that a person brought up in a rural family makes a better farmer than one from the city. For reasons difficult to explain, most people (myself included) find situation A not necessarily unfair but find situation B very unfair. The *E-F conflict* is thus made more acute for the issue of rural–urban residency of an underdeveloped economy like China or India.

Roughly speaking, China (at least pre-reform) opted for control while India opted to have freedom and fairness in the choice of residency. The cost of this freedom and fairness is the overcrowded situation in most Indian cities. The marginal migrants into cities probably contribute negatively to production and also have per capita income below those remaining in the countryside. Nevertheless, they choose to go to the city as there is some chance they may be successful. Each migrant into the city imposes significant external diseconomies on others in terms of the congestion of public facilities and of the reduction in the probability of success (in getting jobs, etc.). The average living standard is much higher in the city than in the countryside due to the choice of most of the well-to-do to live in cities. But the per capita incomes of many of the low income groups may well be not much higher or even lower than of those in the countryside. Given the need for and the usefulness or higher income for urban living, a congestion tax on urban residency sufficiently high to internalize the externality completely may be too high for the low income groups to be deemed 'equitable' (i.e. equalization of the marginal welfare of income).

Given the choice to have freedom and fairness as in India, an optimal policy may be a compromise between equity and efficiency (internalization of externalities). However, given the alternative choice largely to ignore freedom and fairness as in China, an optimal policy may be to have more-or-less complete efficiency (in urban/rural division) and partial equity to partly compensate the rural residents for the unfairness of rural residency imposed on them. That is, rural residents should have incomes high enough to have lower marginal utilities than urban residents. But since their respective marginal utility curves are likely to be roughly as depicted in Figure 3.2, this does not necessarily mean that rural residents should have higher incomes.

The choice whether to opt for freedom or not may be very difficult to make. It may be thought that, if one agrees to the maximization of ex-ante expected utility, then the necessity of sacrificing freedom is obvious where the two conflict. It may thus appear that freedom and fairness have no role to play in a utilitarian or even a more general welfarist (except the extreme Rawlsian) SWF. However, when we consider a broader concept of utility and/or the long-run effects on utilities, the picture is different. This is so because the very lack of freedom may impose a utility loss not captured in a narrow utility analysis of Figure 3.2 or Section 3.3. Moreover, the very choice to ignore freedom and fairness may affect the future prospect by changing institutions and people's attitudes. Thus, the concern for the issues of freedom and fairness need not necessarily be a non-utilitarian one.

3.3   A specific model

To analyse the *E-F conflict* more rigorously in a limited space, we shall deal with a simple model (retaining the simplifying assumptions of identical taste, no disincentive effects, etc.) and ignore many complications discussed informally above.

3.3.1   The model

To facilitate the use of calculus, assume an uncountable number of individuals each being identified by a point on the closed unit interval $(0, 1)$. This assumption (or its relaxation) is innocuous and is used purely for mathematical convenience. The (real-valued) utility of individual i $(0 \geq i \geq 1)$ is denoted U^i. The function that maps each i into u is denoted U, i.e. U maps the unit interval $(0, 1)$ into the set of real numbers, R. Denote as $L(0, 1)$ the set of all such integrable functions. Take social welfare W as a function of all individual utilities. (This common practice is called welfarism and attacked by Sen (1979). For a defence of welfarism against Sen's attack, see Ng 1981, 1985.) This function $W(U)$ maps $L(0, 1)$ into

R. It is thus a functional. However, it differs from a social welfare functional used in the social choice literature. (This maps the *s* individual preference functions into a real-valued social welfare, i.e. the social welfare functional maps the set of all admissible individual preference functions into *R*.) Rather, it is the counterpart (for the case of a continuum of individuals) to the Bergson-Samuelson social welfare function (SWF)

$$W = W(u^1, u^2, ..., u^s) \tag{3.1}$$

where *s* is the number of individuals. In order not to be confused with a social welfare functional in its social choice sense and to emphasize its similar nature with a common SWF, I shall just call the functional *W*( ) a SWF.

Denote x^i as the private-good consumption of individual *i*, and $X \equiv \int_0^1 x^i di$ as the aggregate private-good consumption (= production). Also denote *Y, Z* as the public good provision in the city and in the countryside respectively. Since the population is homogeneous, let the interval (0, *m*) be living in the city and the interval (*m*, 1) be living in the countryside. While individuals have identical welfare functions, their welfare depends on their place of residence. Thus,

$$\begin{aligned} u^i &= u^u(x^i, Y, m) && \text{for } 0 \geq i \geq m \\ &= u^r(x^i, Z, n) && \text{for } m > i \geq 1 \end{aligned} \tag{3.2}$$

where the superscripts *u* and *r* stand for urban and rural respectively, and *n* = *m* − 1.

Ignoring variable intermediate inputs we write the production constraint as follows, since the marginal productivities of urban and rural residents may differ,

$$F(X, Y, Z) = f(m, n) \tag{3.3}$$

3.3.2 Optimality conditions

To derive the conditions for a social welfare maximum, we maximize *W(U)* with respect to *xi, Y, Z,* and *m* subject to (3.3). Assuming that the second-order conditions are satisfied, we concentrate on the following first-order conditions. (See the appendix for their derivation.)

$$W_i u_x^i = W_j u_x^j, \ \forall i,j \tag{3.4}$$

$$\int_{0 \geq i \geq m} \left(\frac{u_Y^i}{u_x^i} \right) di = \frac{F_Y}{F_X} \tag{3.5}$$

$$\int_{m \geq i \geq 1} \left(\frac{u_z^i}{u_x^i} \right) di = \frac{F_z}{F_x} \qquad (3.6)$$

$$\frac{[u^u(x_u^m, Y, m) - u^r(x_r^m), Z, n]}{u_x^m} = \int_{m \geq i \geq 1} \left(\frac{u_z^i}{u_x^i} \right) di - \int_{0 \geq i \geq m} \left(\frac{u_Y^i}{u_x^i} \right) di \qquad (3.7)$$
$$+ (x_u^m - x_r^m) - \frac{(f_m - f_n)}{F_x}$$

where a subscript denotes partial differentiation, e.g. $W_i = \partial W/\partial u^i$, $u_x^i \equiv \partial u^i/\partial x^i$, $F_x \equiv \partial F/\partial X$, etc. except for x_u^m and x_r^m which are the private-good allocations to the marginal resident m, if transferred to the urban area (x_u^m) and if left in the rural area (x_r^m). These two values may differ since the utility of this person m depends on his residence and hence different allocation of the private good may be required to satisfy (3.4). The term $(f_m - f_n)/F_x$ is the difference in marginal productivity between an urban and a rural resident, using as numeraire the marginal cost of the private-good production, F_x which we may normalize to equal unity.

Eq. (3.5) is the Samuelsonian condition for the optimal supply of public goods to the urban area, requiring the equality of $\Sigma MRS = MRT$ or just the marginal cost of providing Y, with F_x normalized to equal one. Eq. (3.6) is the same condition for the rural area.

Eq. (3.4) is the equity (or 'welfare-efficiency') condition in the allocation of the private good, requiring the equality of the marginal (social) welfare significance of the private good across all individuals. Since our *SWF* is Paretian, this welfare significance is through the marginal utility of consumption u_x^i. This condition is usually referred to as the interpersonal *equity* condition. However, since the question of fairness discussed here is quite different to this condition, we may also call Eq. (3.4) the welfare-efficiency condition for the (interpersonal) allocation of the private good. It is an efficiency condition in the maximization of the *SWF* $W(U)$ though the consideration of interpersonal equity could have been reflected in the values of W. If the *SWF* happens to be utilitarian such that $W(U) = \int_{0 \geq i \geq 1} u^i di$, the predominantly welfare-efficiency nature of (3.4) becomes more apparent. Alternatively, following Harsanyi (1953, 1955), we may say that the ex-ante (i.e. before knowledge of which individual one will become) expected utility of an individual has not been maximized unless (3.4) is satisfied, with each W_i a constant.

Eq. (3.7) is the 'club membership' condition concerning the optimal division of the population into the urban and the rural.[4] The LHS is the gain in total utility of the marginal resident transferred from the rural to the urban area with his private-good allocation adjusted in accordance to the requirement of (3.5), i.e. from x_r^m into x_u^m. This gain in utility is measured relative to his marginal utility of the private-good consumption, and is thus in the form of MRS. The first two terms (with integrals) on the RHS measure the cost of the transfer in the form of the cost of increased congestion (assuming $u_m^i < 0$ at the margin) imposed on all urban residents minus the reduction in the congestion in the rural area. The remaining terms in (3.7) measure the cost of the transfer in terms of the increased consumption of the marginal transferee minus his increase in marginal productivity (both of the increases may be negative).

3.3.3 The *E-F conflict*

Whether we assume a centrally directed economy where the government can directly determine each x^i irrespective of the marginal productivity of i, or whether we assume a market economy where the government can impose a different lump-sum tax on each individual, the government has, given the value of X, the same number of instruments (= the number of individuals less one) here as the number of equations to satisfy in (3.4).

While our formal model deals with an uncountable number of individuals to facilitate the use of calculus, the number of individuals is certainly finite in any real economy. If we impose the condition of anonymity such that $W_i = W_j$ if $u_i = u_j$ for all i, j, the number of equations in (3.4) is reduced to one, namely, $W_r u_x^r = W_u u_x^u$, where r and u stand for rural and urban residents respectively, recalling our assumption of identical utility functions (3.2). Given the value of X, the government still has the same number of instrument (one) as the number of equations to satisfy in (3.4). Once the income for either sector is decided, the other follows.

Next, Y and Z can be chosen to satisfy (3.5) and (3.6). (While all these have to be done simultaneously, it is of pedagogic value to proceed one by one.) If, in addition, m is chosen to satisfy (3.7), the production constraint (3.3) determines the value of X. (Recall that $n \equiv 1 - m$.) Thus, there are as many optimality conditions to satisfy as the number of free policy instruments, *only if* the government can also choose m.

If individuals are free to choose their places of residency, it will only be by chance that the welfare optimality conditions can be satisfied. It may be thought that taxes/subsidies can be used to correct for the non-optimality created by individual free choice. For example, if too many individuals choose to reside in the urban area thereby creating excessive congestion, a congestion tax can be imposed on urban residency. The use of such a method can certainly help us to achieve the optimal balance (between urban and rural areas) condition (3.7), but its use precludes the attainment of condition (3.4) except by coincidence. The decision to have freedom of choice of residence thus involves in general one instrument less than the number of optimality conditions. Either some of the efficiency conditions (3.5)–(3.7) or the equity condition (3.4) or both have to be left unsatisfied, except when they are satisfied by coincidence.

3.4 Concluding remarks

As noted at the end of Section 3.2, freedom and fairness may be valued by a purely utilitarian *SWF*, especially in the long run. For those who are willing to value freedom and fairness over and above their contribution to individual welfares (broadly defined), the infringement of freedom and fairness is then doubly 'costly'. Thus, many people may be unwilling to yield an inch in freedom and fairness unless their conflict with equity and efficiency is very strong, i.e. unless the insistence on freedom and fairness will exact a huge loss of equity and/or efficiency.

In principle, we may extend our analysis to many other issues, such as the division between blue and white collar jobs, between different geographical regions, etc. Potential conflict between freedom and fairness with equity and efficiency can still be established for such issues. For most issues, however, the conflict is likely to be minimal relative to the importance of freedom and fairness. It is thus desirable to insist on freedom in all issues except some special issues where the conflict is strong such as the issue of military services due to strong increasing returns.

While it is important to avoid the unjustified infringement of freedom on insufficient grounds, the recognition of the conflict of freedom and fairness with equity and efficiency explains, at least partly, certain social choices (such as conscription) which may appear to economists as irrational because they violate equity, efficiency, freedom, and fairness. Since these objectives cannot all be attained, sacrificing a bit of each and every one of them may yet be an optimal policy.

Appendix 3A

Maximizing $W(U)$ subject to (3.3), we have our Lagrangean

$$L = W(U) - \Theta[F(X, Y, Z) - f(m, n)]$$

where the value of U is specified in (3.2). The first-order conditions with respect to x_i, Y, Z and m are respectively,

$$W_i u_x^i = \Theta F X, \quad \forall i \in (0,1) \tag{3A1}$$

$$\int_{0 \geq i \geq m} W_i u_Y^i di = \Theta F_Y \tag{3A2}$$

$$\int_{m > i \geq 1} W_i u_Z^i di = \Theta F_Z \tag{3A3}$$

$$W_m[u^u(x_u^m, Y, m) - u^r(x_r^m), Z, n] + \int_{0 \geq i \geq m} W_i u_Y^i di - \int_{m > i \geq 1} W_i u_Z^i di \tag{3A4}$$
$$= \Theta F_X(x_u^m - x_r^m) - \Theta(f_m - f_n)$$

where $W_i = \partial W / \partial u^i$, $u_x^i \equiv \partial u^i / \partial x^i$, $F_X \equiv \partial F / \partial X$, etc., and x_u^m is the private good allocated to the marginal resident transferred to the urban area, and x_r^m is his/her allocation if he/she remains in the rural area. These two values may differ since his/her utility depends on his/her residence and hence different allocation of the private good maybe required to satisfy (3A1). The term $(f_m - f_n)$ is the difference in marginal productivity between an urban and a rural resident.

Since $W_i u_x^i$ is equal to ΘF_X for each and every i, we may divide (3A2)–(3A4) through by either $W_i u_x^i$ or $\Theta F x$ to express these conditions in the form of the marginal rates of substitution (MRS), and also rewrite (3A1), yielding (3.4)–(3.7) in the text.

4
Existence of Average-Cost Pricing Equilibria with Increasing Returns

Even in the presence of increasing returns and imperfectly competitive firms, the existence of an average-cost pricing equilibrium that is productively efficient (but in general not Pareto optimal) is demonstrated.

In this chapter, we show the existence of an average-cost pricing equilibrium under the conditions of (possible existence of) increasing returns. It involves some technical maths. Readers finding this too heavy going may skip this chapter without much loss of continuity. The demonstration is based on a standard neoclassical model by Brown and Heal (1983) but generalized to any numbers of individuals, goods, and resources. (On the existence of general equilibrium with increasing returns, see, e.g., Bonnisseau & Meddeb 1999; Brown et al. 1986; Quinzii 1992b; Salchow 2006.)

The set of individuals is taken as given and resources (or factors), including labour, are in fixed supply. This is not really restrictive, as we may view leisure as a good and produced one to one using labour time. Denoting the numbers of individuals, goods (subsuming services), and resources as I, G, and R respectively, we have

$$R_r^1 + R_r^2 + \cdots + R_r^I = R_r; r = 1, \ldots, R \quad \text{(individual ownership of resources)}$$
$$(4.1)$$

where R_r^i is the amount of resource r owned by individual i.

Each individual has a conventional utility function

$$U^i = U^i(G_1^i, G_2^i, \ldots, G_G^i); i = 1, \ldots, I \quad \text{(individual utility functions)} \quad (4.2)$$

where G_g^i is the amount of good g consumed by individual i.[1]

40

Denoting the prices of goods and resources as P_g and W_r respectively, we may write the budget constraint of individuals as

$$\sum_{g=1}^{G} P_g G_g^i = Y^i; \quad i = 1, \ldots, I \quad \text{(individual budget constraints)} \qquad (4.3)$$

Each individual may receive his/her income Y^i from supplying the resources (including labour) owned to the business firms and/or from receiving shares (given) of profits of firms.

$$Y^i = \sum_{r=1}^{R} W_r R_r^i + \sum_{g=1}^{G} S_g^i \left(P_g G_g - \sum_{r=1}^{R} W_r R_{rg} \right) \qquad (4.4)$$

where S_g^i is the share of individual i in the profit of the firm producing good g. Each individual is taken to be small relative to the whole economy and hence takes the prices of goods and resources as well as her profits shares (relatively and absolutely) as given and maximizes (4.2) subject to (4.3) and (4.4) (the latter two equations may be combined into one), giving first-order conditions:

$$\frac{\partial U^i / \partial G_g^i}{\partial U^i / \partial G_G^i} = \frac{P_g}{P_G}; \quad g = 1, \ldots, G-1; \quad i = 1, \ldots, I \quad \text{(utility maximization)} \quad (4.5)$$

These conditions of MRS (marginal rates of substitution) = price ratios, together with the budget constraints above, determine the individual demand functions for the various goods.

Each firm has a production function or equivalently a cost function with conventional properties except that increasing returns are allowed:

$$C^g = C^g(W_1, \ldots, W_R, G_g); \quad g = 1, \ldots, G \quad \text{(cost functions)} \qquad (4.6)$$

The demand for resources by each firm is derived from cost minimization subject to output constraint:

$$\frac{\partial G_g / \partial R_{rg}}{\partial G_g / \partial R_{sg}} = \frac{W_r}{W_s}; \quad r, s = 1, \ldots, R; \quad g = 1, \ldots, G \quad \text{(cost minimization)} \quad (4.7)$$

$$G^g(R_{1g}, \ldots, R_{Rg}) = G_g; \quad g = 1, \ldots, G \quad \text{(production functions)} \qquad (4.8)$$

where R_{rg} is the amount of resource r used in the production of good g. The production functions and resource constraints define the production possibility set and the corresponding production possibility frontier (super-surface) for the economy. This set, while conventional in other aspects (it thus remains homeomorphic to a convex and compact set; conventional assumptions like divisibility in goods and factors, etc. remain), need not be convex (due to the allowance for increasing returns). While we allow for increasing returns in the production of goods and hence do not require perfect competition in all the product markets, we continue to assume perfect competition in the resource markets, i.e. we do not consider monopolistic power in the employment of factors. Thus, we still have the tangency condition between the marginal rates of technical substitution and the resource price ratios which is common to all firms, as specified in (4.7).

Whether a good is produced under the condition of perfect competition or monopolistic competition with free entry, or a public utility constrained to just break even, we have average-cost pricing at the long-run equilibrium:

$$P_g = \frac{C_g(W_1,\ldots,W_R,\ G_g)}{G_g}; \ g = 1,\ldots,G \quad \text{(average-cost pricing)} \quad (4.9)$$

With average-cost pricing from free entry (as in the Dixit–Stiglitz model), the tangency point of the average-cost curve with the demand curve also entails the point of profit maximization as all other points entail negative profits. In all three cases (perfect competition, monopolistic competition, constrained public utility), (4.9) together with (4.7) and (4.8) describe the situation where each firm is in an average-cost pricing equilibrium.

General equilibrium is defined as a set of relative product prices P_1/P_G, a set of relative resource prices W_1/W_R; product demands G_g^i; $i = 1, \ldots, I$; $g = 1, \ldots, G$; resource demands R_{rg}; $r = 1, \ldots, R$, $g = 1, \ldots, G$; and output level G_g; $g = 1, \ldots, G$ such that all individuals are at utility maximization equilibrium and all firms are at average-cost pricing equilibrium described above and all markets clear.

$$G_g^1 + \cdots + G_g^I = G_g; \ g = 1, \ldots, G \quad \text{(product market clearance)} \quad (4.10)$$

$$R_{r1} + \cdots + R_{rG} = R_r; \ r = 1, \ldots, R \quad \text{(resource market clearance)} \quad (4.11)$$

Theorem 4.1 (Brown–Heal generalized): A productively efficient average-cost pricing equilibrium exists.

The general proof of this theorem is not dependent on the graphical presentation for the special case of just two goods for two-dimensional

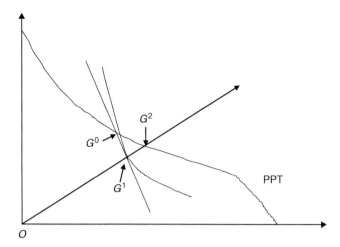

Figure 4.1   Illustrating the continuous transformation

illustration to improve understanding of the general proof. Due to the (possible) presence of increasing returns, the production possibility set need not be convex. However, with the traditional assumptions including divisibility of goods, the set remains homeomorphic (topologically equivalent) to a convex set. Similarly, its outer boundary, the production possibility frontier (PPF) also remains homeomorphic to a convex and compact set. Take any point G^0 on the PPF. (This is illustrated in Figure 4.1 but our argument is more general than the two-goods case of the diagrammatic illustration.) Take the set of resource prices consistent with cost-minimization production at this point and of product prices consistent with average-cost pricing at this point (G^0). Locate the consumption (or product demand) point G^1 of consumer utility maximization at this set of prices (and the corresponding budget constraints). In general, G^1 and G^0 are different points and G^1 need not be on the PPF. Construct a ray from the origin to pass through G^1. The intersection of this ray and the PPF is unique as the PPF is downward-sloping and the ray is upward-sloping. Call this intersection point G^2. This completes the description of the transformation of any point G^0 on the PPF to another point G^2 on the PPF. Under the traditional set of assumptions (including divisibility of goods and continuity of preferences), this transformation is continuous; any point arbitrarily close to G^0 will be transformed (mapped) into a point arbitrarily close to G^4. Since the PPF is homeomorphic to a convex and compact set and since the transformation (mapping) is continuous and maps the set into itself, from Brouwer's fixed point theorem, there exists a fixed point

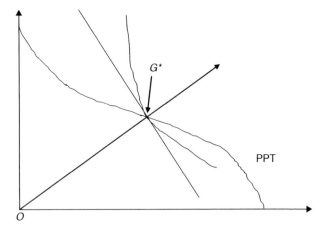

Figure 4.2   Productively efficient general equilibrium under average-cost pricing

that maps into itself. In other words, there exists a point G^* on the PPF where G^0 and G^2 are the same point, i.e. $G^* = G^0 = G^1$. (See Figure 4. 2.) By construction, this point G^* meets the requirements of profit maximization and cost minimization for the firms and utility maximization for the consumers with average-cost pricing for the firms. It is thus an AC-pricing general equilibrium and it is productively efficient as it is on the PPF. A general proof not confined to the two-dimensional illustration follows.

Proof: In our model, while the production possibility set for the economy need not be convex, the production possibility frontier (super-surface) is topologically equivalent to a compact and convex set. From Brouwer's fixed point theorem, any continuous mapping/transformation of a set that is homeomorphic (topologically equivalent) to a compact and convex set into itself possess a fixed point. Thus, any continuous mapping of the production possibility frontier has a fixed point that maps into itself.

Consider the following continuous mapping Φ of PPF into PPF: $(G_1, ..., G_g)^0 \to (W_1/W_R, ..., W_{R-1}/W_R)^0; (P_1, ..., P_G)^0 \to (G_1^d, ..., G_g^d)^1 \to (G_1, ..., G_g)^2$, where

(i) $(G_1, ..., G_g)^0$ is an arbitrary point on the PPF.

(ii) $(W_1/W_R, ..., W_{R-1}/W_R)^0$ is the set of relative resource prices determined by the common (to all firms using the same pair of resources) marginal rates of technical substitution as specified in (4.7) at the point $G^g(R_{1g}, ..., R_{Rg}) = G^{0.}_g$, $g = 1, ..., G$, i.e. the same point as $(G_1, ..., G_g)^0$.

(iii) $(P_1, ..., P_G)^0$ is the set of product prices determined in accordance to the average cost of producing each good g, i.e. $P^0_g = C^g(W_1, ..., W_R, G_g)/G_g$; $g = 1, ..., G$, at the given production levels given by $(G_1, ..., G_g)^0$.

(iv) $(G^d_1, ..., G^d_g)^1$ is the market demand for the various goods, i.e. $G^d_g = G^1_g + ..., G^I_g$; $g = 1, ..., G$, where each G^i_g is the individual utility-maximization quantity of g good demanded by individual i at the set of product prices $(P_1, ..., P_G)^0$ and resource prices $(W_1/W_R, ..., W_{R-1}/W_R)^0$.

(v) $(G_1, ..., G_g)^2$ is the intersection of the ray from the origin through the point $(G^d_1, ..., G^d_g)^1$ and the PPF.

Since the mapping Φ is continuous and the PPF is homeomorphic to a compact and convex set, the mapping has a fixed point which is denoted as $(G_1, ..., G_g)^*$. At this fixed point, $(G_1, ..., G_g)^0 = (G^d_1, ..., G^d_g)^1 = (G_1, ..., G_g)^2 = (G_1, ..., G_g)^*$. Hence, demand for goods $(G_1, ..., G_g)^1$ equals supply $(G_1, ..., G_g)^0$ at the product prices $(P_1, ..., P_G)^*$, the average costs of producing the various goods at $(G_1, ..., G_g)^0$. The equilibrium relative resource prices $(W_1/W_R, ..., W_{R-1}/W_R)^*$ is the common MRTS specified in (4.7). This production point gives equilibrium values of resource demand R_{rg}; $r = 1, ..., R$; $g = 1, ..., G$ satisfying (4.11). Finally, the individual demands for products G^i_g; $i = 1, ..., I$; $g = 1, ..., G$ total to satisfy (4.10). Since the production point is on the PPF, it is productively efficient. This completes the proof.

5
The Efficiency of Encouraging Goods with High Degrees of Increasing Returns

From the viewpoint of Pareto optimality, goods with increasing returns are under-produced relative to those without increasing returns; goods with higher degrees of increasing returns are under-produced relative to those with lower degrees. Ignoring administrative and indirect (such as rent-seeking) costs, subsidies on goods produced under conditions of (high degrees of) increasing returns financed by taxes on goods produced under non-increasing and lower increasing returns may increase efficiency. These results apply even though all goods (including those with increasing returns) are assumed to be produced at prices equaling the average costs of production. This is first shown for a general case in Section 5.1 and next for a specific case in Section 5.2. For the general case, two alternative methods are used, the first establishing a Pareto improvement and the second establishing positive net benefits using a cost-benefit analysis.

5.1 The general case

First, from an average-cost pricing equilibrium as established in the previous chapter, we have, as a condition for market equilibrium,

$$P_g = A_g \quad \text{for all good } g, \tag{5.1}$$

where P_g and A_g are respectively the (producer) price and average cost of good g.

For simplicity, as in the previous chapter, we abstract from the monopsonistic power of producers, i.e. we assume factor-price taking producers. (The absence of monopsonistic power is less unrealistic than that of perfect competition in the output markets.) This allows us to define the (local) degree of increasing returns to scale I_g (for any good g) as the percentage reduction in the average cost due to a one percentage increase in the output, or

$$I_g \equiv -\left(\frac{\partial A_g}{\partial G_g}\right)\frac{G_g}{A_g} \tag{5.2}$$

where G_g is the output level of good g. This definition of the degree of increasing returns describes a situation of constant/decreasing returns as one having a zero/negative degree of increasing returns, as intuitively agreeable. This is convenient as it allows us to compare two goods in terms of their degrees of increasing returns, covering all cases of increasing, constant, and decreasing returns. This definition may be applied either to increasing returns at the firm or industry level, depending on the interpretation of G_g. Since we are mainly concerned with firm-level increasing returns here, G_g is taken as the output level of firm g. (With increasing returns, equilibrium implies a downward-sloping demand curve. Hence it is more appropriate to regard each firm as producing a distinct good, making the distinction of the firm and the industry no longer relevant.)

Each consumer maximizes a utility function

$$U^i = U^i(G^i_1, G^i_2, \ldots, G^i_G); \quad i = 1, \ldots, I \tag{5.3}$$

subject to a budget constraint

$$\sum_{g=1}^{G} P_g G^i_g = 0, \tag{5.4}$$

where some of the gth 'goods' could be the negative amounts of (labour) services performed. (This notational convention differs from that of the previous chapter, but the essential substance does not differ.) The first-order conditions for an interior solution to this maximization problem are

$$\frac{U^i_g}{U^i_h} = \frac{P_g}{P_h}; \quad i = 1, \ldots, I; \quad g, h = 1, \ldots, G, \tag{5.5}$$

where $U^i_g \equiv \partial U^i / \partial G^i_g$ is the marginal utility of good g to individual i. Eq. 5.5 specifies the equality of (absolute) MRS (marginal rate of substitution) for any pair of goods with the price ratio. The second-order conditions are assumed satisfied; similarly for the following maximization problem.

We now turn to the conditions for Pareto optimality (or alternatively optimality in accordance to a Paretian social welfare function). Maximizing the utility of any individual given those of others and subject to the production possibility constraint

$$F(G_1, ..., G_G) = 0, \tag{5.6}$$

where $G_g = \Sigma_{i=1}^I G_g^i$ for each g, the first-order conditions are

$$\frac{U_g^i}{U_h^i} = \frac{F_g}{F_h} = \frac{M_g}{M_h}; \quad i = 1,..., I; \ g, h = 1, ..., G, \tag{5.7}$$

where U_g^i/U_h^i is the marginal rate of substitution (equalling the ratio of marginal utilities) and F_g/F_h is the marginal rate of transformation between g and h and the latter equals the ratio of the marginal costs of producing g and h, M_g/M_h. (The absence of external effects is assumed.)

From (5.1) and (5.5), we have, for a market equilibrium,

$$\frac{U_g^i}{U_h^i} = \frac{A_g}{A_h}; \quad i = 1,..., I; g, \ h = 1,..., G. \tag{5.8}$$

By definition, $A_g \equiv C_g/G_g$ where C_g is the total costs of producing good g. Thus, from (5.2) and from simple differentiation, we have, for all g,

$$I_g \equiv -\left(\frac{\partial A_g}{\partial G_g}\right)\frac{G_g}{A_g} = 1 - \frac{M_g}{A_g}, \tag{5.9}$$

where $M_g \equiv \partial C_g/\partial G_g$ is the marginal cost of producing good g.

From (5.9), we have at any point

$$I_g > I_h \quad \text{iff} \quad \frac{A_g}{A_h} > \frac{M_g}{M_h}. \tag{5.10}$$

Let us now start from any market equilibrium point P. From (5.8) and (5.10), we have for this point P,

$$\text{MRS}_{gh} > \frac{M_g}{M_h} \quad \text{iff } I_g > I_h. \tag{5.11}$$

At this point P, either the economy is on its transformation curve or on production possibility frontier (PPF) or it is inside it. If it is inside it, it is obvious that a Pareto improvement could be made by producing more of some or all goods, including good g. Thus, Theorem 5.1A obviously holds. Thus, let us take the case where the economy is on its PPF. (The existence of increasing returns does not rule out productive efficiency in the sense of producing at the frontier.) In the absence of external effects, the (absolute) slope of the production possibility frontier in the g/h plane (i.e. holding all goods other than g and h unchanged) equals M_g/M_h (with good g on the horizontal axis and good h on the vertical). Thus, from (5.11), if good g has a higher degree of increasing returns than good h, the (absolute) slope of the PPF at P is less steep than the (absolute) MRS_{gh} (slope of the indifference curve which is tangent to the common price line) for all individuals who consume both g and h. Thus, if good g has a higher degree of increasing returns than good h, the market-equilibrium MRS_{gh} is larger than the slope of PPF. Given that both g and h are goods (not bads), both the indifference curve and the PPF at P are downward sloping. Given the usual assumptions about preferences (including local non-satiation), a movement down the (downward-sloping) transformation curve involving a larger amount of good g and a smaller amount of good h must lead to a point of higher indifference curve/surface. We thus have

Theorem 5.1A: At an average-cost pricing market equilibrium, if the degree of increasing returns for good g is larger than that for good h, a point of higher efficiency (Pareto-superiority) could be reached by increasing the output of g and decreasing the output of h (holding the consumption/ production of other goods unchanged).

Note that this theorem is applicable between any two goods of different degrees of increasing returns, including two of both decreasing returns. Efficiency could be increased by increasing/decreasing the good of less/more decreasing returns. It is obvious that, for such two goods, it may be even more efficient to decrease production of both of them and increase production of another (set of) good(s) that has even higher degree of increasing returns than both these two goods, if it exists. The validity of Theorem 5.1A partly depends on the assumed absence of external effects. Obviously, if good g happens to have a large amount of external costs, this may outweigh the efficiency consideration based on increasing returns. The validity of Theorem 5.1A also depends partly on the abstraction away of possible second-best offsetting effects. Holding the consumption/production of other goods unchanged allows us to benefit from the divergence between the MRS and MRT of the relevant pair of goods. If important inefficiencies exist in other goods, the variation in the quantities of these goods as a response to the change in the relative quantities of goods g and h may cause indirect effects that may be reinforcing or offsetting to the direct effects. When we deal with situations in the real economy where it may not be possible to abstract away such second-best complications, it remains true that the efficiency gain of Theorem 5.1A may still be taken as applicable for the benchmark case. When the specific knowledge on how the second-best consideration affects the result is available, we may then combine them to assess the net result. In actual application, the worrisome factors are the likely inefficiencies of incorrect identification, rent-seeking activities, corruption, etc. Thus, unless the divergences involved are very large, a *laissez-faire* policy may still be optimal.

It is tempting but incorrect to make the following inference. Comparing the conditions for Pareto optimality (PO) specified in (5.7) and those for market equilibrium (ME) in (5.8), we have

$$\mathrm{MRS}_{gh}^{PO} > \mathrm{MRS}_{gh}^{ME} \quad \text{iff} \quad \frac{M_g}{M_h} > \frac{A_g}{A_h}. \tag{5.12}$$

From (5.12) and (5.10), it might then be concluded that

$$I_g > I_h \quad \text{iff } \mathrm{MRS}_{gh}^{ME} > \mathrm{MRS}_{gh}^{PO}. \tag{5.13}$$

This inference is incorrect since each of the various inequalities applies to the same point while *ME* and *PO* are at different points. As we move from a *ME* to a *PO* point, the values of goods other than g and h may be changed and this change may (though not necessarily so) affect the validity of (5.13). In particular, suppose there is another good k, which has even a higher degree of increasing returns than g (or some other efficiency reasons like external benefits, if not assumed absent, calling for its increased production), the movement from the original market equilibrium point P to the Pareto-optimal point Q may then involve a much increased output of good k. If k is a close Edgeworth-complement of g, the much higher value of good k may make MRS_{gh}^{PO} larger than MRS_{gh}^{ME} (all in absolute terms) and hence invalidating (5.13).

Next, a cost-benefit analysis is used to show that, ignoring the administrative, transitional, and indirect (e.g. rent-seeking) costs of making the change, the aggregate (over individuals) net benefits of increasing the output of a good (denoted H) with a higher degree of increasing returns made possible by reducing that (L) with a lower degree is positive. In our analysis where external effects and second-best complications (which may go either way) are absent/ignored, the aggregate net benefits of the above change by a marginal amount are measured by: the marginal value of good H times ΔG_H – the marginal costs of good H times ΔG_H – (the aggregate marginal value of good L times ΔG_L – the marginal costs of good L times $|\Delta G_L|$, i.e. the absolute value of the change in good L), or

$$NB = V_H\Delta G_H - M_H\Delta G_H - [V_L|\Delta G_L| - M_L|\Delta G_L|] \qquad (5.14)$$

where NB = aggregate net benefit of the above change, V = marginal value, M = marginal cost. Since the change has to be feasible, the marginal costs of good H times ΔG_H must equal the marginal costs of good L times $|\Delta G_L|$.

$$M_H\Delta G_H = M_L|\Delta G_L| \qquad (5.15)$$

Substitute (5.15) and the value of ΔG_H from (5.15) into (5.14), yielding

$$NB = \left[\frac{V_H M_L |\Delta GL|}{M_H}\right] - (V_L)|\Delta GL| \qquad (5.16)$$

With average-cost pricing and individual utility maximization, we have marginal value = price = average cost. Thus, replacing marginal value V by average cost A, (5.16) becomes

$$NB = \left(\frac{A_H}{M_H} - \frac{A_L}{M_L}\right)M_L |\Delta G_L| \qquad (5.17)$$

Since $M_L|\Delta G_L|$ is positive, the aggregate net benefits of the above change NB are positive if and only if $(A_H/M_H - A_L/M_L)$ is positive. From (5.9) above, a good H has a higher degree of increasing returns than another good L if and only if $(A_H/M_H - A_L/M_L)$. Thus, (5.17) is positive. We thus have

Theorem 5.1B: At an average-cost pricing market equilibrium, if the production/consumption of a good with a lower degree of increasing returns is decreased to allow for a corresponding increase in the production/ consumption of another good with a higher degree of increasing returns, holding the consumption/production of other goods unchanged, the aggregate net benefits of the change is positive.

From Theorems 5.1A and 5.1B, we may state the following

Corollary: A necessary condition for an average-cost pricing market equilibrium to be Pareto optimal is for every good to have the same degree of increasing returns.

However, as noted above, leisure may be regarded as a good that each individual may produce from labour times at the rate of one to one, i.e. with constant returns. Thus, in the presence of increasing returns in the production of some goods, an average-cost pricing market equilibrium cannot be Pareto-optimal, as at least leisure will be over-consumed in comparison to those goods with increasing returns, unless offset by other considerations such as environmental disruption not considered in the above analysis, as traditional.

5.2   A specific case illustrated

As this is just an illustrative specific case, let us opt for simplicity by considering the case of a Cobb–Douglas utility function with three goods (with good Z being leisure/labour) and simple production functions with no intermediate inputs. The representative (atomistic) individual maximizes

$$U = \ln x + \ln y + \ln z \tag{5.18}$$

subject to the budget constraint

$$(p - s)x + (q + t)y = 3 - z \tag{5.19}$$

where x and y are the amounts of the two goods consumed, p and q are the producer prices of these two goods, s and t are the per unit subsidy/tax on X and Y, leisure/labour Z is used as the *numeraire*, and the amount of time endowment is normalized to equal 3 to simplify calculation without affecting the substantive result. The maximization gives the following demand functions

$$x = \frac{1}{(p-s)}; \; y = \frac{1}{(q+t)}; \; z = 1. \tag{5.20}$$

On the supply side, let the production functions of the two goods be

$$x = z_x^2; \ y = z_y; \tag{5.21}$$

to represent the specific case where good X is subject to large increasing returns and Y to constant returns with respect to the amount of labour (only input) used. Average-cost pricing then ensures that the relevant supply functions are

$$x = \frac{1}{p^2}; \ q = 1. \tag{5.22}$$

The equation of supply and demand at each market gives us the equilibrium prices and quantities:

$$x = \frac{1}{(p-s)}; \ p = \frac{[1+(1-4s)^{1/2}]}{2}; \ q = 1; \ y = \frac{1}{(1+t)}. \tag{5.23}$$

The requirement of government budget balance necessitates

$$sx = ty. \tag{5.24}$$

Substituting x (after substituting out p) and y from (5.23) into (5.24), we have

$$t = \frac{2s}{[1+(1-4s)^{1/2} - 4s]}. \tag{5.25}$$

Substitute t from (5.25) into the expression for y in (5.23) and the resulting values for x and y, and also $z = 1$ (from Eq. 5.20) into (5.18), we have U only as a function of s. We may then examine how U varies with s and conclude accordingly. However, mathematically it is more convenient to get the same conclusions by the following alternative method.

Starting from a situation without any subsidy and tax (i.e. $s = t = 0$), we have $x = y = z = 1$, and $U = 0$. Then consider a situation of $s = 0.025$ and $t = 0.027046276$ (which satisfy the requirement of budget balance, as may be verified). We then have, $p = 0.97434165$, $x = 1.05336156$, $y = 0.97366596$, and $U = 0.0786735$ which is an increase from the previous case of no subsidy/tax. However, we could do better in finding out the optimal s and t that satisfy budget balance and maximize U. From (5.19) to (5.22), we may derive the feasible values of x and y as given by

$$y = 2 - x^{1/2}. \tag{5.26}$$

Substituting y from (5.26) and $z = 1$ into (5.18), we may express U as a function of x only.

$$U = \ln x + \ln(2 - x^{1/2}) \tag{5.27}$$

Maximizing this function with respect to x, we have the optimal value of x as $x = 1.77777\ldots$ and the corresponding value of y (from Eq. 5.26) as $y = 0.6666\ldots$. With $z = 1$, this gives the optimized value of U as approximately 0.17. We may then go back to ask for the values of s and t that will both meet the budget balance and achieve these values for x and y, obtaining,

$$s = 0.1875; \ t = 0.5 \tag{5.28}$$

as the optimal tax/subsidy. Of course, these high optimal values of tax/subsidy depend on the unrealistically high degree of increasing returns in the production of X which is not meant to be descriptive.

The above depends on the ability to identify which goods have higher degrees of increasing returns. In the absence of this knowledge or if all goods have the same degree of increasing returns, could taxes/subsidies be used to encourage more production to tap the increasing returns? If we rule out lump-sum taxes and taxes on leisure as impracticable and confine to the normal type of taxes/subsidies on consumption (or production) and income, and require the government to observe the balanced budget requirement, it is not difficult to show that no improvement is possible through taxes/subsidies. The intuitive explanation is that a subsidy on consumption (work) has to be financed by a tax on income (consumption) which exactly offsets the subsidy.

6
Division of Labour: Increasing Returns at the Economy Level

Increasing returns at the economy level through the division of labour is analyzed, focusing on the Yang–Ng framework of inframarginal analysis. The central trade-off is between the economies of specialization and the required higher transaction costs. The resulting higher role of entrepreneurship and importance of organizational (in contrast to allocational) efficiency of the network of division of labour are also discussed. Some welfare economic issues and some policy implications are outlined.

6.1 Introduction: Marginal versus inframarginal analysis

Economic (and in fact many non-economic) decisions may be classified into the marginal decisions regarding how much of a (or a number of) variable one should undertake (buy, sell, produce, invest, etc.) and the inframarginal decisions as to whether to undertake it at all and which one to undertake, e.g. whether to set up a business and in the production of which good? Whether to produce a good or input yourself or to buy it from the market? Whether to get a job and in what occupation? While the marginal decisions on the appropriate value of a variable is also important, it is often the inframarginal decisions of 'whether' and 'which' that are even more decisive in affecting one's success or failure and welfare. Think of your (or your parents') classmates in high school or university, their fortunes now probably depend much more on which degrees they did at the universities, on which lines of business or occupation they took up than on how many hours of study or work they allocate to the various activities.

While inframarginal decisions are very important, orthodox economic analysis after the neoclassical marginalism revolution concentrates on the marginal analysis of resource allocation, largely ignoring the problems of division of labour and specialization emphasized by classical economists. The economies of specialization make all-or-nothing choice sensible. A person who specializes in economics does not teach or does research in biology, physics or chemistry. (I violated this myself, spending, while writing my PhD thesis, two weeks on the theory of relativity, understanding it; two weeks on quantum physics, mystified by it; and, later, publishing a dozen papers in biology, maths, philosophy, and psychology; that is why I am not as good an economist! Ha! This violation may be explained by the preference for diversity on the consumption side and that research is both production and consumption, a complication not yet allowed in our formal analysis.) A farmer does not work in the factory; a factory worker does not grow rice. The values of many variables are zeros. The solution point is at a corner. To compare the desirability of such corner solutions requires something more than just marginal analysis; inframarginal analysis or the comparison of total costs and benefits across different corner solutions is required. When Marshall (1920) synthesized the contributions of neoclassical economics, the use of differential calculus had been introduced in economic analysis with great success. It is very useful in the marginal analysis of resource allocation which involves the comparisons of marginal adjustments. However, Marshall did not have access to such mathematical techniques as the Kuhn-Tucker conditions for handling corner solutions. Marshall avoided the problems created by corner solutions by adopting the dichotomy between pure consumers and pure producers. In the current textbook version, we have the circular flow diagram with the household or consumer sector in one box and the business or producer sector in another box. This dichotomy takes the pattern and degree of division of labour as given and ignores the inframarginal decisions regarding the whether and what business/occupation problems of individuals.

While inframarginal analysis of various decision problems have been done earlier (See Yang & S. Ng 1998 and Yang 2001, 2003 for surveys of these developments), the formal inframarginal analysis of division of labour in a general-equilibrium framework with applications to various economic problems of trade, growth, industrialization, urbanization, economic organizations, property rights, etc. is provided in Yang and Ng (1993). This analysis resurrects the spirit of the classical economics in a modern body of inframarginal analysis, and provides a new framework for the study of many economic problems with new insights. As *Journal of Economic Literature* reviewer Smythe (1994, pp. 691–2) states 'This is an ambitious…interesting and original book. Its motivation is sound, and its fundamental insights are compelling. ... a refreshing new approach to microeconomics, one that has the potential to address many issues that have long resisted formal treatments.'

It may be thought that we are already in a fully specialized economy with virtually everyone having only one job or selling only one product such that the analysis of specialization is no longer relevant. However, even in our era of high specialization, there is still much scope for increasing the degree of the division of labour. First, things done at home are still being increasingly replaced by those done through the market, e.g. take-away food and dining out, specialized carpet cleaning, and gardening. Second, further specialization can take place at the level of input usage by producers with the use of more specialized inputs and more roundabout methods of production. Third, with lower market transaction costs, specialization between firms may replace specialization within a firm. This is especially characteristic of the small- and medium-sized firms in Taiwan and Wenzhou (China), which may specialize in producing a certain input or a particular process, including the final assembly of a product. Thus, improvements in transaction efficiency (expected to accelerate with the development of e-commerce made possible by the internet) could lead to a much higher degree of division of labour and provide benefits through the economies of specialization. This benefit is better analysed by inframarginal analysis.

6.2 Basic inframarginal analysis of division of labour

The essence of the Yang–Ng framework is the trade-off between economies of specialization made possible by the division of labour and the transaction costs of trade necessitated by specialization. If transaction efficiency is low, the economies of specialization are outweighed by transaction costs, so that autarky or a low level of division of labour is efficient and will be chosen. If transaction efficiency is improved, the efficient level of division of labour and the related size of market network will increase.

Figure 6.1 (from Yang & Ng 1993) gives an intuitive illustration of the evolution of the network of division of labour (a type of comparative statics of general equilibrium) where the number of goods and the population are assumed to be four in a symmetric version of the model. The lines in Figure 6.1 denote goods flow. The small arrows indicate the directions of goods flow. The numbers beside the lines signify the goods involved. A circle with number *i* denotes a person selling good *i*. Panel (a) denotes autarky where each person self-provides four goods,

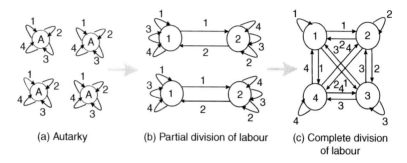

(a) Autarky   (b) Partial division of labour   (c) Complete division
                                                              of labour

Figure 6.1   Evolution of division of labour

due to extremely low transaction efficiency. Panel (b) denotes partial specialization where each person sells one good, buys one good, trades two goods, and self-provides three goods, as an improvement in transaction efficiency generates a partial division of labour. Panel (c) denotes complete specialization where each person sells and self-provides one good, buys three goods, and trades four goods, due to high transaction efficiency and/or large economies of specialization.

A simple mathematical model in the Yang–Ng framework capturing the evolution of division of labour illustrated above is presented in Appendix 6A. A comprehensive textbook covering most major issues of economics using the new framework is Yang (2001). Economies of specialization has been analysed using modern economic tools, in particular by Ethier (1979, 1982; see Francois & Nelson 2002 for a geometrical illustration) by allowing productivity to increase with the number of intermediate goods used. In contrast, Yang and Ng allows for economies of specialization at the individual level and start right from the very basic of individual choices of which goods to produce, trade, etc.

Sun, Yang, and Zhou (2004) provide a theoretical underpinning to the new framework by establishing the equilibrium existence theorem, the first and second welfare theorems, and the core equivalence for a family of general-equilibrium models in the new framework with (possibly) increasing returns and transaction costs. The crux of this demonstration is the use of a model of an uncountable number of individuals. The fact that the real world cannot have even a countably infinite number of individuals means that the results do not apply 100% to the real economy. However, the fact that the equilibrium exists in this model of an uncountable number of individuals suggests that, in the real world of billions of individuals, the approximation to equilibrium may be close, at least in the absence of other factors that may prevent the equilibrium from prevailing.

6.3   Pareto optimality of general equilibrium in the new framework – the higher role of entrepreneurship

In Yang and Ng (1993) where individuals are taken as ex-ante identical, and the general-equilibrium economic structure is defined as one that maximizes the equalized (to ensure equilibrium among identical individuals) utility level, the general equilibrium is Pareto optimal by definition. However, this concept of general equilibrium is somewhat narrow and does not include a situation where the economy is in equilibrium in the sense of not changing and the equilibrium applies to the whole economy (hence general). This narrow versus wider concepts of general equilibrium also applies to the concept of general equilibrium in the traditional (perfect competition) framework.

To see the point, consider Arrow's (1951, p. 528) example of the non-existence of general equilibrium. (The example is more popularly available in Chipman 1965, as reprinted in Townsend 1971/1980.) The economy consists only of two farmers and two goods, meat and vegetables.

> Suppose Farmer Jones has some vegetables which he has grown and wishes to market. Assume that if the price of vegetables is high enough in relation to meat, he will sell some of them and buy meat with the proceeds, but below a certain price he will just consume his own vegetables; finally, if vegetables are free, he will want to consume an indefinitely large quantity of them. On the other hand, suppose Farmer Brown has a small and insufficient supply of meat, but a bumper crop of vegetables, more than he could possibly want for himself. (Chipman 1965, as reprinted in Townsend 1971/1980, pp. 352 and 446)

Then, at any positive price of vegetables relative to meat, there is a negative excess demand for vegetables (as both farmers want to sell vegetables in exchange for meat). At a zero price of vegetables, excess demand for vegetables is infinite. Hence, at no price is the excess demand for vegetables equal to zero. There is no general equilibrium in this sense. However, this does not mean that 'the price of vegetables will oscillate indefinitely' (Chipman as reprinted in Townsend 1980, p. 448). Rather, there will simply be no transaction. The economy will be at equilibrium with each farmer consuming his own endowment.

Since this applies to all markets in the economy, this should be accepted as a 'general equilibrium' in the wider sense. The narrower concept of equilibrium in terms of a set of prices that clears all markets is a Walrasian equilibrium. But not all general equilibria, even if confined to be perfectly competitive, need be Walrasian. Thus, we may have a million identical farmers Jones and a million identical farmers Brown, with each having no appreciable effect on prices. There still does not exist a price at which the excess demand for vegetables is zero. However, the economy will still be at equilibrium with no transaction, with each farmer consuming his own endowment. Thus, we have a non-Walrasian general competitive equilibrium. However, many general-equilibrium theorists seem too much 'captured' by their abstract theories to see this simple real-world possibility. Hence, in the absence of a Walrasian equilibrium set of prices, they think that this must imply that the price will oscillate. The no-transaction equilibrium does not enter the realm of possibility in their minds at all.

Now consider the Yang–Ng framework. Take the simplest case of just two identical individuals J and K and two goods, x and y. If the costs of transaction are very high, it is efficient for each individual to self-produce and consume both goods. We have an autarkic equilibrium. Now suppose that the transaction efficiency has improved to a level making it efficient for each individual to specialize in the production of one good, selling part of the product in exchange for another good from the other individual. With the transaction efficiency and/or the degree of economies of specialization being high enough, specialization is more efficient than autarky. A general equilibrium with the two individuals each specializing in the production of one good exists and is Pareto optimal. However, the existence of equilibrium does not necessarily mean that it will be attained in the real economy. Some coordination is needed to move from the original autarky to the specialization equilibrium. In this simple case of two individuals, the required coordination is very simple. One of the individual could just say to the other, 'Why don't you specialize in producing y and I in x and then we could exchange the goods?' If they do not engage in hard bargaining and agree on the terms of exchange, the new specialization equilibrium will be achieved. However, some coordination is needed. Moreover, this required coordination is over and above those provided by the price system. To see this, assume the existence of a Walrasian auctioneer who announces the most efficient and fair price of one between x and y. Let each individual (or each of the two million individuals) take the price as given and maximize accordingly. Each will decide to specialize in the production of one good only and then try to exchange for another good at this price of one. However, in the complete absence of extra-price coordination, both individuals may produce x with no one producing y. If y is essential for life, we may reach a new equilibrium with both individuals dead!

The fact that some extra-price coordination may be needed does not mean that it is best done by a central planning board. Consider the more general case of the introduction of a new good in a more realistic setting. When the transaction efficiency, population size, technology, etc. have increased to a level making the marketing of a new good efficient, its introduction into the market need not be an instant success, as people have to learn of the new good and perhaps make adjustments accordingly. For example, before the availability of take-away food, eating out was quite expensive and most people cooked their own dinners and packed their own lunches. Then, the introduction of readily available take-away food reduced significantly the costs of eating out. People gradually adjusted to this by reducing home cooking and have more leisure time and/or spend more time working on their specialized activities. However, most new goods need some time for consumers to learn and adjust to them before they become profitable. Thus, even the most successful entrepreneurs may have to sustain substantial initial losses. (This makes wealth a factor for people to become entrepreneurs; cf. the model of entrepreneur–rentier choice of Gabszewicz & Laussel 2007.) To be able to sustain such initial losses is one of the requirements of entrepreneurial success. This also suggests the importance of the existence of big firms and the role of financial institutions in transferring resources from savings into investment. If we compare a centrally planned economy and a free-enterprise market economy in terms of the successful introduction of suitable new goods, the superiority of the latter is even more decisive than in the allocation of resources between existing set of goods. Thus, the need for coordination is largely filled in a market economy by the function of entrepreneurial activities. (On the importance of entrepreneurs and entry in the transitional economies, see McMillan & Woodruff 2002.)

The need for entrepreneurial activities exists even in the traditional framework, as the use of a new lower-cost method of production and the introduction of new goods are by definition the function of entrepreneurship. However, the requirement of entrepreneurship is rather meagre in the traditional framework of perfect competition with no increasing returns. When the technology/demand/transaction conditions have improved to a level such that the demand for and supply of a new good result in the intersection of the downward-sloping demand curve and upward-sloping supply curve at a positive quantity, the introduction of that new good will prove to be profitable. Moreover, whoever first introduces it will reap supernormal profits as the demand price is initially higher than the supply price. In contrast, in the framework of division of labour and increasing returns, someone shifting to the production of a newly marketed good may not even break even until a sufficient number of other individuals stop home-producing that good and buy from him/her instead. There is more need to sustain an initial period of losses.

The need for the entrepreneurial function and perhaps other ways to solve the coordination problem is present even before we consider the indirect network externality discussed in the next section that raises further issues of welfare economics which are only beginning to be addressed. There is much further scope for welfare economic analysis in the new framework. (The problem of coordination in increasing the degree of division of labour is illustrated in a simple model in Appendix 6B. In particular, it is also shown that, in the absence of coordination, a much higher level of transaction efficiency may be needed to achieve a higher degree of division of labour.)

6.4   Some welfare economic issues of division of labour

There are many other welfare economic issues in the new framework. Here, only two examples are considered. A non-mathematical outline is given in this section. Detailed developments of the arguments are presented respectively in Chapters 8 and 10.

6.4.1   Infrastructure improvements and indirect network externalities

Governments have been very active in engaging and in encouraging the improvements in transaction efficiency, including the provision of legal, social, and economic infrastructures. (For the effects of infrastructure on productivity, see World Bank 1994 for a survey; see also Boserup 1981 and Chandler 1990 on the historical perspective and the importance of population size. The empirical evidence of Duggal et al. 2007 shows the presence of increasing returns in public and private infrastructure, with information technology being the largest contributing component to growth during the expansion of the 1990s in the US.) Even free-market economists including Adam Smith find 'the erection and maintenance of the public works which facilitate the commerce of any country, such as good roads, bridges, navigable canals, harbours' desirable and indeed find this as 'evident without any proof' (Smith 1776/1976, II, p. 245). Perhaps this apparently self-evident nature made economists pay little attention to the role of infrastructure until the past two decades. (See Aschauer 1989; Bougheas et al. 2000; Gramlich 1994; La Ferrara 2001).

The need for government involvement may be explained by the public goods nature of infrastructure. This may well be the major part of the explanation for many cases. However, if this is the only reason, there is little reason for encouragement if the items involved are excludable and can be priced as applicable in many cases including instruments for communication such as telephones. Moreover, according to the traditional analysis, even for non-excludable items, there should be no reason for providing them beyond the levels indicated by the equation of (aggregate) marginal benefits and marginal costs, evaluated at the existing structure of economic organizations or the degree of specialization of the whole economy (which is **not** taken as a variable in the traditional analysis). If we take the degree of specialization as endogenous, the provision of infrastructures that decreases transaction costs may produce some indirect network externality. This should be distinguished from the possible network externality of the infrastructure itself, which is well known. For example, the usefulness of a telephone, fax machine, email facility increases as more people are on the phone, etc. This is the direct network externality, which we shall abstract away. Rather, we refer to the following more indirect effects.

The improvement in transaction (including communication and transportation) efficiency may generate benefits in excess of the direct private benefits through the promotion of higher degree of specialization. If transaction efficiency is very low (i.e. transaction costs are very high), it may be optimal for everyone to be in autarky, self-producing all goods needed. As transaction efficiency improves, it may become optimal to buy some goods from others and sell the good one specializes in, but in general some goods are still self-produced and self-consumed (which exist even in modern times, including home cooking, cleaning, gardening, and child minding). As transaction efficiency improves, the set of goods bought from others increases. Thus, the benefits of an improvement in transaction efficiency is not only directly in reducing the costs of transaction, but also indirectly in promoting the degree of division of labour and the consequent tapping of the economies of specialization. Even assuming that the costs of exclusion is negligible and that there is no free-rider problem, a private producer of an improvement in infrastructure that reduces transaction costs may only be able to capture the direct benefits of lowering transaction costs, but not be able to capture the indirect benefits of promoting more specialization (even in the absence of individual differences giving rise to different consumer surpluses). People will just assess the benefits of lower transaction costs given the existing level of specialization of the economy. Not only that the benefits through a higher degree of specialization will occur only in the future contingent on the appearance of new marketable goods, but also this development is taken as not affected by the improvement in the transaction efficiency of an individual himself/herself. It is thus rational even under full knowledge to ignore the indirect benefit of higher transaction efficiency on the level of specialization.

In other words, there are two public-good problems. The improvement in infrastructure to raise transaction efficiency may itself be a public good. However, even if this public-good problem can be overcome through excludability, there is another public-good problem at the level of the increase in the level of specialization that the higher transaction efficiency contributes to. Even with perfect foresight, each individual does not take into account the benefits of a higher level of specialization because that level is determined by the general level of transaction efficiency prevailing in the whole economy, not appreciably affected by that of any single individual. Even if I correctly foresee that the widespread use of a new communication system will promote specialization and make a number of new products available in the market, I will not count the benefits of the availability of the new products in assessing the usefulness of the new communication system to me, as the new products will be available even if I do not use the new communication system but if most others do. This second level of publicness problem is quite impossible to solve through exclusion, as the producers of the new set of products are typically different from the producer of the infrastructure. Thus, the indirect externality of infrastructure may then make the public provision or encouragement desirable. The Yang–Ng framework of inframarginal analysis is used in Ng and Ng (2007) to analyse the case for encouraging improvement in transaction efficiency over and above its direct benefits.[1] Our results are consistent with the empirical evidence that public infrastructure capital has positive long-run effects on output and that 'the short-run rates of return are rather low while the long-run rates of return tend to be quite high' (Demetriades & Mamuneas 2000, p. 689). It takes time for the degree of specialization to develop.

In the demonstration, we also discovered that the lumpiness in investments to improve transaction efficiency also play a role in creating a divergence between social and private benefits. For non-lumpy invest-ments, the divergence is negligible. This may also partly explain why big projects may be regarded as a ground for encouragement. Of course, like all other reasonable justification, this one may also be misused to justify really inefficient projects.

6.4.2 Do the economies of specialization justify the work ethics?

Buchanan (1991, 1994) proposes an interesting hypothesis explaining the prevalence of an ethic encouraging more work. The economies of specialization mean that more division of labour may increase product-ivity. If everyone works more, this increases the extent of the market which enables higher degree of division of labour and hence higher productivity. Individual choice between leisure and work thus results in a sub-optimal level of work. One way to counteract this is to main-tain a work ethic. Economists have not paid much attention to this and similar problems partly, if not mainly, because of the preoccupation with the sectoral resource allocation problem of the neoclassical eco-nomics instead of the division-of-labour problem of the classical eco-nomics. However, even within the traditional framework, the problem of increasing returns has not been completely ignored. A well-known analysis is the Dixit–Stiglitz (1977) model of monopolistic competition. (The model was later adapted by Ethier 1979, 1982 to analyse the num-ber of intermediate goods.) Within the monopolistic competition sector, each firm produces a product with decreasing average costs (a positive fixed cost plus a constant marginal cost). The rest of the economy is lumped into a composite good. To analyse the problem of work ethics, we may regard this composite good as leisure. There is nothing in the model to preclude such an interpretation. We may then directly apply the Dixit–Stiglitz result to assess the validity of Buchanan's hypothesis within such a model. Dixit and Stiglitz compare the market equilibrium (with free entry) with both the case of constrained optimum (where each firm must not make a positive loss) and that of unconstrained optimum (where lumpsum subsidies to firms are allowed). Due to the difficulties of lumpsum subsidies in the real world and to Buchanan's emphasis on realistic market economies, the case of constrained opti-mum is the more relevant one. Dixit and Stiglitz's 'results undermine the validity of the folklore of excess capacity, from the point of view of the unconstrained optimum as well as the constrained one. ...with a constant intra-sector elasticity of substitution, the market equilibrium coincides with the constrained optimum. ...It is not possible to have a general result concerning the relative magnitudes of [leisure]' (Dixit & Stiglitz 1977, pp. 301–2). In other words, even if the unconstrained optimum is feasible, it may involve more or less leisure than the cases of the free-market equilibrium and constrained optimum. This is in contrast to Buchanan's hypothesis on the presumption of over-consumption of leisure. However, this need not be a fatal blow to Buchanan who has in mind not so much the traditional economies of scale but the classical economies of specialization from the division of labour which is better modelled by the Yang–Ng framework. In fact, Buchanan and Yoon (1994a) provide a model with the result of over-consumption of leisure. The higher productivity of a larger market size comes from a larger supportable number of intermediate goods, which is assumed to increase productivity (the Ethier assumption). Ng and Ng (2003) show the possibility in the Yang–Ng framework without using the Ethier mechanism.[2] They provide some support to the Buchanan thesis by showing that the higher the degree of economies of specialization, the larger is the beneficial effect of a higher work ethics on the trading partner. Buchanan's thesis probably has more relevance in ancient times when the work ethics originated but is less significant in the current world of global trade where the billions of individuals involved is largely sufficient to sustain specialization without artificial encouragement of additional work effort. (There are some exceptions to this, including industries with huge economies of scale such as the production of Concordes and the production of knowledge which is a global public good. However, the latter consideration favours more a larger population than more work effort; see Ng 1986b, 2002.) On the contrary, the competition for relative standing, the materialistic bias caused by our accumulation instinct and advertising, and the environmental disruption of material production and consumption suggest that the discouragement of long working week may be more conducive to welfare. (This is discussed in Chapter 10.)

6.5   Some implications

As mentioned above, the new framework has been used to analyse many economic issues, but the welfare implications are only beginning to be discussed. There is much scope for further research. One implication thrown into focus by the new framework is the need to take account of the indirect effects on the structure of economic organization or the network of division of labour. This is involved in the discussion of both issues of infrastructure investment and work ethics above but certainly not confined to them only. Rather, any changes that affect the organizational structure of the economy may have indirect effects which may be ignored if we only have the traditional framework as our model of the economy. The new framework helps not only to explain the trade-off between economies of specialization and transaction costs, but also to focus on the indirect effects of organizational efficiency. The new framework may also make us view certain issues of the real world differently. A bigger role for entrepreneurs has already been noted above (Section 6.3). Another point related to international trade is outlined below.

According to the traditional Ricardian theory of comparative advantage, international trade and globalization may make some groups in some countries worse off, though the (monetary) losses are smaller than the gains of others. For example, the exportation of high-tech and capital-intensive goods from US to China and the importation of labour-intensive goods from China into the US may lower the US prices of labour-intensive goods and hence the wages of unskilled labour in US. Though the gains to other groups (consumers of labour-intensive goods, producers of capital-intensive goods) more than offset the losses at least in monetary terms, unskilled workers in US may not be happy. The argument in Ng (1979, appendix 9A and 1984) for treating a dollar as a dollar in specific issues still suggests that having free trade to maximize the efficiency gains combined with general transfer to help the lower income groups will still achieve a quasi-Pareto improvement. However, people may not see the point or may be worried about the lack of corresponding transfer. This is probably a single most important cause of the movement against globalization. Seen from the US perspective, the opposition to trade may appear to have some moral ground as the unskilled workers are typically of lower incomes. However, the unskilled workers in China are made better off by trade. Since they are much poorer than the unskilled workers in US, seen from the world perspective equality is promoted by trade. (This focuses on the effects of trade as such, ignoring the possible effects of globalization in limiting the pursuit of distributional equality in each country discussed towards the end of chapter 11 in Ng 2004.) However, the point here is rather that, in contrast to the conflict of interest of different groups according to the Ricardian theory of trade, according to the analysis of Adam Smith and Xiaokai Yang, international trade and globalization allows division of labour and specialization to reach higher levels, making all people in all countries better off. If economists can emphasize this Smith–Yang analysis and explain to the public, the noise against globalization may become much smaller (Buchanan & Yoon 2002).

Exogenous comparative advantage, economies of scale at the firm level, and economies of specialization at the economy level are all present in the real world. (Not to mention increasing returns at the world level on which see Ethier 1979; Chandra et al. 2002.) Thus, the different types of analysis are all important. However, traditional trade theory emphasizes too much constant returns and largely ignores the economies of specialization. (On the significance of increasing returns at the firm level and imperfect competition for international trade, see Helpman & Krugman 1985.) This bias should be corrected. Which type of gain from trade is more important in the real world depends on the actual situation. During a seminar presented by Buchanan at Monash University in March 2002, Yang said, according to the Ricardian theory, trade should be mainly between the advanced countries and the developing countries as they have different factor endowments. However, international trade is mainly between the advanced countries themselves with similar technical and endowment conditions. This shows that the gain from specialization must be more important. Buchanan agreed. I think that this provides a *prima facie* case but further studies are needed, as the amount of trade and the gain from trade need not have a constant proportion. This is particularly so since, according to the Ricardian theory, trade between countries of very different factor endowments should provide larger gains.

Some wider conceptual implications of the presence of increasing returns may also be briefly stated. Obviously, if a firm is facing a downward-sloping demand curve for its product, its profit will be increased by any rightward shift in the demand curve at the current (profit-maximizing) price. An increase in aggregate demand in the whole economy may also increase the profits of most firms, if the increase in aggregate output does not push up the costs of most firms significantly, as may well be true in the presence of excess capacity and unemployed resources. (This is true either in the short or long run, defined by the given/variable number of firms; see Section 3.1 and Ng 1986a for details.) With full employment, could welfare be improved by increasing aggregate demand through a nominal increase (such as increasing the money supply or an increase in the willingness to spend), an increase in work effort, or an increase in population? First consider this question in the absence of real external effects (like pollution and conspicuous consumption), imperfect knowledge, and imperfect rationality. With full employment, an increase in nominal aggregate demand is unlikely to be either profit or welfare improving as the costs of firms will likely be increased significantly at higher output levels. This improvement is however not impossible if the response of costs to aggregate output is not large and offset by the economies of larger output levels, including the higher degree of division of labour and the higher economies from knowledge improvements. (An increase in the price elasticity of demand for products of firms, including those caused by more intense competition due to the entry of new firms, may also help to make the improvement possible; see Ng 1986a, chapter 4). Just as the presence of increasing returns at the firm and industry level may make particular firms/industries under-expanded, the presence of increasing returns at the economy level may make the whole economy under-expanded. If this situation does not apply for an increase in nominal aggregate demand, it may still apply for an increase in real aggregate demand through either a population increase (immigration or birth) or a higher work effort (Section 6.4 and Chapter 10 of this book). However, while we are likely to benefit from the increasing returns related to higher specialization or to the lower average costs of providing infrastructure and obtaining new knowledge, we may suffer from the increasing costs of higher environmental disruption. If we also take account of the relative-income effects and the materialistic bias (Ng 2003), it becomes more likely that the discouragement instead of encouragement of work effort may be desirable.

Regarding population size, there is an additional complication. Even if an increase in population will decrease income per capita or even welfare per capita (average welfare), it is not clear that it is a bad thing. The question whether average welfare or total welfare (average welfare times the number of population) should be maximized has been debated by economists and philosophers for a long time without a conclusive answer. My position is that, at the level of ideal morality, total welfare (abstracting away animal welfare) should be maximized but people now may be partial towards their own welfare (Ng 1989).[3]

When economists ignore the real world and focus on the perfectly competitive equilibrium under simplified assumptions, the picture seems so consistent, coherent, and beautiful. Such a simplified general-equilibrium analysis no doubt captures some essential elements of the real economy and represents an important achievement in economic analysis. However, the simple beautiful picture is also far removed from the real world in many important aspects. Just the recognition of increasing returns already causes havoc to many of the established wisdoms. Competition cannot be perfect; equilibrium may not exist and may not be Pareto optimal even if it exists, and so on. The real economy is more likely in a process close to the complicated interactions of millions of individuals and collective profit and utility-seeking activities that are largely efficient (ignoring certain issues like environmental disruption) but never perfectly so. This is much ensured by free exchanges (including employment), free enterprise (including entry/exit), and the rapid advance and utilization of knowledge in consumption and production. Such a complicated process is very difficult to model precisely. The traditional simple general-equilibrium analysis captures some important elements of it, the Austrian school (see, e.g., Kirzner 1997; Vaughn 1994) emphasizes different important aspects (including adjustments out of equilibrium and the importance of entrepreneurial discovery of previously unthought-of knowledge) of it, the information economics (see Stiglitz 2002) focuses on other complications (including informational asymmetry), and the Yang–Ng framework captures the classical emphasis on the division of labour, not to mention such more radical departures from rational economic behaviour examined by experimental and behavioural economists and others, as well as studies on the importance of institutional, cultural, and historical factors. While a synthesis may be desirable, it could be very difficult to achieve in a formal analysis. Nevertheless, at least we need to have some overall balanced view, if not a complicated mathematical model.

Appendix 6A: A simple model of the Yang–Ng framework of division of labour[4]

It is assumed that the economy consists of M ex-ante identical consumer-producers and m consumer goods. Denoting the self-provided amount of good i as x_i, the amount purchased from the market of good i as x_i^d, the amount of good i consumed is $x_i + k\,x_i^d$, where $k x_i^d$ is the amount an individual obtains when he/she purchases x_i^d, $1 - k$ being the transaction cost coefficient and k the transaction efficiency coefficient.

A Cobb–Douglas utility function is adopted to reflect the preference for diverse consumption.

$$u = \prod_{i=1}^{m} (x_i + k x_i^d) \tag{6A1}$$

Each consumer-producer also has a system of production functions

$$x_i + x_i^s = l_i^a \quad i = 1, \dots, m; \quad a > 1 \tag{6A2}$$

where x_i^s is the amount of good i sold to the market and $x_i + x_i^s$ is the amount of good i produced and l_i the amount of labour used in producing good i. The assumption that $a > 1$ (Note that this is a, not alpha.)

captures the economies of specialization, making the labour productivity in the production of each good increase with the individual's level of specialization in its production, measured by the labour time used. Apart from the per unit transaction cost $1 - k$, a fixed cost (measured by labour time) for the purchase of each good c is also assumed. With $n - 1$ goods purchased from the market, the endowment constraint of an individual is given by

$$c(n-1) + \sum_{i=1}^{m} l_i = 1; \quad 0 \le li, \quad c(n-1) \le 1 \tag{6A3}$$

where the total amount of labour time has been normalized to unity. The budget constraint of the individual is given by

$$p_i x_i^s = \sum_{r \in R} p_r x_r^d \tag{6A4}$$

where p_i is the price of good i, R is a set of all goods purchased. In (6A4), only one good is supplied to the market by an individual since, from $a > 1$, it can be shown that an individual sells only one good at most (see Lemma 2.1 in Yang and Ng 1993). Each individual (effectively) takes the market prices as given either because the population is large relative to the number of goods and thus the number of individuals producing each good i, M_i, is large and/or due to the coincidence with the Walrasian regime in the multilateral bargaining game of the Yang–Ng model (1993, chapter 3). (However, see Section 6.3 in the text on some problems of coordination.)

Each individual is then allowed to maximize utility by allotting his/her fixed amount of time to the production and purchase of different goods, balancing the trade-off between economies of specialization ($a > 1$) on the one hand and the costs of market transaction (c, $1-k > 0$) on the other. Each individual is allowed not only to choose the quantities of the various goods consumed but also to choose what goods to self-provide and sell to the market. If an individual buys a good, he/she does not sell it and vice versa.

Next, market equilibrium in terms of the equality of the amount of each good supplied and demanded in the market is then imposed.

$$M_i x_i^s = \sum_{r \in R} M_r x_{ri}^d \tag{6A5}$$

where M_i is the number of individuals selling good i, x_{ri} is the amount of traded good i purchased by individuals selling good r, it can then be shown that (proposition 5.1 of Yang and Ng) if the transaction efficiency and/or the degree of economies of specialization are very low, the equilibrium is autarky. Every individual self-provides all goods. As the transaction efficiency improves (i.e. k increases and/or c decreases), each individual sells a good to the market and buys some other goods in exchange. (See Figure 6.1 in the text.) The number of goods purchased from the market, division of labour, and income all increase with transaction efficiency. When each person's number of goods purchased from the market is small, trade occurs within a small local community. When the number of goods purchased from the market becomes larger and larger due to the increase in transaction efficiency and endogenous increase in comparative advantage through learning by doing (Yang & Borland 1991; Yang & Ng 1993, chapter 7), trade expands to unify the national market and then to involve international trade (which is discussed in Chapter 11).

The simple analysis has been extended to cover many more complicated issues like the endogenous choice of the number of goods, the use of intermediate inputs, or more roundabout methods of production, the emergence of middlemen, firms, urbanization, industrialization, money, investment, etc; see Yang and Ng (1993), Yang (2001, 2003), Cheng and Yang (2004).

Appendix 6B: Division of labour, coordination, and entrepreneurship[5]

In this appendix, the problem of coordination in increasing the degree of division of labour is illustrated in a simple model. It is also shown that, in the absence of coordination, a much higher level of transaction efficiency may also lead to a higher degree of division of labour. However, the level of transaction efficiency needed to achieve this is higher than that with coordination.

Using a model similar to that in Chapter 8, we have in equilibrium (see Chapter 8 for derivation)

$$u = A^m n^{(a-1)n} k^{n-1} \tag{6B1}$$

where $A \equiv \{[1 - c(n - 1)]/m\}^a$, m = number of all goods, n = number of goods traded, a = degree of economies of specialization, k = coefficient of transaction efficiency ($1 - k$ is the transaction costs of trade).

From (6B1), it seems that the maximization of u with respect to n yields the optimal number of goods purchased. The optimal value n^* is the integer in the neighbourhood of n^{**} that is given by the first-order condition $\partial u/\partial n = 0$. (It is assumed that c is of sufficient high value to ensure the satisfaction of the second-order condition.) This is in fact the case when everyone in the economy has adjusted to the given set of parametric values (particularly k, c, and a) with no further opportunity for improvement. However, when a parameter just changes its value, the desired adjustment of an individual is subject to the market opportunity at the time. For example, as the transaction efficiency coefficient k increases, each individual may wish to increase the number of goods purchased from others. However, this desire may not be realized before the additional marketable goods are supplied to the market. This problem is especially serious in a realistic model where goods are not symmetrical. Then, goods (that would have been purchased) may not be supplied in the market soon after an increase in transaction efficiency but before the organizational structure of the whole economy adjusts to the new situation. For example, with higher transaction efficiency, people may want to buy take-away meals and spend less time doing home cooking (a good in the set J) but may not be able to do so before some take-away meals are sold in the market. However, in time, some entrepreneurs will see the opportunity. Here we consider a simplified case with only one individual being entrepreneurial. All other individuals still use the level of division of labour (sets of goods self-provided, bought, etc.) consistent with the original level of transaction efficiency.

Initially, at $k = 0.9$, (with $m = 50$, $a = 1.215$, $c = 0.0092$ throughout), optimal $n = 44$. Now let k increase to a higher value (e.g. 0.94) such that a larger n is optimal. But suppose that no one specializes in the production of the new (45th) good for sale. Everyone still adopts the level of division of labour with only 44 marketable goods ($n = 44$), except one entrepreneurial person. For simplicity, suppose she also keeps her former production, sale, purchase, and consumption of the 44 goods unchanged but just 'partially' specializes in the production of the 45th good (formerly in the set J of everyone) and sell part of it at a price P (using the 46th good that she buys in exchange as the numeraire) to $N (= n - 1)$ other individuals that she already traded with. She also continue to produce goods 47–50 for own consumption. ('Specialization' in the production of one of the 44 goods and partially 'specializing' in this additional 45th good cannot be a final optimal situation. However, as we just want to show the tendency to deviate from the former equilibrium of $n = 44$, we are examining the disequilibrium adjustments. This is similar to the fact that we may use the existence of coalition B to block an allocation A to show that A is not in the core, even if the resulting allocation of coalition B itself is also not in the core.)

Each of the trading partner of this entrepreneur maintains his production, sale and purchase corresponding to $n = 44$ unchanged. He also still produces the original set of goods in J (45th to 50th goods) for self-consumption. However, he now has the additional option of buying the 45th good at the price P from the entrepreneur in exchange for giving up some of his self-produced 46th good). Again, with this opportunity, he will want to readjust his other plans (e.g., spending more time producing the 46th good or even specializing in the production of this 46th good) to further increase his utility. However, even before he can make such further improvements, we may show that both the entrepreneur and her trading partners can increase their utility. Each of the trading partners is thus faced with the utility function

$$u = x_i \prod_{r \in R_i} k\, x_r^d \prod_{j \in J_i} x_j$$
$$= An^{(a-1)}[kAn^{(a-1)}]^{n-1} A^{m-n-2}[A+kx][A-px] \tag{6B2}$$

where x_i is the quantity of good i retained by individual i for self-consumption, x_i^d is the amount of good i purchased, R_i is the set of goods purchased from other individuals, J_i is the set of self-provided goods, x is the amount of the 45th good he buys from the entrepreneur. (Note: all other x's carry some subscripts.) Since his production, exchange, and consumption choices of other goods other than the 45th and 46th goods are given, we may consider his utility maximization behaviour with respect to the choice of x as the maximization of

$$U = [A + kx]\,[A - Px] \tag{6B2a}$$

Assuming that he take the price P fixed by the entrepreneur as given, his choice of the amount of the 45th goods bought from the entrepreneur x is given by

$$x = \frac{(k-P)}{2kP} \tag{6B3}$$

Given this demand function from each of her N trading partner, the entrepreneur maximizes with respect to P,

$$(B - Nx)kNPx \tag{6B4}$$

where $B \equiv \{2[1 - c(n - 1)]/m - d\}^a$ is the output of her partially special-ized good (the 45th). She originally had $[1 - c(n - 1)]/m$ amount of time devoted to the production of each of the 45th and the 46th good. Since she is now no longer producing the 46th good, she can devote twice that amount, less any costs d of trading an additional good including the possible additional costs of making her offer known to her trading partner. The optimal P is given by

$$P\star = \left\{ \frac{NAk}{[2B+(NA/k)]} \right\}^{1/2} \tag{6B5}$$

With the specific numerical example of $k = 0.9$ (with $m = 50$, $a = 1.215$, $c = 0.0092$ throughout), optimal $n = 44$. When k increases to 0.94, the optimal P (of only a single entrepreneur under the specification of everyone else adopting the old level of specialization mentioned above) equals 0.916 which is lower than the new value of k at 0.94. (In the additional transaction with the entrepreneur, the trading partners are using the higher value of k as the guide.) This makes it advantageous for each trading partner to buy the 45th good from the entrepreneur. The optimal amount bought at this price is $x = 0.000065162$. After this transaction with all her 43 trading partners, the entrepreneur's 'sub' utility (i.e. the part in his/her utility function accounted by the 45th and 46th goods only; since the consumption of all other goods are unchanged before and after the increase in k and the same for all individuals under our simplified comparison, we need only to compare this 'sub' utility) equals $(2^a B - xN)kxNP$ and equals 25.01 (using units of 10^{-6} for all 'sub' utility numbers). This is larger than her 'sub' utility before her entrepreneurial trade; the latter being the same as that of all other individuals before the additional trade and equals A^2 or 21.8836 units. Each of the trading partner's 'sub' utility also increases from A^2 to $(A - xP)(A + kx)$ or 21.8873 units.

We may further ask what is the value of k that just makes the above add-itional trade between the entrepreneur and her trading partners mutu-ally beneficial as described. It turns out that this value of k is larger than the value of k which just makes the optimal n under full coordination equal 45. It can be shown that, with all other parameters unchanged, if k increases to about 0.9143, the optimal n under full coordination increases from 44 to 45. However, in the absence of coordination to adjust the pro-duction all around, even if k is as high as 0.92, the partial specialization with additional trade by an entrepreneur as described above is not pos-sible as the entrepreneur will end up with a lower utility level.

7
The Smith Dilemma and Its Resolution

The Smith dilemma refers to the inconsistency ('strictly an error') between the Smith theory on the efficiency of the market based on the absence of increasing returns and the Smith theorem on the facilitation of the economies of specialization (which gives rise to increasing returns) by the extent of the market. This chapter argues that, despite the prevalence of increasing returns, Adam Smith was largely right on the efficiency of the invisible hand and hence the Smith dilemma does not really exist. Ignoring separate issues such as environmental disruption, the market is very efficient in coordinating the allocation of resources even in the presence of increasing returns. The efficiency due to the automatic and incentive-compatible adjustments, free trade, and enterprise (entry/exit) largely prevails. The Dixit–Stiglitz model shows that the free-entry market equilibrium coincides with the (non-negative profit) constrained optimum when the elasticity of substitution between products is constant. For non-constant elasticities, the divergences between the market equilibrium and the constrained optimum in output levels, in the numbers of firms, and in utility levels are shown to be small.

Many important insights in economics can be traced to Adam Smith (1776), if not earlier. For example, the crowning jewel on the Pareto optimality of a competitive equilibrium is a formal proof of the Smith theory on the efficiency of the invisible hand of the market.[1] (For a much earlier but less detailed case for this, see Si-ma (104 BC)). For another example, the recent emphasis on the economies of specialization (see Chapter 6 in this book and the survey by Cheng & Yang 2004) is a formal analysis (though also with many new results) of the Smith theorem on the facilitation of the economies of specialization by the extent of the market through the division of labour.

However, since the Pareto optimality of a competitive equilibrium depends on the absence of increasing returns and since the division of labour gives rise to increasing returns through the economies of specialization, we have the Smith dilemma: 'The inconsistency of the efficiency of the invisible hand (the Smith theory) based on the absence of increasing returns with the facilitation of the economies of specialization (which gives rise to increasing returns) by the extent of the market (the Smith theorem).' (See Stigler 1951.) In fact, Heal (1999, p. xiii) regards this as an inconsistency ('strictly an error') of Smith. (Compare the 'conflict' discussed by Winch 1997.) This chapter argues that, interpreted in a practical sense, Smith was in fact correct on both points. Section 7.1 presents a verbal argument on the resolution of the Smith dilemma. Section 7.2 uses the Dixit–Stiglitz model to support the argument in Section 7.1.

7.1 Towards a resolution of the Smith dilemma

First-year economics allows us to see the incompatibility of increasing returns with perfect competition. A perfectly competitive firm faces a horizontal demand curve for its product and also cannot influence input prices. In the presence of increasing returns, its average cost is falling and its marginal-cost curve lies below its AC curve. If this situation persists and the price is high enough such that some production is better than no production, the firm will keep increasing its profit by increasing output. Eventually, it must become too large to remain perfectly competitive. As early as the early twentieth century (Marshall 1920), attempts have been made to save perfect competition from the devastation of increasing returns by confining increasing returns to those resulting from external effects between the production processes of different firms rather than from the internal economies within the firm. Each firm sees its average cost as not falling with its output, though the average costs of all firms fall as the whole industry expands. We may then have a competitive equilibrium though, without tackling the external economies, Pareto optimality is absent in general. (See Chipman 1970; Romer 1986; Suzuki 1996 for formal analysis). More importantly, while such external economies capture an important aspect of the real economy, the equally important factors of internal economies and product differentiation have been abstracted away.

Buchanan and Yoon (1999) attempt to resolve the Smith dilemma; their basic point is this. If the increasing returns are due to the facilitation of more economies of specialization by a larger market, it is generalized increasing returns at the level of the whole economy or the whole network of division of labour. This type of increasing returns may be consistent with perfect competition. Will it be Pareto optimal in the absence of other problems? Buchanan believes that the market equilibrium is sub-optimal with respect to the amount of work. This issue is discussed in Section 6.4 and Chapter 9. Here, ignoring work-leisure choice as well as external economies, consider the implications of increasing returns from internal economies.

Strictly speaking, the existence of a (perfectly) competitive equilibrium in practice is clearly impossible. The prevalence of increasing returns rules out the universality of perfect competition and the virtual universality of product differentiation makes perfect competition a rare exception. Marginal-cost pricing equilibrium is also impractical as, in the presence of increasing returns, it involves losses. Thus, in a sense, Heal is correct in saying that the Smith theory on the efficiency of the invisible hand is inconsistent ('strictly an error', Heal 1999, p. xiii) with the Smith theorem on the economies of specialization. However, it may be reasonably argued that Smith was correct both on the efficiency of the invisible hand and on the economies of specialization, at least to a very large extent.

Ignoring external effects, ignorance/irrationality, and occasional major failures like financial crisis and depressions (and possibly as caused by informational asymmetry on which see Stiglitz 2002), which are issues largely separate from the consistency between the efficiency of the invisible hand and increasing returns, the real market economy is very efficient (though not 100% efficient) in coordinating the separate activities of individual decision-makers in the economy despite the widespread prevalence of increasing returns and the rarity of perfect competition. The economies of specialization (especially with the additional power of learning by doing and exogenous technical progress) made possible by the division of labour also do lead to increasing returns at the economy level and propel economic growth and the evolution of economic organization. Provided that Smith did not intend to mean that the invisible hand is 100% efficient (in the same sense of the perfect Pareto efficiency of an Arrow–Debreu model of perfect competition which has never existed 100% in the real world), he was correct both in the Smith theory and the Smith theorem! The real market economy is characterized by high (even if imperfect) efficiency and increasing returns; there is really no Smith dilemma. In this perspective, it is misleading to say that 'the fact that a competitive equilibrium has a desirable property is of no significance if such an equilibrium does not exist' (Vohra 1994, p. 102). Even if a competitive equilibrium does not exist, many features that define a competitive equilibrium largely exist in the real market economy and these features make the real economy largely efficient. (Our remark here and below refers to most advanced countries with free enterprise, property rights, and the rule of law.)

The features that make both the real economy and the imaginary perfectly competitive economy efficient include the use of the price system, automatic market coordination, incentive-compatible decisions through the utility and profit maximization of individual consumers and producers, free trade and free enterprise (entry/exit). Compared to the real economy, the imaginary economy has the additional feature of perfect competition, making it perfectly efficient (ignoring problems like external effects). Largely speaking, the real economy possesses all these features except perfect competition. However, due to free entry/exit, competition remains high, making it largely efficient. (More on this is discussed in the rest of this section and the following section.)

The above-given common-sense point is very difficult to establish rigorously since it applies only 'largely speaking', not perfectly. Not only small inefficiencies exist as remarked above, but occasional large inefficiencies also cannot be ruled out, especially when the dynamic perspective is explicitly taken into account. In the presence of increasing returns, 'A technology that improves slowly at first but has enormous long-term potential could easily be shut out, locking an economy into a path that is both inferior and difficult to escape' (Arthur 1994, p. 10). The real case of the elimination of the technically superior Beta by VHS in video cassettes may also be recalled. (On path-dependency, see also Gallo 2006. Compare analyses of a complex adaptive system from an evolutionary and complexity perspective, either involving or not involving increasing returns; see, e.g., Beinhocker 2006; Gintis 2007.)

It may be thought that, even ignoring such occasional large inefficiencies (which may become more frequent in the future with the increase in importance in the role of knowledge and increasing returns in the economy), the remaining inefficiencies may still be large. For a firm with a high degree of monopolistic power (or in the presence of perfect contestability, for a firm with a high degree of increasing returns), if it were willing to increase output, efficiency would be significantly improved. So, how could the initial situation with $MR = MC < MV = AC$ be said to be highly efficient? This alleged high inefficiency is based on comparing the actual situation with some infeasible situation. If we are confined to feasible situations, the degree of inefficiency will be much less. It is true that the market solution need not even be (non-negative profit) constrained optimal. But the divergence, if any, of the market solution from the constrained optimum is much less than that from the unconstrained optimum. For the case of a constant elasticity of substitution, Dixit and Stiglitz (1977) show that the market equilibrium in fact coincides with the constrained optimum, irrespective of the degree of the constant elasticity of substitution. This result may be roughly explained intuitively. The higher the elasticity of substitution (the more the product of one producer is substitutable to that of another) the more price elastic is the demand for the product of any one producer. Profit maximization thus results in less mark-up of price above marginal cost. Thus, the larger is the output per producer and the lower is the number of producers. However, the higher the elasticity of substitution also means that it is less important to have a large number of producers/products. This makes the requirement of constrained optimality coincide with that of MR = MC of profit maximization. For the case of a variable elasticity of substitution, precise optimality cannot be ensured. Dixit and Stiglitz show that no general conclusion could be obtained. (The lack of definite general conclusions is also obtained by other analysts; see, e.g., Hart 1985; Ireland 1985; Lancaster 1979; Spence 1976.) Nevertheless, it is our contention that, since we have precise optimality for the case of constant elasticity, the divergence in terms of welfare losses for the general case is unlikely to be very large for most cases, as they are unlikely to diverge from the case of a constant elasticity (at whatever value) by a big margin. This point is shown more rigorously in the next section not only for absolute and relative welfare losses but also for output levels and the number of firms.

7.2   The efficiency of the market: A simulation using the Dixit–Stiglitz model

Dixit and Stiglitz (1977) show that the market equilibrium in fact coincides with the constrained optimum in the case of a constant elasticity of substitution (irrespective of the degree of this constant elasticity), but they did not coincide in the case of a variable elasticity of substitution. In this section, we show that the divergences in the output level, the number of firms, and in utility between the market equilibrium and the constrained optimum are very small both absolutely and relative to the divergences with the unconstrained optimum in the case of a variable elasticity of substitution.

The utility function is

$$u = x_0^{1-\gamma} \left\{ \sum_i v(x_i) \right\}^{\gamma}$$

with v increasing and concave, $0 < \gamma < 1$. Following Dixit and Stiglitz (1977), we define

$$\frac{1+\beta(x)}{\beta(x)} = -\frac{v'(x)}{xv''(x)}$$

$$\rho(x) = \frac{xv'(x)}{v(x)}$$

$$\omega(x) = \frac{\gamma\rho(x)}{[\gamma\rho(x)+(1-\gamma)]}$$

We can write the DD curve and the demand for the *numeraire* as

$$x = \frac{I}{np}\omega(x), \quad x_0 = I[1-\omega(x)]$$

Three equilibria are considered: the Chamberlinian equilibrium (i.e. market equilibrium with free entry/exit), the constrained optimum, and the unconstrained optimum. Denote p as the price of product, x as the output level, n as the number of firms, I as income. These equilibria results are following.

For the Chamberlinian equilibrium, x_e is defined by

$$\frac{cx_e}{a+cx_e} = \frac{1}{1+\beta(x_e)},$$

and

$$pe = c[1+\beta(x_e)],$$
$$n_e = \frac{I\omega(x_e)}{a+cx_e}$$
$$u_e = x_0^{1-\gamma}[n_e v(x_e)]^{\gamma}$$

where a is the fixed cost, c is marginal cost, subscript e stands for the Chamberlinian equilibrium.

For the constrained optimum, x_c is defined by

$$\frac{cx_c}{a+cx_c} = \frac{1}{1+\beta(x_c)} - \frac{\omega(x_c)x_c\rho'(x_c)}{\gamma\rho(x_c)}$$

and

$$p_c = c[1 + \beta(x_c)]$$

$$n_c = \frac{I\omega(x_c)}{a + cx_c}$$

$$u_c = I\gamma^\gamma (1-\gamma)^{1-\gamma} \frac{\left[\dfrac{\rho(x_c)v(x_c)}{a + cx_c}\right]^\gamma}{\gamma\rho(x_c) + (1-\gamma)}.$$

Where the subscript c stands for the constrained optimum. For the unconstrained optimum, x_u is defined by

$$\frac{cx_u}{a + cx_u} = \rho(x_u),$$

and

$$p_u = c$$

$$n_u = \frac{I\gamma}{a + cx_u}$$

$$u_u = [nv(x_u)]^\gamma \left[\frac{1 - n_u(a + cx_u)}{I}\right]^{1-\gamma} I^{1-\gamma}.$$

Where the subscript u stands for the unconstrained optimum.
   If we specify $v(x) = e^{-0.1x}x^a$, $\alpha = 0.5$, $c = 1$, $a = 100$, $\gamma = 0.5$, $I = 10000$, we have following simulation results, they are summarized in Table 7.1.
   From Table 7.1, we can see that the divergences in output level, in the number of firms, and in welfare (utility) between the market

Table 7.1   Simulation results for three equilibria

	Output level	Number of firms	Utility
The Chamberlinian equilibrium	$x_e = 1.31221$	$n_e = 26.5932$	$u_e = 441.799$
The constrained optimum	$x_e = 1.82918$	$n_e = 23.6421$	$u_e = 449.656$
The unconstrained optimum	$x_e = 4.56356$	$n_e = 47.8178$	$u_e = 568.865$

equilibrium with free entry/exit (the Chamberlinian equilibrium) and the constrained optimum are very small and relative to the divergences with the unconstrained optimum. To examine the sensitivity of the results, we undertake the following comparative statics analysis for various parameters. First, for a given set of parameters, $\alpha = 0.5$, $c = 1$, $\gamma = 0.5$, $I = 10000$, we examine how an increase in fixed cost a affects the various endogenous variables n, x, u for the three equilibria, $u_c - u_e$ and $(u_c - u_e)/u_u - u_c)$, the results are shown in Table 7.2.

Where $a = 2500$ is the critical value to make $u_c \approx u_e$, $n \approx 1$. We can see that the welfare levels between the market equilibrium and the constrained optimum converge as the fixed cost a increases; there is a critical value for a to make welfare between the market equilibrium and the constrained optimum equal.

Next, let us examine the comparative statics for the income parameter I. For a given set of parameters, $\alpha = 0.5$, $c = 1$, $a = 100$, $\gamma = 0.5$, we see how an increase in income I affects the various endogenous variables n, x, u for the three equilibria, $u_c - u_e$ and $(u_c - u_e)/(u_u - u_c)$, the results are showed in Table 7.3.

From Table 7.3, we can see that the difference in welfare between the market equilibrium and the constrained optimum is very small but this difference increases as income increases, but the ratio $(u_c - u_e)/(u_u - u_c)$ remains constant. This constancy result is interesting and comes from the fact that income I is only a scale factor which does not affect the elasticity of demand. (In the model here, income I may be taken as the product of per-capita income times the number of individuals.)

Table 7.2 Comparative statics for fixed cost a

a	100	200	300	400	1000	2500
x_e	1.31221	1.32579	1.3304	1.33272	1.33692	1.33861
x_c	1.82918	1.84977	1.85676	1.86027	1.86664	1.8692
x_u	4.56356	4.76719	4.84119	4.87948	4.95074	4.98012
n_e	26.5932	13.3463	8.90882	6.68586	2.67743	1.07147
n_c	23.6421	11.8681	7.92272	5.94608	2.38136	0.953015
n_u	47.8178	24.418	16.402	12.3494	4.97537	1.99602
u_e	441.799	313.722	256.63	222.322	140.793	89.092
u_c	449.656	319.401	261.19	226.371	143.369	90.6943
u_u	568.865	406.809	333.462	289.364	183.225	116.341
$u_c - u_e$	7.857	5.679	4.56	4.049	2.576	1.6023
$\dfrac{u_c - u_e}{u_u - u_c}$	0.066	0.065	0.063	0.064	0.065	0.062

Table 7.3 Comparative statics for income I

I	1000	5000	9000	10,000	11,000	15,000
x_e	1.31221	1.31221	1.31221	1.31221	1.31221	1.31221
x_c	1.82918	1.82918	1.82918	1.82918	1.82918	1.82918
x_u	4.56356	4.56356	4.56356	4.56356	4.56356	4.56356
n_e	2.65932	13.2966	23.9339	26.5932	29.2526	39.8898
n_c	2.36421	11.8211	21.2779	23.6421	26.0063	35.4632
n_u	4.78178	23.9089	43.036	47.8178	52.5996	71.7267
u_e	44.1799	220.9	397.62	441.799	486.01	662.7
u_c	44.9656	224.828	404.691	449.656	494.622	674.485
u_u	56.8866	284.433	511.979	568.865	625.752	853.298
$u_c - u_e$	0.7857	3.928	7.071	7.857	8.621	11.784
$\dfrac{u_c - u_e}{u_u - u_c}$	0.066	0.066	0.066	0.066	0.066	0.066

Table 7.4 Comparative statics for marginal cost c

c	0.1	0.2	0.3	0.5	1	1.5	2
x_e	1.33692	1.33412	1.33132	1.32579	1.31221	1.299	1.28614
x_c	1.8664	1.86239	1.85816	1.84977	1.82918	1.80912	1.78956
x_u	4.95074	4.90289	4.8564	4.76719	4.56356	4.3831	4.22144
n_e	26.8556	26.7537	26.7333	26.6927	26.5932	26.4963	26.4019
n_c	23.8136	23.794	23.7764	23.7362	23.6421	23.5509	23.4625
n_u	49.7537	49.5145	49.282	48.8359	47.8178	46.9155	46.1072
u_e	445.901	444.838	444.451	443.685	441.799	439.958	438.159
u_c	449.619	449.627	449.634	449.645	449.656	449.646	449.614
u_u	567.823	568.063	568.266	568.574	568.865	568.631	568.015
$u_c - u_e$	3.718	4.789	5.183	5.96	7.857	9.688	8.215
$\dfrac{u_c - u_e}{u_u - u_c}$	0.031	0.040	0.043	0.050	0.066	0.081	0.068

Third, let us examine the comparative statics for the marginal-cost parameter c. For a given set of parameters, $\alpha = 0.5$, $a = 100$, $\gamma = 0.5$, $I = 10000$, we see how an increase in marginal cost c affects the various endogenous variables n, x, u for the three equilibria, $u_c - u_e$ and $(u_c - u_e)/(u_u - u_c)$, the results are showed in Table 7.4.

It can be seen that, while the relevant divergences change as c changes, the divergences between the market equilibrium and the constrained optimum remain low in output levels, the numbers of firms, and in utility levels, both absolutely and relative to the divergences with the unconstrained optimum.

Fourth, for a given set of parameters, $c = 1$, $a = 100$, $\gamma = 0.5$, $I = 10000$, we see how a change in sub-utility parameter α affects the various endogenous variables n, x, u for the three equilibria, $u_c - u_e$ and $(u_c - u_e)/(u_u - u_c)$, the results are shown in Table 7.5. Finally, let us examine the comparative statics for the utility parameter γ. For a given set of other parameters, $\alpha = 0.5$, $c = 1$, $a = 100$, $I = 10000$, we see how a change in utility parameter γ affects the various endogenous variables n, x, u for the three equilibria, $u_c - u_e$ and $(u_c - u_e)/(u_u - u_c)$, the results are shown in Table 7.6.

These results show that, under a wide range of parametric values, the divergences in the output level, the number of firms, and in utility

Table 7.5 Comparative statics for sub-utility parameter α

α	0.2	0.4	0.6	0.8
x_e	0.288131	0.920343	1.74101	2.68545
x_c	0.364064	1.25895	2.45623	3.8357
x_u	1.82114	3.64804	5.48043	7.31809
n_e	14.5745	23.3307	29.3577	33.7951
n_c	14.0083	21.2461	25.538	28.3139
n_u	49.1057	48.2402	47.4022	46.5905
u_e	307.034	396.708	491.192	609.772
u_c	307.968	401.2461	502.885	631.901
u_u	478.861	530.132	616.627	742.134
$u_c - u_e$	0.934	4.5381	11.693	22.129
$\dfrac{u_c - u_e}{u_u - u_c}$	0.0055	0.035	0.1028	0.2

Table 7.6 Comparative statics for utility parameter γ

γ	0.2	0.4	0.6	0.8
x_e	1.31221	1.31221	1.31221	1.31221
x_c	1.68756	1.7708	1.90628	2.17959
x_u	4.56356	4.56356	4.56356	4.56356
n_e	8.33191	19.4781	35.1542	58.8259
n_c	7.52067	17.3274	31.1038	51.8804
n_u	19.1271	38.2542	57.3814	76.5085
u_e	2258.98	723.342	283.339	137.577
u_c	2268.19	731.725	290.969	146.563
u_u	2541.52	896.492	375.804	187.215
$u_c - u_e$	9.21	8.383	7.03	8.986
$\dfrac{u_c - u_e}{u_u - u_c}$	0.0337	0.0509	0.082	0.22

between the market equilibrium and the constrained optimum are very small both absolutely and relative to the divergences with the unconstrained optimum. They also show how the various endogenous variables change with respect to the changes in the various parametric variables.

7.3 Concluding remarks

This chapter argues that, despite the prevalence of increasing returns, Adam Smith was largely right on the efficiency of the invisible hand and hence the Smith dilemma does not really exist. Ignoring separate issues such as environmental disruption, the market is very efficient in coordinating the allocation of resources even in the presence of increasing returns. The efficiency due to the automatic and incentive-compatible adjustments, free trade, and enterprise (entry/exit) largely prevails. To a large extent, Heal is likely to concur, as he writes

> It is puzzling that although economies of scale are undoubtedly important in reality, our belief in the invisible hand, in the efficiency of competition, seems verified by observation and experience, although not supported by current theory. This suggests that our understanding of economies with increasing returns is far from complete: there may be a role for competition and markets in allocating resources in the presence of increasing returns that we have not yet understood. (Heal 1999, p. xvi)

We certainly agree that more research on increasing returns is needed but the 'puzzle' may also be partly explained by the high degree of efficiency of the market economy as argued above. It may be added that this high degree of efficiency is to a large extent due to the presence of largely free entry/exit of producers. (Nevertheless, free entry/exit contributes to efficiency only in the absence of artificial price maintenance. A combination of price maintenance and free entry could lead to a very inefficient situation.) The importance of this can already be seen in the traditional analysis. The role of the market in coordinating not only the resource allocation problems of an economy of a given network of division of labour but also in coordinating the pattern of division of labour itself is further shown in a framework designed to analyse the division of labour (Yang & Ng 1993), though this coordination is not only done by the price system as such but also by the important function of entrepreneurs, as discussed in the previous chapter. Thus, the generalized increasing returns at the economy level due to the economies of specialization at the individual level can be largely realized through the division of labour facilitated by market coordination. However, the increasing returns at the firm level and the associated efficiency problems have yet to be analysed further in the new framework. (See Chapters 8 and 10 on the analysis of infrastructure investment and work ethics respectively.) Other related issues such as path-dependency (and thus the importance of history) due to increasing returns (as ably analysed by Arthur 1994; see also Dixit & Stiglitz 1977; Arrow 2000) also remain to be further explored.

8
Why Should Governments Encourage Improvements on Infrastructure? Indirect Network Externality of Transaction Efficiency

Governments have been very active in engaging and in encouraging the improvements in transaction efficiency, including the provision of legal, social, and economic infrastructure. While this may partly be explained by the public goods nature, the presence of indirect network externalities (or a second-level publicness) due to the economies of specialization may also be important. The improvement in transaction (including communication and transportation) efficiency may generate benefits in excess of the direct private benefits through the promotion of division of labour that leads to more economies of specialization and the availability of more goods in the market. This is shown in the Yang–Ng framework of inframarginal analysis.

8.1 Why should governments encourage improvements in transaction efficiency?*

Governments have been very active in engaging and in encouraging the improvements in transaction efficiency, including the provision of legal, social, and economic infrastructure. (For the effects of infrastructure on productivity, see World Bank 1994 for a survey; see also Boserup 1981 and Chandler 1990 on the historical perspective and the

*Section 8.1 is a reproduction of 6.4.1 and readers who have read the latter may wish to skip 8.1.

importance of population size.) Even free-market economists including Adam Smith find 'the erection and maintenance of the public works which facilitate the commerce of any country, such as good roads, bridges, navigable canals, harbours, etc.' desirable and indeed find this as 'evident without any proof' (Smith 1776/1976, II, p. 245). Perhaps this apparently self-evident nature made economists pay little attention to the role of infrastructure in either theoretical or empirical studies until the late 1980s. (See Gramlich 1994 for a survey.) This interest is mainly concerned with the relationship of infrastructure investment and economic growth and development or the related issue of the productivity of public capital (e.g. Aschauer 2001; Batina 2001; Bougheas et al. 2000; Brox & Fader 2005; Esfahani & Ramirez 2003; Evans & Karras 1994; Fernand 1999; Haughwout 2002; Holtz-Eakin 1994; Paul et al. 2004; Pereira 2001; Röller & Waverman 2001; Wang 2002).[1] While these issues are also related to the theme of this chapter, the latter is more concerned with the specific point as to the reasons why the involvement of the government is needed.

The need for government involvement may be explained by the public goods nature of infrastructure. This may well be the major part of the explanation for many cases. However, if this is the only reason, there is little reason for encouragement if the items involved are excludable and can be priced as applicable in many cases including communications. Moreover, according to the traditional analysis, even for non-excludable items, there should be no reason for providing them beyond the levels indicated by the equation of (aggregate) marginal benefits and marginal costs, evaluated at the existing structure of economic organizations or the degree of specialization of the whole economy (which is **not** taken as a variable in the traditional analysis). In this chapter, it is argued that, if we take the degree of specialization as endogenous, the provision of infrastructure that decreases transaction costs may produce some indirect network externality by enhancing the network of social division of labour. This should be distinguished from the possible network externality of the infrastructure itself, which is well known. For example, the usefulness of a telephone, fax machine, email facility increases as more people are on the phone, etc. This is the direct network externality, which we shall abstract away. Rather, we refer to the following more indirect effects.[2]

The improvement in transaction (including communication and transportation) efficiency may generate benefits in excess of the direct private benefits through the promotion of higher degrees of specialization. If transaction efficiency is very low (i.e. transaction costs are very high), it may be optimal for everyone to be in autarky, self-producing all goods (taken to include services) needed. As transaction efficiency improves, it may become optimal to buy some goods from others and sell the good one specializes in, but in general some goods are still self-produced and self-consumed. (This is true even in modern times, including home cooking, cleaning, child-care and gardening). As transaction efficiency improves, the set of goods bought from others increases. Thus, the benefits of an improvement in transaction efficiency consist not only in directly reducing the costs of transaction, but also in indirectly promoting the degree of specialization and the consequent tapping of the economies of specialization. Even assuming that the costs of exclusion is negligible and that there is no free-rider problem, a private producer of an improvement in infrastructure that reduces transaction costs may only be able to capture the direct benefits of lowering transaction costs, but not be able to capture the indirect benefits of promoting more specialization (even in the absence of individual differences giving rise to different consumer surpluses). People will just assess the benefits of lower transaction costs given the existing level of specialization of the economy. Not only that the benefits through a higher degree of specialization will occur only in the future contingent on the appearance of new marketable goods, but also this development is taken as not affected by the improvement in the transaction efficiency of an individual himself/herself. It is thus rational even under full knowledge to ignore the indirect benefit of higher transaction efficiency on the level of specialization.

In other words, there are two public-good problems. The improvement in infrastructure to raise transaction efficiency may itself be a public good. However, even if this public-good problem can be overcome through excludability, there is another public-good problem at the level of the increase in the degree of specialization that the higher transaction efficiency contributes to. Even with perfect foresight, each individual does not take into account the benefits of a higher degree of specialization because that degree is determined by the general level of transaction efficiency prevailing in the whole economy, not appreciably affected by that of the individual. Even if, especially after writing this chapter, I correctly foresee that the widespread use of a new communication system will promote specialization and make a number of new products available in the market, we will not count the benefits of the availability of the new products in assessing the usefulness of the new communication system to us, as the new products will be available even if I do not use the new communication system but if others do. This second level of publicness problem is quite impossible to solve through exclusion, as the producers of the new set of products are typically different from the producer of the infrastructure. Thus, the indirect externality of infrastructure may then make the public provision or encouragement desirable. The Yang–Ng framework of inframarginal analysis is used in the next section to analyse the case for encouraging improvement in transaction efficiency over and above its direct benefits.[3] Our results are consistent with the empirical evidence that public infrastructure capital has positive long-run effects on output and that 'the short-run rates of return are rather low while the long-run rates of return tend to be quite high' (Demetriades & Mamuneas 2000, p. 689). It takes time for the higher degree of specialization to develop.

In the demonstration, we also discovered that the lumpiness in investments to improve transaction efficiency also play a role in creating a divergence between social and private benefits. For non-lumpy investments, the divergence is negligible. This may also partly explain why big projects may be regarded as a ground for encouragement. Of course, like all other reasonable justifications, this one may also be misused to justify really inefficient projects. Also, the case for government involvement in some cases does not rule out the role of private initiatives in infrastructure (see Berg et al. 2002).

8.2   A perspective from the Yang–Ng framework

In contrast to the modelling of specialization at the individual level (detailed below), the earlier papers of Ethier (1982) and Romer (1987) take the output of a final good as a function of intermediate inputs more of which increases productivity but for the fixed costs of their production. Specialization increases the number of intermediate inputs and may increase productivity but this has to be traded off with the fixed costs. Bougheas et al. (2000) extend Romer's model to allow a role for infrastructure by assuming that 'the fixed costs of producing intermediate inputs vary inversely with the stock of public capital *relative to the size of the economy*' (p. 509, italics original). The resource costs of the public capital may then make the relationship between infrastructure and growth an inverted U-shaped one, as supported by the empirical evidence presented. (At the earlier range where the negative effect of resource costs is more than offset by the positive effect of infrastructure investment, a higher level of public capital increases growth. At the range when the reverse is true, further investment in infrastructure decreases growth.) In contrast, the analysis below allows a role for infrastructure by letting it affect the transaction efficiency. Different methods of modelling and different focuses of the same issue may provide different but all useful perspectives.

Partly for simplicity and partly to show the non-reliance on exogenous heterogeneity of individuals (and the resulting exogenous comparative advantage), Yang and Ng (1993) assume that the economy consists of M ex-ante identical consumer-producers and m consumer goods.[4] Denoting the self-provided amount of good i as x_i, the amount purchased from the market of good i as x_i^d, the amount of good i consumed is $x_i + k\,x_i^d$, where kx_i^d is the amount an individual obtains when he/she purchases x_i^d, $1 - k$ being the transaction cost coefficient and k the transaction efficiency coefficient. Here, transaction costs include all costs (including time in finding or going to the market, negotiation, transportation, etc.) incurred due to the need for the individual to engage in trade with others. If the individual self-produces all goods he/she needs, she can avoid all these costs of trade or transaction. However, having to produce all needed goods leads to no specialization or a low level of specialization and hence low productivity. If he/she partially specializes to produce a few goods or fully specialize to produce only one good, he/she has higher productivity due to the economies of specialization (doubling the time to produce one good more than doubling the output). As he/she needs to consume other goods, he/she has to exchange her specialized good with other individuals, incurring transaction costs as a result. The central trade-off in this analysis is the choice of an optimal degree of specialization taking the economies of specialization on the one hand and the required transaction costs on the other.

A Cobb–Douglas utility function is adopted to reflect the preference for diverse consumption. (Other utility functions are also used in Yang & Ng 1993 without changing the main results. General utility functions and more general production functions are used in the proof of existence of equilibrium in the Yang–Ng framework in Sun et al. 2004.)

$$u = x \prod_{r \in R_i} k\,x_r^d \prod_{j \in J_i} x_j \tag{8.1}$$

where x_i is the quantity of good i retained by individual i for self-consumption,[5] R_i is the set of goods purchased from other individuals, $1 - k$ is the transaction costs of trade, and J_i is the set of self-provided goods. Each consumer-producer also has a system of production functions,

$$x_i + x_i^s = l_i^a$$
$$x_j = l_j^a \ \forall \ j \in J_i \tag{8.2}$$

where x_i^s is the amount of good i sold to the market and $x_i + x_i^s$ is the amount of good i produced and l_i the amount of labour used in producing good i. The assumption of $a > 1$ captures the economies of specialization, making the labour productivity in the production of each good increase with the individual's level of specialization in its production, measured by the labour time used. Apart from the per unit transaction cost $(1 - k)$, a fixed cost (measured by labour time) for the purchase of each good c is also assumed. The endowment constraint of the individual is given by

$$c(n-1)+l_i+\sum_{j\in J_i}l_j = 1 \tag{8.3}$$

where the total amount of labour time has been normalized to unity. The budget constraint of the individual is given by

$$p_i x_i^s = \sum_{r\in R} p_r x_r^d \tag{8.4}$$

where p_i is the price of good i, R is a set of all goods purchased. In (8.4), only one good is supplied to the market by an individual since, from $a > 1$, it can be shown that an individual sells only one good at most (see Lemma 2.1 in Yang and Ng, 1993 and generalizations by Wen 1998; Yao 2002; Diamantaras & Gilles 2004). Each individual (effectively) takes the market prices as given either because the population is large relative to the number of goods and thus the number of individuals producing each good i, M_i, is large and/or due to the coincidence with the Walrasian regime in the multilateral bargaining game of the Yang–Ng model (1993, chapter 3).

Each individual is then allowed to maximize utility by allotting his/her fixed amount of time to the production and purchase of different goods, balancing the trade-off between economies of specialization $(a > 1)$ on the one hand and the costs of market transaction $(1 - k > 0, c > 0)$ on the other. Each individual is allowed not only to choose the quantities of the various goods consumed but also to choose what goods to self-provide and sell to the market. If an individual buys a good, he/she does not sell it and vice versa.

Next, market equilibrium in terms of the equality of the amount of each good supplied and demanded in the market is imposed.

$$M_i x_i^s = \sum_{r\in R} M_r x_{ri}^d \tag{8.5}$$

where M_i is the number of individuals selling good i, x_{ri} is the amount of traded good i purchased by individuals selling good r, it can then be shown that (proposition 5.1 of Yang and Ng) if the transaction efficiency and/or the degree of economies of specialization are very low, the equilibrium is autarky. All individuals self-provide all goods. As the transaction efficiency improves (i.e. k increases), each individual sells a good to the market and buys some other goods in exchange. The number of goods purchased from the market, division of labour, and income all increase with transaction efficiency.

The requirements of market equilibrium (8.5) and utility equalization to ensure a general equilibrium in the model of *ex-ante* identical individuals and symmetrical production functions for all goods ensure that all prices are equal and may be taken as unity. Thus, maximizing (8.1) subject to (8.2)–(8.4), we have (the detailed working is available with the author).

$$x_i = \left\{ \frac{[1 - c(n-1)]}{m} \right\}^a n^{(a-1)} \tag{8.6}$$

$$x_j = \left\{ \frac{[1 - c(n-1)]}{m} \right\}^a \tag{8.7}$$

$$u = \left\{ \frac{[1 - c(n-1)]}{m} \right\}^{am} n^{(a-1)n} k^{n-1} \tag{8.8}$$

From (8.8), it seems that the maximization of u with respect to n yields the optimal number of goods purchased. The optimal value n^* is the integer in the neighbourhood of n^{**} that is given by the first-order condition $\partial u / \partial n = 0$. (It is assumed that c is of sufficient high value to ensure the satisfaction of the second-order condition.) This is in fact the case when everyone in the economy has adjusted to the given set of parametric values (particularly k, c, and a) with no further opportunity for improvement. However, when a parameter just changes its value, the desired adjustment of an individual is subject to the market opportunity at the time. For example, as the transaction efficiency coefficient k increases, each individual may wish to increase the number of goods purchased from others. However, this desire may not be realized before the additional marketable goods are supplied in the market.

This problem is especially serious in a realistic model where goods are not symmetrical. Then, goods (that would have been purchased) may not be supplied in the market soon after an increase in transaction efficiency but before the organizational structure of the whole economy adjusts to the new situation. For example, with higher transaction efficiency, people may want to buy take-away meals and spend less time doing home cooking (a good in the set J) but may not be able to do so before some take-away meals are sold in the market. However, in time, some entrepreneurs will see the opportunity. (Consult Section 6.3 and Appendix 6B for more analysis.) For example, the McDonald's restaurant was launched with great success. This changes the structure of economic organization of the society and increases the degree of specialization. People can then spend less time doing home cooking and more on the specialized profession. However, before the new goods are offered for sale in the market, it is quite impossible that people (including firms) will take account of the specialization-enhancing effect through organizational changes of the whole society in assessing the benefits of higher transaction efficiency. Even assuming that the costs of exclusion is negligible and that there is no free-rider problem, a private producer of infrastructure that reduces transaction costs may not be able to capture the indirect benefits of promoting more specialization (even in the absence of individual differences giving rise to different consumer surpluses). People will just assess the benefits of lower transaction costs given the existing level of specialization of the economy.

In the framework presented above, it means that people will assess the benefits of a higher k or lower c at given n. Not only that the benefits through a higher n will occur only in the future contingent on the appearance of new marketable goods, but also this development is taken as not affected by the improvement in the transaction efficiency of each individual himself/herself. It is thus rational even under full knowledge to ignore the indirect benefit of higher transaction efficiency on the level of specialization. In other words, there are two public-good problems. The improvement in infrastructure to raise transaction efficiency may itself be a public good. However, even if this public-good problem can be overcome through excludability, there is another public-good problem at the level of the increase in the level of specialization that the higher transaction efficiency contributes to. Even with perfect foresight, each individual does not take into account the benefits of higher level of specialization because that level is determined by the general level of transaction efficiency prevailing in the whole economy, not appreciably affected by that of a particular individual. In considering whether to buy a mobile phone, an individual only assesses the benefits the phone will bring, given the range of marketable goods available. He/she does not take into account that, if most people have mobile phones and the (full, inclusive of convenience) costs of communication are lower, this may trigger an increase in the range of marketable goods available. This increase depends on the general availability of phones, not on whether he/she has one. Thus, the general possession of phones that reduces communication costs (part of transaction costs) is a public good that may help to increase the level of division of labour. It is this second public-good aspect that this chapter is emphasizing, not the possibly public-good nature of the infrastructure investment itself.

In terms of (8.8), the **individual** benefit of an improvement in transaction efficiency is the increase in utility as either k increases or c decreases. The social benefits include the individual benefits plus the increase in utility from a higher n induced by the increase in k or the reduction in c or both. Consider first an increase in k only; the individual benefit is, from (8.8),

$$\left(\frac{\partial u}{\partial k}\right)_{|n|} = (n-1)\left\{\frac{[1-c(n-1)]}{m}\right\}^{am} n^{(a-1)n} k^{n-2} \tag{8.9}$$

If we treat n as a continuous variable, the social benefit of an increase in transaction efficiency k is given by

$$\frac{\partial u}{\partial k} = \left(\frac{\partial u}{\partial k}\right)_{|n|} + \left(\frac{\partial u}{\partial n}\right)\left(\frac{dn}{dk}\right) \tag{8.10}$$

If we start from a position where individuals have already adjusted to the given level of k in their choice of n (making $\partial u/\partial n$ approximately zero) and for a marginal change in k, the application of the envelope theorem implies that the social benefit is equal to the individual benefit (with of course appropriate summation over the relevant set of individuals where publicness is involved). However, developments in infrastructure are typically lumpy and changes in n can only take on integer values. For such changes, social and individual benefits may diverge significantly. Note that lumpiness as such is insufficient to give rise to the divergence. If there is no publicness in the network of specialization, the individual will take account of the indirect benefit of a higher k through n, i.e. $(\partial u/\partial n)(dn/dk)$ in the right hand side of (8.10) in evaluating the benefits of a higher k. Thus, it is the combination of lumpiness and publicness that causes the divergence between individual and social benefits. Since n can only assume integer values, strictly speaking we cannot really use (8.10) which may however be taken as indicative of the various effects involved.

Let us use illustrative examples involving numerical values for the variables involved. For example, if we take $m = 50$, $a = 1.215$, $k = 0.9$, $c = 0.0092$, it can be calculated that the integer value of n that maximizes the utility value as given in (8.8) is 44, yielding a value (in units of 10^{-104}) 12.093. An improvement in transaction efficiency in the form of a reduction of c to 0.009, with all other parameters held unchanged, increases the utility value to 28.529 at unchanged value of n. However, with the value of n adjusted to the lower c (n^* increases from 44 to 47), the utility value increases further to 30.134. So the social benefits of the reduction in c exceeds the individual benefits by $30.134 - 28.529 = 1.605$ units. The divergence of social and individual benefits associated with an increase in k may be similarly illustrated.

The analysis above examines the willingness to pay for improvements in transaction efficiency without explicitly modelling the financing or resource implication of the investment to improve the transaction efficiency. To do this in a simple example, suppose that a private firm can produce a device that improves the transaction efficiency by reducing c (or increasing k). The device can be sold to all individuals in exchange for a certain amount of their labour time l^d (d for device) which can be used to produce the device. Thus, we assume that there is no public-good free-riding problem for the device. The model above may be revised to account for this by replacing (8.3) with

$$c(n-1)+l^d +l_i+\sum_{j\in J_i}l_j = 1 \qquad (8.3')$$

and with c (or k) dependent on whether l^d is incurred or not. Correspondingly, (8.8) is replaced by

$$u = \left\{\frac{[1-c(n-1)-l^d]}{m}\right\}^{am} n^{(a-1)n}k^{n-1} \qquad (8.8')$$

Let us start with $m = 50$, $a = 1.215$, $k = 0.9$, $c = 0.0092$, $l^d = 0$, $n = 44$, and (in units of 10^{-104}) $u = 12.093$. Now, suppose that a lumpy investment costing a per capita labour time of $l^d = 0.018$ would increase the transaction efficiency k to 0.93927. Even if there is no public-good problem in getting everyone to pay the 0.018, the improvement may not be feasible. Evaluated at the existing level of division of labour with $n = 44$, the higher transaction efficiency does not justify the required cost. With the values of other parameters unchanged but with $l^d = 0.018$, $k = 0.93927$, and $n = 44$, it can be calculated from (8.8') that $u = 12.089466$, lower than the original value of 12.093. However, if the lumpy investment is undertaken, the lower value of k will increase the

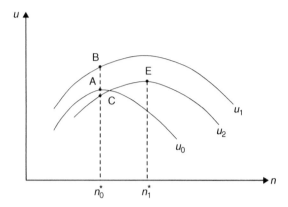

Figure 8.1   The effect of transaction efficiency on the optimal number of traded goods

optimal level of specialization. If the value of n is increased to its new optimal value of 45, the value of u increases to 12.18331, making the investment well worth undertaking.

The argument above may be illustrated partially in Figure 8.1. The curve u_0 relates the utility level of the individual at different values of n at the original parametric values. Ignoring the relevant costs, an improvement in transaction efficiency may lift the curve to u_1. At the original level of specialization represented by n_0^*, the gain is AB. If this gain is less than the costs, the net-of-cost curve u_2 passes below A. However, there is an additional gain as the level of specialization increases to n_1^*, possibly making the new optimal point E higher than the original point A. However, evaluating the improvement at the original level of specialization, the private market may not sanction the improvement even if there is no difficulty in overcoming the first public-good problem of getting everyone to pay for the change.

8.3   Introducing the role of the government

In this section, let us introduce the role of the government. To concentrate on the issue of infrastructure, we ignore all other roles of the government except raising taxes to provide for infrastructure investment that increases transaction efficiency. Instead of (8.4) above, the budget constraint of an individual is now given by

$$(1-t)p_ix_i^s = \sum_{r \in R_i} p_r x_r^d \qquad (8.4')$$

where t is the tax rate on sales revenue. We assume that the government invests all tax revenue into infrastructure to improve transaction efficiency. The relationship between the transaction efficiency coefficient k and investment in infrastructure is assumed as follows.

$$k = 1 - \frac{1}{\alpha \sum_i M_i tp_i x_i^s + A} \tag{8.11}$$

where $\Sigma_i M_i tp_i x_i^s$ is total tax revenue collected by the government, α is a parameter which represents the level of efficiency of investment in infrastructure, A is a parameter (to avoid a negative k when infrastructure investment is low).

With other aspects of the model unchanged from Section 8.2, the maximization of (8.1) subject to (8.2), (8.3), and (8.4'), we have (the detailed working is available with the author)

$$x_i = \left[\frac{1 - c(n-1)}{m} \right]^a n^{a-1} \tag{8.6'}$$

$$x_j = \left[\frac{(1 - c(n-1))}{m} \right]^a \tag{8.7'}$$

$$u = \left[1 - \frac{1}{\alpha t M (n-1) n^{a-1} \left(\dfrac{1 - c(n-1)}{m} \right)^a + A} \right]^{n-1} (1-t)^{n-1} n^{(a-1)n} \left[\frac{1 - c(n-1)}{m} \right]^{am} \tag{8.8''}$$

To show the possibility of utility-increasing taxation to provide for infrastructure investment after a higher degree of division of labour (reflected in our model by an increase in n^*, the optimal number of traded goods) even if it is utility-decreasing at the existing level of division of labour, we shall use an illustrative example involving numerical values for the variables involved. Let us start with $m = 50$, $a = 1.215$, $A = 10$, $c = 0.0092$, $\alpha = 0.00991$, $M = 100000$, $t = 0$, it can be calculated that the integer value of n that maximizes the utility value as given in (8.9) is 44, yielding a value (in units of 10^{-104}) 12.093. Now, suppose that the tax rate is positive, for example, $t = 0.08$, if the existing level of division of labour $n = 44$ is unchanged, it can be calculated from (8.9) that $u = 12.0871$, lower than the original value of 12.093. However, the increase of transaction efficiency (due to the investment in infrastructure from tax revenue) will increase the optimal level of specialization. If the value of n increases to its new optimal value of 45, the value of u increases to 12.0973. This possibility can be similarly illustrated by reference to Figure 8.1 as done in the previous section.

8.4   Concluding remarks

Our analysis is mainly illustrative. The simple functional forms assumed are mainly for simplicity and analytical manageability. They may under or overestimate the situations in the real world. Thus, the quantitative values have no particular real-world significance. For the latter, we have to undertake specific quantitative estimates of the real economies, which is beyond the scope of this chapter and the competence of its author. Nevertheless, our analysis does provide a possible ground for the encouragement in lumpy improvements in transaction efficiency, including the provision of infrastructure. More specific policy implications may be obtained after further developments and applications to ascertain the actual situation and estimate the relevant values.

9

Average-Cost Pricing, Increasing Returns, and Optimal Output: Comparing Home and Market Production

A model with both market production and home production is used to show that, ignoring administrative costs and indirect effects (such as rent-seeking), even if both the home and the market sectors have the condition of increasing returns and there are no pre-existing taxes, it is still efficient to tax the home sector to finance a subsidy on the market sector to offset the under-production of the latter. This under-production is due to the failure of price-taking consumers to take account of the effects of higher consumption in reducing the average costs and hence prices, through increasing returns or the publicness nature of fixed costs. Within market production, it is efficient to subsidize more the sector with a higher fixed cost, a lower elasticity of substitution between goods (higher value of diversity), and a lower degree of importance in preference which all increases the degree of increasing returns.

A popular model with increasing returns is that of Dixit and Stiglitz (1977) with symmetrical monopolistic-competitive firms with free entry and the product is produced with a fixed cost and a constant marginal cost (cf. Spence 1976). Although a special case, this model captures an important aspect of reality, since much of increasing returns at the firm level may be traced to some big fixed-cost components (a piece of land for farming, a factory for manufacturing production, a shop for retailing, learning costs for many skilled activities, etc.) and the variable costs (raw materials, intermediate goods purchased, stocks ordered, etc.) are largely constant within a wide range.

While the Dixit–Stiglitz model captures much of increasing returns at the firm level, those at the economy level arising from the economies of specialization made possible by the division of labour are analysed by Yang and Ng (1993) and discussed in Chapter 6. This latter framework starts from the most basic level of individual decisions on what activities (home production, trade, employment, consumption, etc.) to undertake to maximize utility and the interaction of the activities of individuals and their implications on economic organization, trade, growth, etc. Though the emergence of firms and other issues (including the choice of the variety of products; see Yang & Shi 1992) are also analysed, the economies of specialization is confined to the individual level. In principle, one may use this framework to model increasing returns at the firm level through the complicated interaction between different individuals within the firm and their interaction with other factors employed by the firm, but the complication involved may raise issues of manageability. There are also models that analyse increasing returns from employing production methods with more intermediate goods (e.g. Ethier 1979; Romer 1986; Buchanan & Yoon 1994a; on the role of intermediate inputs in the presence of increasing returns for trade patterns, see Chakraborty 2003). However, there are advantages in directly allowing for increasing returns at the firm level from the fixed-cost components as in the Dixit–Stiglitz model. Moreover, the majority of production in most advanced economies is undertaken by firms with increasing returns prevailing over the completely relevant range of production, but with individual home production still taking place.

The present chapter combines the analysis of economies of specialization at the individual level by Yang and Shi (1992) and Yang and Ng (1993) with the Dixit and Stiglitz (1977) analysis of the market production by monopolistic-competitive firms. (For an earlier model combining home production with market production by firms emphasizing the role of the number of intermediate goods and different stages of production, see Locay 1990. Here, the complications due to intermediate goods and stages in production are ignored.) This combination may move a step closer to the real economy with both home and firm/market production. It allows us to compare home and market production and gives new results not obtained before. The model developed in Section 9.1 could be used to analyse problems other than those discussed in this chapter. Here we aim to analyse the role played by commodity taxation in an economy with both home production and market production, where both types of production exhibit increasing returns to scale and the latter is characterized by imperfect competition.

Many authors have studied the corrective role of commodity taxation in economies with imperfect competition. Keen (1998) gives a comprehensive survey which focuses on the balance between specific and *ad valorem* taxes. For other literature on the effects of taxation with imperfect competition readers may refer to Besley 1989, Delipalla and Keen 1992, Myles 1987, 1989, 1995.

Despite the increasing importance of market production, one cannot ignore the importance of home production as we still spend a sizable amount of our time on home-cooking, gardening, cleaning, child-caring, etc., even if we do not include such activities as sleeping as a form of home production. Home production has been analysed of course since the time of Becker (1965). More recently, home production has been analysed (e.g. Benhabib et al. 1991; Einarsson & Marquis 1997; Greenwood & Hercowitz 1991; Locay 1990; Perli 1998) mainly in relation to its role in the business cycle. Sandmo (1990) uses a model with both home production and market production to analyse optimal taxation. Anderberg and Balestrio (2000) analyse the effect of different tax structures on economic efficiency. Here, we concentrate on the implications of increasing returns for *efficient* allocation. (On the trade-off between equity and efficiency in the presence of increasing returns, see Vohra 1992.) We also concentrate on the division of labour between individuals/households; for the division of labour and bargaining within a household, see Fafchamps and Quisumbing 2003; McElroy 1997.

It is shown in Section 9.1 that it is efficient to tax the home sector to finance a subsidy to the market sector to offset the under-production of the latter. This is so even if both the home and the market sectors have the production condition of increasing returns and there are no pre-existing taxes (including income taxes) on the market sector. (Leisure is assumed not taxable.) The home sector is not under-produced because increasing returns are fully taken into account by the individuals/households. In the production by firms for the market, as the output is priced at average cost and each consumer takes the price as given, the effect of higher consumption in reducing the price through increasing returns is not taken into account. Viewed differently, the fixed cost of production possesses the characteristic of publicness, causing under-production. However, the taxation of the home sector may not be practically feasible. Section 9.2 allows the market production to have two sectors and shows that it is efficient to tax the sector with a lower fixed cost, a higher elasticity of substitution between goods (lower value of diversity), and a higher degree of importance in preference (as all these factors contribute to a lower degree of increasing returns) and subsidize the other sector. Qualifications on the applicability of these results in the real economy are discussed in the concluding Section 9.3.

9.1   A model with home and market production

9.1.1   The model

Consider an economy with M identical consumers. Each of them has the following decision problem for consumption, working, and home production.

$$\text{Max: } u = l^{1-\alpha-\beta}\left[\sum_{r=1}^{n} x_r^{\rho_1}\right]^{\alpha/\rho_1}\left[\sum_{j=1}^{m} x_j^{\rho_2}\right]^{\beta/\rho_2} \quad \text{(utility function)}$$

$$\text{s.t. } \sum_{r=1}^{n} p_r x_r = w\left(1-l-\sum_{j=1}^{m} l_j\right) \quad \text{(budget constraint)} \qquad (9.1)$$

$$x_j = \frac{l_j - a}{c} \quad \text{(home production function)}$$

where p_r is the price of good r which are market goods, w is the price of labour, x_r is the amount of good r that is purchased from the market, n is the number of market goods, x_j is the amount of good j which is home good, l_j is the amount of labour used in producing home good j, $a < 1$ is the fixed cost of producing a home good, c is the marginal cost in home production, m is the number of home goods, l is leisure, $(1 - l - \sum_{j=1}^{m} l_j)$ is the amount of labour hired by firms, $\rho_i \in (0, 1)$ (open interval; i.e., $1 > \rho_i > 0$) is a parameter related to the elasticity of substitution between each pair of consumption goods (this is inversely related to the value of diversity; see Krugman 1982, p. 240), α, β are preference parameters, and u is the utility level. It is assumed that each consumer is endowed with one unit of labour, which is the *numeraire*, so $w = 1$. Each consumer is a price taker and his/her decision variables are m, l, l_j and x_r. It is assumed that the elasticity of substitution $1/(1 - \rho_i) > 1$, or $1 > \rho_i > 0$ for both $i = 1, 2$.

By symmetry, the budget constraint can be rewritten as follows:

$$\sum_{r=1}^{n} p_r x_r + m l_h + l = 1 \qquad (9.2)$$

where l_h is labour used in the production of each home good.

The optimization problem gives the following solutions:

$$l_h = \frac{a}{1-\rho_2}$$

$$l = \frac{\rho_2(1-\alpha-\beta)}{\rho_2 + \beta(1-\rho_2)} \qquad (9.3)$$

$$m = \frac{\beta(1-\rho_2)}{a[\rho_2 + \beta(1-\rho_2)]}$$

$$x_r = \frac{\alpha\rho_2}{[\rho_2 + \beta(1-\rho_2)]p_r^{\frac{1}{1-\rho_1}} \left(\sum_{s=1}^{n} p_s^{\frac{\rho_1}{\rho_1-1}} \right)}$$

Before we consider the behaviour of firms, let us first get the own price elasticity of demand for good r, using the last equation in (9.3), we have

$$\frac{\partial \ln x_r}{\partial \ln p_r} = \frac{\rho_1 - n}{n(1-\rho_1)} \tag{9.4}$$

This is the Yang–Heijdra formula (Yang & Heijdra 1993).

Next, we consider the firms' decision problems. We assume that the market structure is monopolistic competition. Each firm produces a good under the condition of increasing returns to scale. Because of global increasing returns to scale, only one firm can survive in the market for a good. If there are two firms producing the same good, one of them can always increase output to reduce price by utilizing further economies of scale, thereby driving the other firm out of the market. Therefore, the monopolist can manipulate the interaction between quantity and price to choose a profit-maximizing price. Free entry into each sector is, however, assumed. Free entry will drive the profit of a marginal firm that has the lowest profit to zero. Any positive profit of the marginal firm will invite a potential entrepreneur to set up a new firm to produce a differentiated good. For a symmetric model, this condition implies zero profit for all firms.

Assume that the production function of good r is $X_r = (l_r - A)/b$. So the labour cost function of good r is

$$l_r = bX_r + A \tag{9.5}$$

where A is the fixed cost and b the constant marginal cost. The first-order condition for the monopolist to maximize profit with respect to output level or price implies that

$$MR = p_r \left[1 + \frac{1}{(\partial \ln x_r / \partial \ln p_r)} \right] = MC = b \tag{9.6}$$

where MR and MC stand for marginal revenue and marginal cost, respectively. Inserting the expression for the own price elasticity of demand $\partial(\ln x_r)/\partial(\ln p_r)$ in (9.4) into (9.6), we have

$$p_r = \frac{b(n - \rho_1)}{\rho_1(n - 1)} \tag{9.7}$$

The zero-profit condition implies

$$p_r X_r = b X_r + A \tag{9.8}$$

9.1.2   General equilibrium and comparative statics

Since market goods are symmetric, we have $X_r = X_s = X$, $x_r = x_s = x$, $p_r = p_s = p$, r, $s = 1, 2, ..., n$. In addition, home goods are also symmetric, so we have $l_j = l_k = l_h$, $x_j = x_k = x_h$, j, $k = 1, 2, ..., m$. The general equilibrium is given by (9.3), (9.7), (9.8) and the market clearing condition $Mx = X$, which involve the unknowns p, n, m, l, l_h, x, X. Here, the subscripts of variables are skipped because of symmetry. Hence, the general equilibrium values of the various variables are

$$
\begin{aligned}
p &= \frac{b(n - \rho_1)}{\rho_1(n - 1)}, \\[4pt]
X &= \frac{\rho_1 A(n - 1)}{bn(1 - \rho_1)}, \\[4pt]
x &= \frac{\rho_1 A(n - 1)}{bn(1 - \rho_1)M}, \\[4pt]
l &= \frac{\rho_2(1 - \alpha - \beta)}{\rho_2 + \beta(1 - \rho_2)}, \\[4pt]
l_h &= \frac{a}{1 - \rho_2}, \\[4pt]
l_r &= \frac{A(n - \rho_1)}{n(1 - \rho_1)}, \\[4pt]
n &= \frac{M\alpha\rho_2(1 - \rho_1)}{A[\rho_2 + \beta(1 - \rho_2)]} + \rho_1, \\[4pt]
m &= \frac{\beta(1 - \rho_2)}{a[\rho_2 + \beta(1 - \rho_2)]}.
\end{aligned}
\tag{9.9}
$$

In the above solution, it can be checked that the aggregate employment of labour by firms is consistent with supply as $l + ml_h + nl_r/M = 1$.

After obtaining explicit solutions for the general equilibrium values of the variables as functions of the parameters, we may next examine the comparative statics by examining the effects of a change in some parameter on the equilibrium values of the variable, as given below:

$$\frac{\partial n}{\partial M} = \frac{\alpha \rho_2 (1-\rho_1)}{A[\rho_2 + \beta(1-\rho_2)]} > 0,$$

$$\frac{\partial n}{\partial A} = -\frac{M \alpha \rho_2 (1-\rho_1)}{A^2[\rho_2 + \beta(1-\rho_2)]} < 0,$$

$$\frac{\partial n}{\partial \alpha} = \frac{M \rho_2 (1-\rho_1)}{A[\rho_2 + \beta(1-\rho_2)]} > 0,$$

$$\frac{\partial n}{\partial \beta} = -\frac{M \alpha \rho_2 (1-\rho_1)(1-\rho_2)}{A[\rho_2 + \beta(1-\rho_2)]^2} < 0,$$

$$\frac{\partial n}{\partial \rho_1} = 1 - \frac{M \alpha \rho_2}{A[\rho_2 + \beta(1-\rho_2)]} < 0 \qquad (9.10)$$

$$\frac{\partial n}{\partial \rho_2} = \frac{M \alpha \beta (1-\rho_1)}{A[\rho_2 + \beta(1-\rho_2)]^2} > 0$$

$$\frac{\partial m}{\partial \beta} = \frac{\rho_2 (1-\rho_2)}{a[\rho_2 + \beta(1-\rho_2)]^2} > 0,$$

$$\frac{\partial m}{\partial a} = -\frac{\beta(1-\rho_2)}{a^2[\rho_2 + \beta(1-\rho_2)]} < 0,$$

$$\frac{\partial m}{\partial \rho_2} = \frac{-\beta}{a[\rho_2 + \beta(1-\rho_2)]^2} < 0,$$

The signs of the above comparative-statics results are all straightforward except for $\partial n/\partial \rho_1$. It appears to be ambiguous. However, if we substitute the solution for n into the solution for x in (9.9), we have the value of x as given in (9.11). Since the denominator is positive and $\rho_1 A$ in the numerator is also positive, the remaining part $\{M\alpha\rho_2 - A[\rho_2 + \beta(1 - \rho_2)]\}$ in the numerator must also be positive for x to be positive. As x has to be positive for n to be meaningful, the sign of $\partial n/\partial \rho_1$ is in fact unambiguously negative.

The comparative-statics results above may be seen to be intuitively agreeable, though not obvious. For example, an increase in population size M increases the number of market goods n as it allows the sharing of the fixed costs over more individuals. An increase in the fixed cost A has the reverse effect of reducing the number of market goods. Similarly, the same applies to the fixed cost of home production a on the number of home goods m. An increase in preference (represented by α) for the market goods increases the number n of market goods and an increase in preference (represented by β) for the home goods decreases the number of market goods. An increase in the elasticity of substitution between different market goods (represented by ρ_1)

decreases the number of market goods, as it is less important to have different goods. In contrast, an increase in the elasticity of substitution between different home goods (represented by ρ_2) increases the number of market goods, as it decreases the number of home goods m and hence allows the individual to be able to consume more market goods.

To calculate the equilibrium level of utility, first we get the equilibrium values of l, x, x_h, n, m. We have

$$l = \frac{\rho_2(1-\alpha-\beta)}{\rho_2 + \beta(1-\rho_2)}$$

$$x = \frac{\rho_1 A[M\alpha\rho_2 - A(\rho_2 + \beta(1-\rho_2))]}{bM[M\alpha\rho_2(1-\rho_1) + A\rho_1(\rho_2 + \beta(1-\rho_2))]}$$

$$x_h = \frac{a\rho_2}{c(1-\rho_2)} \tag{9.11}$$

$$n = \frac{M\alpha\rho_2(1-\rho_1)}{A[\rho_2 + \beta(1-\rho_2)]} + \rho_1$$

$$m = \frac{\beta(1-\rho_2)}{a[\rho_2 + \beta(1-\rho_2)]}$$

Inserting these values into utility function in (9.1), we have

$$u_e = l^{1-\alpha-\beta} n^{\frac{\alpha}{\rho_1}} x^\alpha m^{\frac{\beta}{\rho_2}} x_h^\beta$$

$$= \rho_2^{1-\alpha} \rho_1^\alpha \beta^{\frac{\beta}{\rho_2}} b^{-\alpha} M^{-\alpha} a^{\beta-\frac{\beta}{\rho_2}} c^{-\beta} A^{\alpha-\frac{\alpha}{\rho_1}} \left(1-\rho_2\right)^{\frac{\beta}{\rho_2}-\beta}$$

$$\times (1-\alpha-\beta)^{(1-\alpha-\beta)} \left[\rho_2 + \beta(1-\rho_2)\right]^{\alpha-\frac{\alpha}{\rho_1}+\beta-\frac{\beta}{\rho_2}-1}$$

$$\times [M\alpha\rho_2 - A(\rho_2 + \beta(1-\rho_2))]^\alpha \{M\alpha\rho_2(1-\rho_1)$$

$$+ A\rho_1[\rho_2 + \beta(1-\rho_2)]\}^{\frac{\alpha}{\rho_1}-\alpha}$$

9.1.3 Optimal output

To analyse the welfare properties, we introduce the government to the model. We let the government to tax home production and subsidize market production. This is not restrictive as the tax rate and the subsidy rate may be either positive or negative. Assume that the tax rate of per unit home labour is τ, and then consumer's problem is

$$\text{Max: } u = l^{1-\alpha-\beta} \left[\sum_{r=1}^{n} x_r^{\rho_1}\right]^{\alpha/\rho_1} \left[\sum_{j=1}^{m} x_j^{\rho_2}\right]^{\beta/\rho_2} \quad \text{(utility function)} \tag{9.12}$$

s.t. $\sum_{r=1}^{n} p_r x_r + \tau \sum_{j=1}^{m} l_j = w\left(1 - l - \sum_{j=1}^{m} l_j\right)$ (budget constraint)

$x_j = \dfrac{l_j - a}{c}$ (production function)

The equilibrium values for above problem are

$$l_h = \frac{a}{1 - \rho_2}$$

$$l = \frac{\rho_2(1 - \alpha - \beta)}{\rho_2 + \beta(1 - \rho_2)}$$

$$m = \frac{\beta(1 - \rho_2)}{a(\tau + 1)[\rho_2 + \beta(1 - \rho_2)]}$$ (9.13)

$$x_r = \frac{\alpha \rho_2}{[\rho_2 + \beta(1 - \rho_2)] p_r^{\frac{1}{1 - \rho_1}} \left(\sum_{s=1}^{n} p_s^{\frac{\rho_1}{\rho_1 - 1}}\right)}$$

In addition, denoting the subsidy rate per unit of market product as σ, the zero-profit condition for each firm is

$$p_r X_r = (b - \sigma) X_r + A$$ (9.14)

We recalculate the equilibrium values of the various variables to obtain

$$p = \frac{(b - \sigma)(n - \rho_1)}{\rho_1(n - 1)}$$

$$X = \frac{\rho_1 A(n - 1)}{(b - \sigma)n(1 - \rho_1)}$$

$$x = \frac{\rho_1 A(n - 1)}{(b - \sigma)n(1 - \rho_1)M}$$

$$x_h = \frac{a \rho_2}{c(1 - \rho_2)}$$

$$l = \frac{\rho_2(1 - \alpha - \beta)}{\rho_2 + \beta(1 - \rho_2)}$$ (9.15)

$$l_h = \frac{a}{1 - \rho_2}$$

$$l_r = \frac{A(n - \rho_1)}{n(1 - \rho_1)}$$

$$n = \frac{M\alpha\rho_2(1-\rho_1)}{A[\rho_2 + \beta(1-\rho_2)]} + \rho_1$$

$$m = \frac{\beta(1-\rho_2)}{a(\tau+1)[\rho_2 + \beta(1-\rho_2)]}$$

Finally, by requiring a balanced budget for the government, we have

$$Mm\tau l_h = n\sigma X \tag{9.16}$$

Using the information above, we can obtain the equilibrium level of utility as

$$u_e = l^{1-\alpha-\beta} n^{\frac{\alpha}{\rho_1}} x^\alpha m^{\frac{\beta}{\rho_2}} x_h^\beta$$

$$= \rho_2^{1-\alpha}\rho_1^\alpha \beta^{\rho_2}(b-\sigma)^{-\alpha}(\tau+1)^{-\frac{\beta}{\rho_2}} M^{-\alpha} a^{\beta-\frac{\beta}{\rho_2}} c^{-\beta} A^{\alpha-\frac{\alpha}{\rho_1}}(1-\rho_2)^{\frac{\beta}{\rho_2}-\beta}$$

$$\times(1-\alpha-\beta)^{(1-\alpha-\beta)}[\rho_2 + \beta(1-\rho_2)]^{\frac{\alpha}{\rho_1}+\beta-\frac{\beta}{\rho_2}-1} \tag{9.17}$$

$$\times[M\alpha\rho_2 - A(\rho_2 + \beta(1-\rho_2))]^\alpha\{M\alpha\rho_2(1-\rho_1) + A\rho_1[\rho_2 + \beta(1-\rho_2)]\}^{\frac{\alpha}{\rho_1}-\alpha}$$

$$= B(b-\sigma)^{-\alpha}(\tau+1)^{-\frac{\beta}{\rho_2}}$$

where

$$B \equiv \rho_2^{1-\alpha}\rho_1^\alpha \beta^{\rho_2} M^{-\alpha} a^{\beta-\frac{\beta}{\rho_2}} c^{-\beta} A^{\alpha-\frac{\alpha}{\rho_1}}(1-\rho_2)^{\frac{\beta}{\rho_2}-\beta}(1-\alpha-\beta)^{(1-\alpha-\beta)}$$

$$\times[\rho_2 + \beta(1-\rho_2)]^{-\frac{\alpha}{\rho_1}+\beta-\frac{\beta}{\rho_2}-1}[M\alpha\rho_2 - A(\rho_2 + \beta(1-\rho_2))]^\alpha$$

$$\times\{M\alpha\rho_2(1-\rho_1) + A\rho_1[\rho_2 + \beta(1-\rho_2)]\}^{\frac{\alpha}{\rho_1}-\alpha}$$

is independent of the tax and subsidy rates τ and σ. The effect of a change in tax rate τ on the equilibrium value of utility with respect to the tax rate, and with the subsidy rate at whatever level that is allowed by the government budget constraint (9.16) as τ varies, evaluated at $\tau = 0$, is given by

$$\left.\frac{du_e}{d\tau}\right|_{\tau=0} = \frac{Bb^{-\alpha}\beta[\alpha M\rho_2(1-\rho_1) + A\rho_1(\rho_2 + \beta(1-\rho_2))]}{\rho_1\rho_2[M\alpha\rho_2 - A(\rho_2 + \beta(1-\rho_2))]} > 0 \tag{9.18}$$

where we have considered the relationship between τ and σ through the government budget constraint in equation (9.16), and it can be expressed explicitly as follows:

$$\sigma = \frac{bM\beta\tau}{(\tau+1)\rho_1[M\alpha\rho_2 - A(\rho_2 + \beta(1-\rho_2))] + M\beta\tau}$$

The positivity of (9.18) means that, starting from the original position without any tax/subsidy, a tax on home production which finances for a subsidy on market production increases utility, ignoring administrative costs and any possible side effects, such as rent-seeking activities triggered by the subsidy. Since all firms just break-even in equilibrium, we may base our welfare comparisons simply on the utility levels alone. We thus have,

> *Proposition 9.1: In our model with both home and market production under the conditions of increasing returns and average-cost pricing, the inefficiency in the market sector due to imperfect competition, i.e. under consumption/production, can be offset by providing subsidies to such a sector financed by a tax on the home sector even if the initial position involves no tax distortion, ignoring administrative costs and any possible side effects.*

In other words, the equilibrium with commodity taxation is a Pareto improvement with respect to the equilibrium without taxation. The possibility for efficiency improvements through some tax/subsidy means that the original equilibrium is not perfectly efficient. What is the source of this imperfect efficiency? We view the imperfect efficiency as a result of the combination of increasing returns and average-cost pricing in market goods. In the model, there are also increasing returns in home production. However, since the individual/household concerned makes the decision to produce/consume, the implications of increasing returns are taken into account and hence the optimizing choice in the home sector does not result in any inefficiency. However, market goods produced by firms are sold to individuals at average costs. Since each consumer takes the price of each of this good as given, the demand functions for these market goods do not take the implications of increasing returns into account. Each consumer assumes that, no matter how much he/she buys, the price will not be affected. However, if all consumers buy more of a market good, the fixed-cost component of producing this good will spread over a larger number of units, resulting in a lower average cost and hence lower price for every consumer. This effect is not taken into account and hence we have the under-production of the market goods. Subsidizing market goods financed by taxing home production may thus be utility increasing. In other words, the fixed-cost component of a market good may be viewed as possessing a publicness characteristic since it is shared by all consumers. The under-consumption/production of market goods may be related to the public-good nature of the fixed-cost components.

The taxing of home production may not be practically feasible and a lump-sum tax or poll tax may not be politically feasible or distributionally desirable. The subsidy on market production may thus be impracticable. However, if we allow for different degrees of increasing returns between different market goods, it may be feasible to tax market goods with lower degrees of increasing returns and subsidize market goods with higher degrees of increasing returns, as the next section shows.

9.2   A model with home and differentiated market production

In this section, the model of the previous section is extended to allow for different sectors of market goods that may have different degrees of elasticity of substitution and different degrees of increasing returns (through different values of the fixed cost and marginal cost). Instead of (1), we now have

$$\text{Max: } l^{1-\alpha_1-\alpha_2-\beta}\left[\sum_{r=1}^{n_1} x_r^{\rho_1}\right]^{\alpha_1/\rho_1}\left[\sum_{k=1}^{n_2} x_k^{\rho_2}\right]^{\alpha_2/\rho_2}\left[\sum_{j=1}^{m} x_j^{\rho}\right]^{\beta/\rho} \quad \text{(utility function)}$$

$$\text{s.t. } \sum_{r=1}^{n_1} p_r x_r + \sum_{k=1}^{n_2} p_k x_k = w\left(1-l-\sum_{j=1}^{m} l_j\right) \quad \text{(budget constraint)} \qquad (9.1')$$

$$x_j = \frac{l_j - a}{c} \quad \text{(home production function)}$$

where two types of market goods are allowed, with n_1 and n_2 as the numbers of the first and second types and p_r, p_k their prices and x_r, x_k their quantities consumed/demanded by the representative individual respectively. Other aspects, variables, and parameters in (9.1') are similar to those in (9.1). For example, $\rho_i \in (0, 1)$ is the parameter of elasticity of substitution between each pair of the same type market goods, $\rho \in (0, 1)$ is the parameter of elasticity of substitution between each pair of home goods. Each consumer is a price taker and his/her decision variables are m, l, l_j and x_r, x_k.

For the budget constraint, instead of (9.2), we have

$$\sum_{r=1}^{n_1} p_r x_r + \sum_{k=1}^{n_2} p_k x_k + ml_h + l = 1 \tag{9.2'}$$

For the new maximization problem, we can get the following solutions:

$$l_h = \frac{a}{1-\rho}$$

$$l = \frac{\rho(1-\alpha_1-\alpha_2-\beta)}{\rho+\beta(1-\rho)}$$

$$m = \frac{\beta(1-\rho)}{a[\rho+\beta(1-\rho)]} \tag{9.3'}$$

$$x_r = \frac{\alpha_1\rho}{[\rho+\beta(1-\rho)]p_r^{\frac{1}{1-\rho_1}}\left(\sum_{s=1}^{n_1} p_s^{\frac{\rho_1}{\rho_1-1}}\right)}$$

$$x_k = \frac{\alpha_2\rho}{[\rho+\beta(1-\rho)]p_k^{\frac{1}{1-\rho_2}}\left(\sum_{s=1}^{n_2} p_s^{\frac{\rho_2}{\rho_2-1}}\right)}$$

From the last two equations in (9.3'), we have

$$\frac{\partial \ln x_r}{\partial \ln p_r} = \frac{\rho_1 - n_1}{n_1(1-\rho_1)}, \quad r = 1,2,\dots,n_1 \tag{9.4'}$$

$$\frac{\partial \ln x_k}{\partial \ln p_k} = \frac{\rho_2 - n_2}{n_2(1-\rho_2)}, \quad k = 1,2,\dots,n_2 \tag{9.4''}$$

Let the labour cost functions of market goods be

$$l_r = b_1 X_r + A_1 \tag{9.5'}$$

$$l_k = b_2 X_k + A_2 \tag{9.5''}$$

The zero-profit condition gives

$$p_r X_r = b_1 X_r + A_1 \tag{9.8'}$$

$$p_k X_k = b_2 X_k + A_2 \tag{9.8''}$$

Similar to the derivation of (9.9), we may derive

$$p_1 = \frac{b_1(n_1 - \rho_1)}{\rho_1(n_1 - 1)}$$

$$p_2 = \frac{b_2(n_2 - \rho_2)}{\rho_2(n_2 - 1)}$$

$$X_1 = \frac{\rho_1 A_1(n_1 - 1)}{b_1 n_1(1 - \rho_1)}$$

$$X_2 = \frac{\rho_2 A_2(n_2 - 1)}{b_2 n_2(1 - \rho_2)}$$

$$x_1 = \frac{\rho_1 A_1(n_1 - 1)}{b_1 n_1(1 - \rho_1)M}$$

$$x_2 = \frac{\rho_2 A_2(n_2 - 1)}{b_2 n_2(1 - \rho_2)M}$$

$$l = \frac{\rho(1 - \alpha_1 - \alpha_2 - \beta)}{\rho + \beta(1 - \rho)}$$

$$l_h = \frac{a}{1 - \rho} \tag{9.9'}$$

$$x_h = \frac{a\rho}{c(1 - \rho)}$$

$$l_1 = \frac{A_1(n_1 - \rho_1)}{n_1(1 - \rho_1)}$$

$$l_2 = \frac{A_2(n_2 - \rho_2)}{n_2(1 - \rho_2)}$$

$$n_1 = \frac{M\alpha_1\rho(1 - \rho_1)}{A_1[\rho + \beta(1 - \rho)]} + \rho_1$$

$$n_2 = \frac{M\alpha_2\rho(1 - \rho_2)}{A_2[\rho + \beta(1 - \rho)]} + \rho_2$$

$$m = \frac{\beta(1 - \rho)}{a[\rho + \beta(1 - \rho)]}$$

Their comparative statics are

$$\frac{\partial n_1}{\partial M} = \frac{\alpha_1\rho(1 - \rho_1)}{A_1[\rho + \beta(1 - \rho)]} > 0$$

$$\frac{\partial n_1}{\partial A_1} = -\frac{M\alpha_1\rho(1 - \rho_1)}{A_1^2[\rho + \beta(1 - \rho)]} < 0$$

$$\frac{\partial n_1}{\partial \alpha_1} = \frac{M\rho(1 - \rho_1)}{A[\rho + \beta(1 - \rho)]} > 0 \tag{9.10'}$$

$$\frac{\partial n_1}{\partial \beta} = -\frac{M\alpha_1\rho(1-\rho_1)(1-\rho)}{A_1[\rho+\beta(1-\rho)]^2} < 0$$

$$\frac{\partial n_1}{\partial \rho_1} = -\frac{M\alpha_1\rho}{A_1[\rho+\beta(1-\rho)]} + 1 < 0$$

$$\frac{\partial n_1}{\partial \rho} = \frac{M\alpha_1\beta(1-\rho_1)}{A_1[\rho+\beta(1-\rho)]^2} > 0$$

Similarly, $\dfrac{\partial n_2}{\partial M} > 0,\ \dfrac{\partial n_2}{\partial A_2} < 0,\ \dfrac{\partial n_2}{\partial \alpha_2} > 0\ \dfrac{\partial n_2}{\partial \rho_2} < 0,\ \dfrac{\partial n_2}{\partial \rho} > 0$

$$\frac{\partial m}{\partial \beta} = \frac{\rho(1-\rho)}{a[\rho+\beta(1-\rho)]^2} > 0$$

$$\frac{\partial m}{\partial a} = -\frac{\beta(1-\rho)}{a^2[\rho+\beta(1-\rho)]} < 0$$

$$\frac{\partial m}{\partial \rho} = \frac{-\beta}{a[\rho+\beta(1-\rho)]^2} < 0$$

The qualitative results of the comparative statics are again consistent with intuition.

To analyse the welfare properties, we introduce the government to the model and allow the government to tax or subsidize market production but not home production. Denote the tax/subsidy rate of per unit of each market good in set one as τ_1 (positive if tax; negative if subsidy) and that on set two as τ_2. Then, the zero-profit conditions for firms are

$$p_r X_r = (b_1 + \tau_1)X_r + A_1 \tag{9.14'}$$

$$p_k X_k = (b_2 + \tau_2)X_k + A_2 \tag{9.14''}$$

The equilibrium values of the various variables are given by

$$p_1 = \frac{(b_1 + \tau_1)(n_1 - \rho_1)}{\rho_1(n_1 - 1)}$$

$$p_2 = \frac{(b_2 + \tau_2)(n_2 - \rho_2)}{\rho_2(n_2 - 1)}$$

$$X_1 = \frac{\rho_1 A_1(n_1 - 1)}{(b_1 + \tau_1)n_1(1 - \rho_1)}$$

$$X_2 = \frac{\rho_2 A_2(n_2 - 1)}{(b_2 + \tau_2)n_2(1 - \rho_2)}$$

$$x_1 = \frac{\rho_1 A_1(n_1 - 1)}{(b_1 + \tau_1)n_1(1 - \rho_1)M}$$

$$x_2 = \frac{\rho_2 A_2 (n_2 - 1)}{(b_2 + \tau_2) n_2 (1 - \rho_2) M}$$

$$l = \frac{\rho(1 - \alpha_1 - \alpha_2 - \beta)}{\rho + \beta(1 - \rho)}$$

$$l_h = \frac{a}{1 - \rho}$$

$$x_h = \frac{a\rho}{c(1 - \rho)}$$ (9.15')

$$l_1 = \frac{A_1(n_1 - \rho_1)}{n_1(1 - \rho_1)}$$

$$l_2 = \frac{A_2(n_2 - \rho_2)}{n_2(1 - \rho_2)}$$

$$n_1 = \frac{M\alpha_1\rho(1 - \rho_1)}{A_1[\rho + \beta(1 - \rho)]} + \rho_1$$

$$n_2 = \frac{M\alpha_2\rho(1 - \rho_2)}{A_2[\rho + \beta(1 - \rho)]} + \rho_2$$

$$m = \frac{\beta(1 - \rho)}{a[\rho + \beta(1 - \rho)]}$$

The balanced budget requirement for the government gives

$$n_1\tau_1 X_1 + n_2\tau_2 X_2 = 0$$ (9.16')

The equilibrium utility value is given by

$$u_e = l^{1 - \alpha_1 - \alpha_2 - \beta} n_1^{\frac{\alpha_1}{\rho_1}} x_1^{\alpha_1} n_2^{\frac{\alpha_2}{\rho_2}} x_2^{\alpha_2} m^\rho x_h^\beta$$

$$= \left(\frac{\rho(1 - \alpha_1 - \alpha_2 - \beta)}{\rho + \beta(1 - \rho)} \right)^{1 - \alpha_1 - \alpha_2 - \beta} \left\{ \frac{M\alpha_1\rho(1 - \rho_1)}{A_1[\rho + \beta(1 - \rho)]} + \rho_1 \right\}^{\frac{\alpha_1}{\rho_1}}$$

$$\times \left\{ \frac{\rho_1 A_1[M\alpha_1\rho - A_1(\rho + \beta(1 - \rho))]}{M[M\alpha_1\rho(1 - \rho_1) + A_1\rho_1(\rho + \beta(1 - \rho))]} \right\}^{\alpha_1} \left\{ \frac{M\alpha_2\rho(1 - \rho_2)}{A_2[\rho + \beta(1 - \rho)]} + \rho_2 \right\}^{\frac{\alpha_2}{\rho_2}}$$

$$\times \left\{ \frac{\rho_2 A_2[M\alpha_2\rho - A_2(\rho + \beta(1 - \rho))]}{M[M\alpha_2\rho(1 - \rho_2) + A_2\rho_2(\rho + \beta(1 - \rho))]} \right\}^{\alpha_2}$$

$$\times \left\{ \frac{\beta(1 - \rho)}{a[\rho + \beta(1 - \rho)]} \right\}^{\frac{\beta}{\rho}} \left[\frac{a\rho}{c(1 - \rho)} \right]^\beta (b_1 + \tau_1)^{-\alpha_1} (b_2 + \tau_2)^{-\alpha_2}$$

$$= B(b_1 + \tau_1)^{-\alpha_1} (b_2 + \tau_2)^{-\alpha_2}$$

(9.17')

where

$$B \equiv \left(\frac{\rho(1 - \alpha_1 - \alpha_2 - \beta)}{\rho + \beta(1 - \rho)} \right)^{1 - \alpha_1 - \alpha_2 - \beta} \left\{ \frac{M \alpha_1 \rho(1 - \rho_1)}{A_1[\rho + \beta(1 - \rho)]} + \rho_1 \right\}^{\frac{\alpha_1}{\rho_1}}$$

$$\left\{ \frac{\rho_1 A_1 [M \alpha_1 \rho - A_1(\rho + \beta(1 - \rho))]}{M[M \alpha_1 \rho(1 - \rho_1) + A_1 \rho_1(\rho + \beta(1 - \rho))]} \right\}^{\alpha_1} \left\{ \frac{M \alpha_2 \rho(1 - \rho_2)}{A_2[\rho + \beta(1 - \rho)]} + \rho_2 \right\}^{\frac{\alpha_2}{\rho_2}}$$

$$\left\{ \frac{\rho_2 A_2 [M \alpha_2 \rho - A_2(\rho + \beta(1 - \rho))]}{M[M \alpha_2 \rho(1 - \rho_2) + A_2 \rho_2(\rho + \beta(1 - \rho))]} \right\}^{\alpha_2} \left\{ \frac{\beta(1 - \rho)}{a[\rho + \beta(1 - \rho)]} \right\}^{\frac{\beta}{\rho}} \left[\frac{a\rho}{c(1 - \rho)} \right]^{\beta}$$

is independent of the tax/subsidy rates. We calculate the derivative of equilibrium utility level with respect to the tax rate τ_1, with the value of τ_2 given by the government budget constraint (9.16') as τ_1 varies, evaluated at $\tau_1 = 0$, $\tau_2 = 0$, yielding

$$\left. \frac{du_e}{d\tau_1} \right|_{\tau_1 = 0} = \frac{B\{\rho_1 \alpha_2 \{M \alpha_1 \rho - A_1[\rho + \beta(1 - \rho)]\} - \rho_2 \alpha_1 \{M \alpha_2 \rho - A_2[\rho + \beta(1 - \rho)]\}\}}{b_1^{\alpha_1 + 1} b_2^{\alpha_2} \rho_2 \{M \alpha_2 \rho - A_2[\rho + \beta(1 - \rho)]\}}$$

(9.18')

From (9.18'), it can be seen that

$$\left. \frac{du_e}{d\tau_1} \right|_{\tau_1 = 0} > 0 \qquad\qquad (9.19')$$

$$\text{if } \frac{\rho_1[M \alpha_1 \rho - A_1(\rho + \beta(1 - \rho))]}{\alpha_1} > \frac{\rho_2[M \alpha_2 \rho - A_2(\rho + \beta(1 - \rho))]}{\alpha_2}$$

To see the meaning of this condition, consider the following three simple cases:

1. The case of $\rho_1 = \rho_2$ and $\alpha_1 = \alpha_2$ when the condition collapses into $-A_1 > -A_2$, or $A_1 < A_2$. This means that, *ceteris paribus,* if the fixed-cost component in the production of market goods of sector one is smaller than that of sector two, it is efficient to tax sector one and subsidize sector two.
2. The case of $\alpha_1 = \alpha_2$ and $A_1 = A_2$ when the condition collapses into $\rho_1 > \rho_2$. This means that, *ceteris paribus,* if the elasticity of substitution between goods within sector one is larger than that within sector two, it is efficient to tax sector one and subsidize sector two.
3. The case of $\rho_1 = \rho_2$ and $A_1 = A_2$ when the condition collapses into $\alpha_1 > \alpha_2$. This means that, *ceteris paribus,* if the preference of individuals is such that goods in sector one is regarded as more important than

those in sector two, it is efficient to tax sector one and subsidize sector two.

The intuitive reasons for the three separate points above may be briefly explained. The first point relates to the degree of increasing returns; the higher the fixed cost, the higher the degree of increasing returns and the larger is the publicness characteristic. The elasticity of substitution between goods (second point) is also relevant. The more substitutable are goods within a sector, *ceteris paribus*, the less number of goods of that sector will be produced and the more of each good will be produced. (This point is confirmed below.) Then, given that the fixed cost is the same, the degree of increasing returns is lower at higher output. (Defining the degree of increasing returns as the negative of the elasticity of average cost with respect to output, this point may be verified simply by differentiation.) Thus, the sector with a higher elasticity of substitution between goods within that sector has lower degree of increasing returns. A tax on the sector with higher elasticity of substitution and a subsidy on the sector with lower elasticity of substitution are thus taxing the sector with lower degree of increasing returns and subsidizing the sector with a higher degree of increasing returns. Our results here are thus consistent with the general result of the efficiency of producing more of a good with a higher degree of increasing returns obtained in Chapter 5.

The point that, *ceteris paribus*, higher elasticity of substitution leads to a lower number of goods and higher output for each good may be verified. The effect on the number of goods is given by $\partial n_i / \partial \rho_i$ being negative in (9.10'). The effect on output can be obtained by first substitute the solution for, say, n_1 into that for X_1 from (9.15'), obtaining

$$X_1 = \frac{\rho_1 A_1 \{M\alpha_1\rho - A_1[\rho + \beta(1-\rho)]\}}{b_1\{M\alpha_1\rho(1-\rho_1) + A_1\rho_1[\rho + \beta(1-\rho)]\}}$$

Partial differentiation gives

$$\frac{\partial X_1}{\partial \rho_1} = b_1 M\alpha_1\rho\{M\alpha_1\rho - A_1[\rho + \beta(1-\rho)]\} > 0$$

where the positivity follows from the numerator in the expression for X_1 above.

We may now consider the third point above on the effect of the degree of preference. The more important is a sector regarded by individuals (the higher is α_i), the more of the goods in that sector are consumed.

This again results in a higher output level for goods in that sector, i.e. a higher X_i. This again leads to a lower degree of increasing returns. Thus, *ceteris paribus*, a tax on this sector and a subsidy on a sector with lower importance will be efficient (This is in line with the results of Heal 1980 that large markets are over-served and small markets are under-served). Thus, all the three elements of fixed cost, elasticity of substitution, and preference importance parameters are relevant and they all relate to the degree of increasing returns. When more than one of these three elements differ, their effects intertwine and the net effects are as given in (9.19'). Our results may be summarized as

Proposition 9.2: In our model with both home and market production under the conditions of increasing returns and average-cost pricing with two sectors of different fixed costs, elasticities of substitution, and degrees of importance in preference, ceteris paribus, it is efficient to tax the sector with lower fixed costs, or higher elasticity of substitution (lower value of diversity) or higher degree of importance in preference and subsidize the other in accordance to (9.19').

Here again, we may interpret according to the overshifting effect of subsidizing and taxing market goods. This can be seen in the following inequalities.

$$\frac{\partial p_1}{\partial \tau_1} = \frac{M\alpha_1\rho}{\rho_1[M\alpha_1\rho - A_1(\rho + \beta(1-\rho))]} > 1$$

$$\frac{\partial p_2}{\partial \tau_2} = \frac{M\alpha_2\rho}{\rho_2[M\alpha_2\rho - A_2(\rho + \beta(1-\rho))]} > 1$$

where we have used expressions of p_1 and p_2 in (9.15'). Overshifting is occurring in both kinds of market goods. However, corresponding to three simple cases discussed above, in each case we have

$$\frac{\partial p_1}{\partial \tau_1} < \frac{\partial p_2}{\partial \tau_2}$$

This means that welfare can be improved by taxing the sector with lower fixed costs, or a higher elasticity of substitution (lower value of diversity) or a higher degree of importance in preference and subsidizing the other.

Our first result in this proposition is related to some results in Myles (1987) and the second result in this proposition is related to some results in Doi and Futagami (2004). Myles (1987) shows that under certain conditions it is welfare-improving to tax the competitive industry and subsidize the imperfectly competitive industry where the two industries are connected via consumers who view the outputs as perfect substitutes at a taste-dependent rate of transformation. Doi and Futagami (2004) use a monopolistic competition model to show that goods with higher elasticity of substitution should be taxed heavier. However, our results can be regarded as an extension of their results. Although we both use a similar model and similar taxation set up, here we use the Yang–Heijdra formula of the own price elasticity of demand rather than Dixit–Stiglitz formula; the result in Doi and Futagami (2004) is a special case of our results. The detailed difference between Yang–Heijdra formula and Dixit–Stiglitz formula can be found in Yang and Heijdra (1993). As discussed in Doi and Futagami (2004), our second result is also opposed to the Ramsey inverse elasticity rule. (Compare also the case for subsidizing labour market participation by Booth & Coles 2007.)

9.3 Concluding remarks

Despite the straightforward nature of our results as summarized in the two propositions, the applicability to the real economy is subject to important qualifications. First, the government may not have the information to differentiate which goods should be taxed (and by how much) and which subsidized. Allowing differential tax/subsidies may open a floodgate of rent-seeking activities causing more waste than the efficient gain that could be obtained. Second, we have not considered other factors causing imperfect efficiency in the real economy. One important factor is environmental disruption of many production and consumption activities. If the degrees of such disruption are not related to whether a good is home produced or produced for the market, our conclusions may not be much affected. However, there may be some presumption that home production activities are generally less environmentally disruptive than market production. Most of home production consists of home-cooking, cleaning, washing, gardening, and childcare, which are largely non-disruptive except for the energy and detergents used. (Some people may also regard some of these activities/goods as involving some merit-good aspect due to the effects on children.) Thus, on the environmental issue, it may be the case that market production should be taxed instead. However, this consideration is largely offset by the pre-existence of general taxation including income taxes and value-added or goods and services taxes. These taxes do not fall upon home production (the intermediate goods used in home production are produced for the market). If we view these general taxes as largely offsetting to the higher degrees of environmental disruption of most market goods, then the differential degrees of disruption between home and market goods no longer affect our conclusion on the efficiency of subsidizing market goods with higher degrees of increasing returns. The desirability of doing so is then mainly qualified by the first consideration on the lack of information and the promotion of rent-seeking activities.

10
Do the Economies of Specialization Justify the Work Ethics? An Examination of Buchanan's Hypothesis

Buchanan (1991, 1994) proposes an interesting hypothesis explaining the prevalence of an ethic encouraging more work. Economies of specialization mean that more division of labour may increase productivity. If everyone works more, it increases the extent of the market which enables higher degree of division of labour and hence higher productivity. Individual choice between leisure and work thus results in a sub-optimal level of work. One way to counteract this is to maintain a work ethic. This chapter examines the validity and significance of this hypothesis in the Yang–Ng framework of inframarginal analysis. A simultaneous artificial decrease in preference for leisure by all individuals decreases intrinsic utility evaluated at the original preference. However, using a more realistic model allowing for both home and firm/market production developed by Ng and Zhang (2005), and discussed in Chapter 9, a strong support is provided for Buchanan's hypothesis as a shift in preference by everyone from leisure to market goods produced under increasing returns; average-cost pricing increases utility even if evaluated in accordance with the original preference. Buchanan's thesis probably has more relevance in ancient times when the work ethics originated but is less significant in the current world of global trade where the billions of individuals involved is sufficient to sustain specialization without artificial encouragement of additional work effort. On the contrary, the competition for relative standing, the materialistic bias caused by our accumulation instinct and advertising, and the environmental disruption of material production and consumption suggest that the discouragement of long working week may be more conducive to welfare.

10.1 Introduction

Buchanan (1991, 1994) proposes an interesting hypothesis explaining the prevalence of an ethic encouraging more work. The economies of specialization mean that more division of labour may increase productivity. If everyone works more, it increases the extent of the market which enables higher degree of division of labour and hence higher productivity. Individual choice between leisure and work thus results in a sub-optimal level of work. One way to counteract this is to maintain a work ethic. This chapter examines the validity and significance of this hypothesis.

Economists have not paid much attention to this and similar problems partly, if not mainly, because of the preoccupation with the sectoral resource allocation problem of the neoclassical economics instead of the division-of-labour problem of the classical economics. Yang and Ng (1993) attempt to shift the attention back to specialization, using formal models of optimization and equilibrium to analyse the classical problem of division of labour. It is interesting to see the significance of Buchanan's hypothesis in this new framework.

Even within the traditional framework, the problem of increasing returns has not been completely ignored. A well-known analysis is the Dixit–Stiglitz (1977) model of monopolistic competition. Within the monopolistic competition sector, each firm produces a product with decreasing average costs (a positive fixed cost plus a constant marginal cost). The rest of the economy is lumped into a composite good. To analyse the problem of work ethics, we may regard this composite good as leisure. There is nothing in the model to preclude such an interpretation. We may then directly apply the Dixit–Stiglitz result to assess the validity of Buchanan's hypothesis within such a model. Dixit and Stiglitz compare the market equilibrium (with free entry) with both the case of constrained optimum (where each firm must not make a positive loss) and that of unconstrained optimum (where lump sum subsidies to firms are allowed). Due to the difficulties of lump sum subsidies in the real world and to Buchanan's emphasis on realistic market economies, the case of constrained optimum is the more relevant one. Dixit and Stiglitz's 'results undermine the validity of the folklore of excess capacity, from the point of view of the unconstrained optimum as well as the constrained one. ... with a constant intrasector elasticity of substitution, the market equilibrium coincides with the constrained optimum. ... It is not possible to have a general result concerning the relative magnitudes of [leisure]' (Dixit & Stiglitz 1977, pp. 301–2). In other words, even if the unconstrained optimum is feasible, it may involve more *or* less leisure than the cases of the free market equilibrium and constrained optimum. This is in contrast to Buchanan's hypothesis on the presumption of over-consumption of leisure. However, this need not be a fatal blow to Buchanan who has in mind not so much the traditional economies of scale but the classical economies of specialization from the division of labour which is better modelled by the Yang–Ng framework. Therefore, we shall mainly examine the Buchanan hypothesis on work ethics in this latter framework. To do so in an intuitively more obvious way of graphical presentation, we first discuss the consumption constraint (partly for its own interest) faced by an individual in the Yang–Ng framework in the next section, before examining the issue of work ethics. In fact, Buchanan and Yoon (1994a) provide a model with the result of over-consumption of leisure. The higher productivity of a larger market size comes from a larger supportable number of intermediate goods, which is assumed to increase productivity (the Ethier–Romer assumption). In Section 10.3, we show the possibility without using this mechanism. Appendix 10A examines the problem more formally, providing some support to the Buchanan thesis. Section 10.4.1 shows that a simultaneous artificial decrease in preference for leisure **by all individuals** decreases intrinsic utility evaluated at the original preference. However, using a more realistic model allowing for both home and firm/market production developed by Ng and Zhang (2005), a stronger support is provided for Buchanan's hypothesis in Section 10.4.1, as a shift in preference by everyone from leisure to market goods produced under increasing returns and average-cost pricing increases utility even if evaluated in accordance with the original preference. However, the concluding Section 10.5 discusses some offsetting considerations. Briefly, Buchanan's thesis probably had more relevance in ancient times when the work ethics originated but is less significant in the current world of global trade where the billions of individuals involved are sufficient to sustain specialization without artificial encouragement of additional work effort. On the contrary, the competition for relative standing, the materialistic bias caused by our accumulation instinct and advertising, and the environmental disruption of material production and consumption suggest that the discouragement of long working week may be more welfare conducive.

10.2   Specialization and consumption constraints

In the traditional framework discussed in all economics textbooks, the consumption constraint faced by an individual/household who can buy at given prices is linear. In the case of Robinson Crusoe, it coincides with the production possibility curve which is concave (the production set is convex). In the Yang–Ng's framework, the production set is

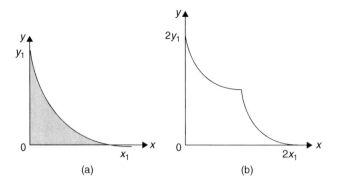

Figure 10.1 Production possibility

non-convex both for the case of Robinson Crusoe and for the case of a multi-person economy. Due to the economies of specialization, the production set is as depicted in Figures 10.1a and 10.1b, respectively for the cases of a single person and two persons.

In the single person case, obviously, the consumption constraint coincides with the production set. For the case of zero transactions costs with an infinite number of individuals offering unlimited trading possibilities (unlimited in the sense of eliminating the integer problem of finding a willing partner to exchange goods each specializes in, not in the sense of the absence of constraints on the price-ratio), the picture is also simple and similar to the traditional case. The individual will be able to trade at the given equilibrium price-ratio and hence face a linear consumption constraint. For the case of individuals with similar production abilities/functions, they all have the same production set and hence the equilibrium price-ratio is determined by the (absolute) slope of the line y_1x_1 in Figure 10.2, since a different price-ratio will be unable to induce any individual to produce one of the goods. Neither the similarity in preferences between individuals nor the symmetry in preferences between the goods is needed for this result. For simplicity and without loss of generality, normalize the units of the goods such that the value of each good produced by one person is equal. (In Figure 10.1a and Figure 10.2, $x_1 = y_1$.) At the equilibrium price-ratio of the line in Figure 10.2, if the aggregate amount of good X demanded relative to that of good Y is a/b, $[a/(a + b)]\%$ of people produce good X and $[b/(a + b)]\%$ produce good Y. Each individual just chooses a point on the line to reach his/her highest indifference curve as in the textbook. His/her production point is at either x_1 or y_1 depending on whether he/she

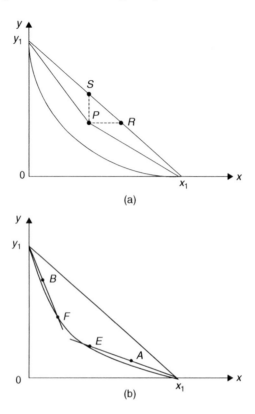

Figure 10.2 Consumption possibility – many individuals

produces X or Y. We have here the complete division of labour (each person produces no more than one good) with free exchange unfettered by the integer problem due to a large number of individuals relative to the number of goods.

The introduction of transactions costs makes the consumption constraint different from the line x_1y_1. For simplicity, consider the case of a proportional transactions cost (i.e. the ice-block effect, with a constant percentage of the good bought from the market melted before consumption; as a larger block of ice will have a smaller percentage melted, the ice-block is not a perfect example of this case of proportional transactions costs). If the transactions costs are small relative to the degree of economies of specialization such that it is always more efficient to specialize in the production of one good, the situation is as depicted in Figure 10.2a where the consumption constraint becomes x_1Py_1. If the highest indifference curve is reached along the segment x_1P, the individual produces at x_1 and exchanges up from x_1 along x_1S, but with the proportionate transactions cost reducing the consumption point to the segment x_1P. (With transactions costs, it is not efficient for a producer of X to exchange beyond this point S; if an individual prefers to consume more of good Y than the point P, he/she should produce y instead of x, and *vice versa* for the producer of Y with respect to the point R.) However, if the transactions cost is large relative to the degree of economies of specialization, the consumption possibility set is Ox_1AEFBy_1 in Figure 10.2b. The individual may produce at either x_1 or y_1; other points on his/her PPC are inefficient except possibly the segment EF. The cases of fixed transactions costs, combined transactions costs, etc. may be similarly analysed.

For the case where the number of individuals is not large relative to the number of goods, the situation is quite different and much more complicated. As a simple example, consider the case of two individuals (Arthur and Betty) with two goods (X and Y). Assuming similar production possibilities, their aggregate production set is as depicted in Figure 10.1b. But what is the consumption constraint of each? First, each individual always has the autarky alternative to fall back on. Hence, the consumption possibility set cannot be smaller than the production set of autarky (i.e. the shaded area Ox_1y_1 in Figure 10.1a). It is well known that, in the case of bilateral bargaining situation, the outcome is indeterminate and depends on the bargaining skills of the persons involved. So, let us abstract away this aspect of the problem by assuming that the two persons are similar in bargaining skills (or both insist on some form of fairness) or by assuming a Nash bargaining outcome. The two individuals will reach an outcome that is somewhat equally advantageous to both (hence, effectively also eliminating the possibility of a stalemate). The situation remains complicated.

If we further assume that the two individuals have identical preferences and that transactions costs are zero, the consumption possibility set faced by each person is Ox_1Qy_1, i.e. the aggregate production set divided by two, as shown in Figure 10.3. For example, the point P on the consumption constraint is reached with one person producing at x_1 and the other producing at P'', reaching the aggregate production point P' whose equal division gives the point P. If viewed alternatively, the person producing at x_1 exchange Tx_1 amount of X for PT amount of Y. (Hence, we may note that, unlike the case of many individuals, here the equilibrium exchange ratio is dependent on preferences, even under the assumption of similar preferences and equal bargaining skills. In

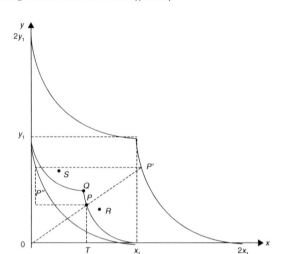

Figure 10.3 Consumption possibility – two individuals

Yang and Ng (1993), the simplifying assumption of symmetry in preferences between goods ensures that point Q instead of any other point in the consumption constraint is selected.)

Note that points on the line $x_1 Q y_1$, except the three points x_1, Q, and y_1, that are feasible in the case of Figure 10.2 (with many individuals and with zero transactions costs) are no longer feasible in this case of Figure 10.3 (with only two individuals and identical preferences) and hence not drawn. For example, if Arthur prefers a point like R to Q and wants to produce at x_1 and exchanges up $x_1 Q$ to reach R, this is possible only if Betty produces at y_1 and exchanges to reach S. However, with the usual convexity of preferences, if R is preferred to Q, Q is preferred to S and hence, *a fortiori*, R is preferred to S. With our assumption of equal bargaining skill and similar preferences, Betty will not agree to settle at S, with Arthur reaching a much superior position R. Of course, if S is still superior to all point in the autarky production set and if Arthur is better in bargaining than Betty, then R may be feasible. This illustrates the dependence of the feasible consumption set on bargaining. And of course, the introduction of transactions costs further complicates the identification of the consumption set, as we discussed for the case of many individuals illustrated in Figure 10.2. However, instead of discussing this complication, we move to the introduction of leisure.

For simplicity, Yang and Ng (1993) do not consider leisure as a variable. Lio (1996) has considered leisure in the new classical framework of inframarginal analysis. In our graphical approach here, leisure necessitates an additional axis as illustrated in Figure 10.4 for the case of an infinite number of individuals with no transactions costs. The introduction of leisure allows the question of work ethics to be analysed, as done in the next section.

10.3 Does the economy of specialization make work ethics welfare-improving? A terms-of-trade approach

It may first be noted that, in the case of an infinite number of individuals and in the absence of ignorance, irrationality, tax distortion, and external effects (on which see Section 10.5), the artificial encouragement of work ethics cannot increase, but will likely decrease, welfare, ignoring possibly some freak second-best and/or distributional effects. In this case, the advantage of specialization can be fully realized without artificial encouragement of work ethics (in the absence of significant transactions costs whose presence complicates the graphical illustration without affecting the conclusion). Each individual reaches his/her highest indifference surface by rational choice depending on his/her true preference between leisure and goods. In Figure 10.4, suppose point

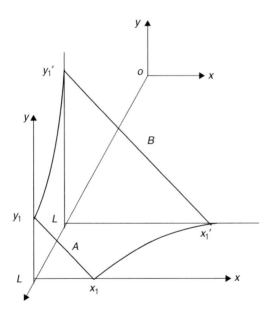

Figure 10.4 Leisure choice – many individuals

A touches the highest indifference surface and the individual chooses to have *OL* amount of leisure. The artificial encouragement (including through work ethics) to work more may make the individual choose a point like *B* and a smaller amount of leisure *OL'*. However, evaluated at his/her undistorted preference, he/she is better off at A than at B. This is so despite the fact that his/her labour productivity is higher at B (with the production point at either x_1' or y_1') than at A (with the production point at either x_1 or y_1) due to the economies of specialization. True, 10% more work may produce 15% more product. However, if the individual prefers the consumption point A to B, it is better to have lower productivity and more leisure. Thus, the study by Lio (1996) which addresses the question of productivity but not the question of preference or welfare, while yielding some interesting results, does not answer the question regarding the desirability of encouraging work.

However, in the case of a small number of individuals, it is not difficult to construct examples to show that a decrease in the preference for leisure (higher level of work ethics) by an individual may benefit others through more opportunities for trade and specialization. This effect is similar to the network externality. However, this extra-trade effect is present even in the absence of the economies of specialization. This is illustrated in Figure 10.5 for the simple case of two individuals with exogenous comparative and absolute advantage, constant returns to scale, linear transformation curve (between good *X* and good *Y*; i.e. constant marginal rate of transformation, but a diminishing MRT may also be allowed), and absence of transactions costs. Arthur has a comparative advantage in producing *X*; spending PR amount of time working, his production possibility curve for the two goods is indicated by the line x_1y_1', in contrast to that of x_2y_2' for Betty. Arthur would like to sell *X* for *Y* if the price of *X* in terms of *Y* is larger than 1/2. However, if Betty prefers to have 24 hours of leisure a day, choosing the corner solution at P even if she is offered two units of *X* for each unit of *Y*, Arthur is stuck with his production possibility set. However, if a higher level of work ethics makes Betty willing to spend *PQ* amount of time working to produce at 1/2 and exchange (drawn as one to one, but could be more favourable) to reach the point *A*, this will allow Arthur to reach *B* which may be preferable to all points on his production set. Thus, Arthur is made better off by Betty's higher level of work ethics due to the increased opportunity for exchange. While goods are tradable, leisure is not. (The possibility of joint usage of leisure and/or the externality in leisure is not considered here.) Betty's preference for the corner solution at *P* may be regarded as rather extreme. However, even at less extreme

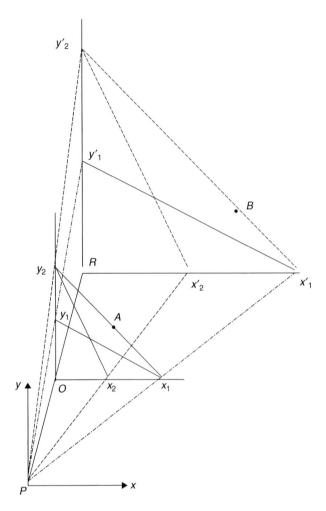

Figure 10.5 Trade opportunity

choice, Betty's strong preference for leisure may still leave Arthur with little opportunity to trade, such as being able to move up from x'_1 only a very small distance, instead of to point B or beyond. That the opportunity for trade of an individual is increased by the lower preference for leisure is shown more formally in Appendix 10A which allows for different degrees of economies of specialization and shows that the higher the degree of economies of specialization, the larger is the beneficial effect of a higher work ethics on the trading partner.

However, the gain of Arthur from the higher work ethics of Betty is at the expense of the latter. In terms of her intrinsic preference (her preference unaffected by the work ethics), Betty must be worst off at the point A. (Rationality and the absence of ignorance are assumed here. For relaxation of these, see the next section.) Otherwise, Betty could be persuaded by Arthur to produce at 1/2 and trade to and consume at A, even without the artificial work ethics.

It may be noted that the case for the work ethics on the ground of economies of specialization should be based on the evaluation in accordance with the original preferences. For example, the case for taxing pollution is justified on the ground that individuals will be better off with the tax according to the given preferences, though each individual prefers to pollute. If the case for the work ethics were based on some irrationality of preferences, then the evaluation might be made with respect to certain more rational preferences if such could be justified. Since the case is not based on some problem with the original preferences but purely on the economies of specialization, one must be able to show that, due to the working of these economies, some artificially higher level of work ethics may yet lead to a superior situation even according to the original preferences. If one could base the case on the new preferences, one could argue for changing the preference for x over y into y over x for any x and y at all. However, it is true that, since economic analysis is based on a given set of preferences, when preferences change, especially if exogenously, economists have really no widely accepted criteria to judge desirability. Nevertheless, I have argued elsewhere (Ng 2003) that happiness should then be used as a valid cross-preference criterion since happiness is our ultimate objective and that remains unchanged as preferences change. However, the case for the work ethics does not pretend to be based on a higher happiness level even if the resulting situation is lower in terms of the original preference. Thus, we need not be concerned with this issue here.

A question arises: Does Arthur gain more than marginally at only a marginal loss to Betty? If so, the artificial encouragement of the work ethics may still be desirable from a social point of view. The answer is negative. At the exchange ratio of one-to-one illustrated in Figure 10.5, it is true that the gain to Arthur may be larger than marginal even only for a small amount of exchange undertaken. It is also possible for the loss in intrinsic preference to Betty to be only marginal. However, if this is the case, Arthur should be able to persuade Betty to undertake some production and some exchange at a more favourable ratio to Betty such that the whole change is Pareto optimal according to the intrinsic preferences of both individuals. The fact that this is not possible and an artificial work ethics is needed means that, if the change is more than marginally beneficial to Arthur, it must also be more than marginally detrimental to Betty according to the intrinsic preferences.

While the economy of specialization is not necessary to make work ethics possibly welfare-improving for others due to higher trading opportunity, it should increase this welfare-improving effect as it increases the gain from specialization and trade. In this sense, the Buchanan thesis on work ethics has some validity. However, its quantitative significance is unlikely to be large. This is so since there are millions of individuals in the real world and the costs of long-distance trade are decreasing due to improved transportation and communication. Hence, in the real world, we are more characterized by the case of Figure 10.4 than by that of Figure 10.5, or the generalization of Figure 10.5 to cover the presence of economies of specialization.

While the network or trading externality may exist for the case of a small number of individuals (in either the presence or absence of the economy of specialization, as shown above), it need not always exist even for the case of just two individuals. This is shown in Figure 10.6

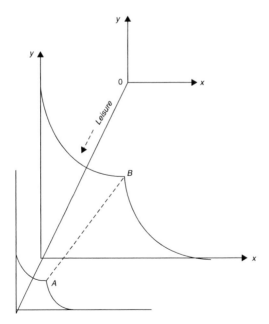

Figure 10.6 Leisure choice

for the case of two identical (in productivity, preference, and bargaining skills) individuals with the presence of economies of specialization. (Figure 10.6 is the extension of the case of Figure 10.3 to include leisure as a variable.) Suppose that the consumption feasibility set (only shown partially in Figure 10.6) touches the highest indifference surface (in accordance to the intrinsic preference) at *A*; the artificial encouragement of work ethics shifts the solution to *B*. Similar to the case of Figure 10.4, this shift is again a deterioration according to the intrinsic preference. The expanded extent of the market does not help in this case (Figure 10.6) as the economy of specialization has already been fully utilized at the original point A where each individual specializes in the production of only one good. Even if there are more goods than individuals such that each individual has to produce more than one good, a higher degree of specialization can be better facilitated by a larger number of individuals than by a longer working week. Moreover, the globalization of the economy means that we have billions of individuals, a number well in excess of the number of goods.

10.4 Does the economy of specialization make work ethics welfare-improving? Further investigations

In the previous section and in more detail in Ng and Ng (2003), the validity and significance of Buchanan's hypothesis is examined. Instead of modelling the work ethics as an additional constraint, it examines the effect of a higher preference for work (or a lower preference for leisure). It concludes with a qualified support for the Buchanan hypothesis by showing that a decrease in preference for leisure (a higher work ethics) by an individual benefits his/her trading partners by improving the terms of trade of the latter. Moreover, the higher the degree of the economies of specialization, the larger is this beneficial effect on others (Appendix 10A). It suggests that the Buchanan hypothesis probably has more relevance in ancient times when the work ethics originated but is less significant in the current world of global trade where the billions of individuals involved is sufficient to sustain specialization without artificial encouragement of additional work effort.

Essentially, the artificial decrease in the preference for leisure (and the correspondingly higher production and hence higher desire to trade) by an individual may benefit his/her trading partners but actually harms the individual, at least if valued at his/her original or intrinsic preference. Thus, it is unclear that this benefit (even if it is larger at a higher degree of economies of specialization) justifies the work ethics. This is not pursued in Ng and Ng (2003) which focuses on the effect on the terms of trade rather than on utility or welfare to avoid the tricky questions of interpersonal comparisons of utility and welfare evaluation in the presence of preference changes. In this section, a way is found to do the analysis despite these tricky questions.

Section 10.4.1 shows that a simultaneous artificial decrease in preference for leisure **by all individuals** decreases the intrinsic utility (the utility derived from using the original utility function with the new set of objective variables) of all individuals in a simple model of ex-ante identical individuals. (In a model of heterogeneous individuals, it is possible to construct specific cases where some individuals may gain but usually others will lose more, still failing to provide a case for the artificial encouragement of work ethics at the societal level.) Rather, if the original population size is not large enough to allow full specialization, an increase in population increases utility by allowing more specialization.

Moreover, using a more realistic model allowing for both home and firm/market production developed by Ng and Zhang (2005) and discussed in Chapter 9, a stronger support is provided for Buchanan's hypothesis by showing that a shift in preference by everyone from leisure to market goods produced under increasing returns and average-cost pricing increases utility even if evaluated in accordance with the original preference (Section 10.4.2). However, a shift in preference from leisure to home goods (even if also produced under increasing returns) decreases utility evaluated in accordance with the original preference. The contrast between market and home goods is due to the fact that the effect of increasing returns in home production is already fully taken into account by each individual (or household) while that of firm production has not been fully taken into account. Market goods are priced at average costs, consisting of the average fixed cost plus a constant marginal cost. This makes the fixed cost component possess some publicness aspect which is not fully accounted for by individual maximization. This contrast is explained in detail in Section 10.5.

Like the papers by Buchanan and Yoon, Ng and Ng, the present chapter is only concerned with the potential benefits of having a work ethic but not concerned with the coordination and/or game-strategic process in arriving at the accepted ethic, work or otherwise. On some aspects of the latter and related issues, see, e.g. Gauthier (1986) who argues that ethics may emerge from the agreement by rational individuals based on the mutual interest of observance. Similarly, the present study is not concerned with the crowding-out of intrinsic motivation by incentive payments or other aspects of the principal-agent problem; on this crowding-out of work ethics, see Grepperud and Pedersen (2001).

10.4.1   Division of labour by identical individuals

Since Buchanan relates work ethics to economies of specialization from the division of labour, his case is examined by using models (the previous section and Appendix 10A use a most simple model of two symmetrical goods and two ex-ante identical individuals with no non-labour inputs) of a framework designed for analysing the division of labour by Yang and Ng (1993), but with leisure added to examine the role of work ethics. In this section, that model is expanded to allow for three goods (in addition to leisure) X, Y, and Z (to examine the role of population size later; the number of individuals remains at two at the moment; we can easily collapse this model into the one of two goods similar to Section 10.3 by taking Z out of the utility function and make l_z, the amount of labour used to produce Z, equal to zero.) It will be shown in this model of division of labour with economies of specialization that an artificial shift in preference from leisure to goods by all individuals decreases the utility of the representative individual evaluated at the original preference.

Each individual has T units of time which may be used for leisure or the production of either one or more of the three goods X, Y and Z. Thus, each individual is faced with time constraint

$$T = \ell + l_x + l_y + l_z \qquad (10.1)$$

where ℓ = leisure time, l_i is the amount of time used in the production of good i. The production functions are

$$X = l_x^a;\ Y = l_y^a;\ Z = l_z^a \qquad (10.2)$$

where $a > 1$ indicates the presence of economies of specialization. Individuals are taken as ex-ante identical and production functions are symmetrical to emphasize the point that gain from trade may arise from the economies of specialization alone.

A Cobb–Douglas utility function is used for simplicity. Since we are considering a change in preference only for leisure, we let only leisure to carry a preference variable. Those for x, y, and z (using lower case to indicate the amount consumed) may be normalized to unity by scaling the utility function since the preferences are symmetric over the goods.

$$U = xyzl^\alpha \qquad (10.3)$$

Consider first the case of autarky where the individual self-produces all goods. The maximization of (10.3) subject to (10.1) and (10.2) gives the solution[1]

$$l_x = l_y = l_z = \frac{aT}{(3a + \alpha)}$$

$$\ell = \frac{T}{(3a + \alpha)} \tag{10.4}$$

$$U^A = a^{3a} \alpha^\alpha \left[\frac{T}{(3a + \alpha)} \right]^{3a + \alpha}$$

where the superscript A indicates autarky.

Now consider the case of specialization where an individual specializes in producing either X or Y and exchange with the other individual who specializes in the other good, and both individuals self-produce and consume Z. Due to symmetry, we need to consider only the case where the individual specializes in X. From his/her output of X, he/she supplies x^s in exchange for y at a price of p (price of X in terms of Y). However, market transactions are supposed to incur a transactions cost of $1 - k$. Thus, while the amount of Y he/she bought is equal to px^s, the amount he/she actually consumes equals only kpx^s. His/her utility function may thus be written as

$$U = [(T - \ell - l_z)^a - x^s] \, kpx^s l_z^a \, \ell^\alpha \tag{10.5}$$

The maximization of (10.5) with respect to ℓ, l_z and x^s gives the following solution

$$\ell = \frac{\alpha T}{(3a + \alpha)}$$

$$l_x = \left[\frac{2aT}{(3a + \alpha)} \right]^a$$

$$x = x^s = \frac{[2aT/(3a + \alpha)]^a}{2} \tag{10.6}$$

$$y = kp \frac{[2aT/(3a + \alpha)]^a}{2}$$

$$U_2^D = 2^{2(a-1)} kp a^{3a} \alpha^\alpha \left[\frac{T}{(3a + \alpha)} \right]^{3a + \alpha}$$

where the superscript D indicates division of labour and the subscript 2 indicates the number of individuals or the number of traded goods.

From (10.5) and (10.6), we have for the symmetrical case with $p = 1$ (as required by the assumption of free choice of occupation with initially identical individuals),

$$\frac{U_2^D}{U_A} = 2^{2(a-1)}k \tag{10.7}$$

Thus, division of labour yields a higher utility if and only if $2^{2(a-1)}k > 1$, i.e. if the economies of specialization (measured by $a - 1$) is sufficiently large to offset the effect of transactions costs (measured by $1 - k$). For example, if $a = 1.1$, k has to be no smaller than 0.87055 for division of labour to dominate autarky in this simple model. It may be noted that, in this model, the relative superiority of division of labour versus autarky does not depend on the preference for leisure. However, if division of labour is chosen, then the willingness to trade decreases with higher preference for leisure; x^s is a decreasing function of α. Thus, to the extent that other people may benefit from one's willingness to trade, a higher degree of work ethics (reduced preference for leisure) may be regarded as favourable. This may be shown more formally by bringing in the other person who produces Y into the picture. His/her situation is exactly the same as the person producing X depicted above, except that his/her preference parameter for leisure is indicated by β. Then his/her supply y^s is the same as the third equation in (10.6) for x^s except that α is replaced by β. Then, from the market equilibrium requirement $px^s = y^s$ (since the price of Y in terms of X is the inverse of the price of X in terms of Y), we may solve for the equilibrium price of X in terms of Y as

$$p = \left[\frac{(3a + \alpha)}{(3a + \beta)}\right]^a \tag{10.8}$$

which clearly increases with α and decreases with β. Thus, the person producing X benefits from the higher work ethics of the person producing Y and vice versa.

Now, let us examine the effect of a higher degree of the economies of specialization (a larger a) on the benefits of the higher work ethics of others. To concentrate on the increase in work effort rather than the complication of an initial interpersonal difference in preferences for leisure, we evaluate the effect of an increase in a on the effect of a change in α (or β, the two are symmetrical) on p at an initial position when $\alpha = \beta$. We then have,

$$
\frac{\partial^2 p}{\partial \alpha \partial a} = \frac{(3a+\alpha)^{a-1}}{(3a+\beta)^a} \left\{ 1 - \frac{3a}{3a+\alpha} + a[\ln(3a+\alpha) \right.
$$
$$
\left. - \ln(3a+\beta) - \frac{3a^2(\alpha-\beta)}{(3a+\alpha)(3a+\beta)} \right\}
$$

(10.9)

Since a, α, and β are all positive, the right hand side of (10.9) is positive at $\alpha = \beta$. This means that, the higher the degree of economies of specialization, the larger is the beneficial effect of a higher work ethics on the trading partner. From this (but using a model of only two goods; see Appendix 10A) Ng and Ng (2003) conclude that Buchanan's conjecture has validity and is related to the economies of specialization. However, as already noted in the previous section, the artificial decrease in the preference for leisure by an individual actually harms the individual himself/herself, at least if valued at his/her original or intrinsic preference. Thus, it is unclear that this benefit (even if it is larger at a higher degree of economies of specialization) justifies the work ethics. To support Buchanan's hypothesis, we need to show that, if all individuals decrease their preference for leisure, they will all benefit in accordance to their original preference, at least in a model of identical individuals. A way of examining whether this is true is provided below. The use of a model of identical individuals not only abstracts away the complications of interpersonal differences, but it also allows us to avoid having to make interpersonal utility comparisons.

Using the above model (the same result obtains when using a similar model with different numbers of individuals and goods, including the simpler model of two goods used in Ng & Ng), we let each individual adopt objective variables ℓ, x, etc. in accordance to those that would obtain if the preference for leisure parameter α were lower at α'. (Since we are now letting all or both individuals adopt this change simultaneously, we do not have to distinguish two different preference-for-leisure parameters α and β). From (10.6), but replacing α by α', we have

$$
\ell' = \frac{\alpha'T}{(3a+\alpha')}
$$
$$
x' = x^{s'} = \frac{[2aT/(3a+\alpha')]^a}{2}
$$

(10.6')

$$y' = kp \frac{[2aT/(3a + a')]^a}{2}$$

$$U' = 2^{2(a-1)} kpa^{3a}(a') \left[\frac{T}{(3a + a')} \right]^{3a+a}$$

where U' is the value of utility if the values of leisure x and y are given by ℓ', x', y' respectively but the utility function remains at the original (10.3), in particular with the preference for leisure parameter still at α. Define $U'/U \equiv R$, where U is as given in (10.6) with variables in accordance to the original preference, we have

$$R = (\alpha')^\alpha \frac{(3a + \alpha)3a + \alpha}{[\alpha^\alpha(3a + \alpha')]^{3a+\alpha}} \qquad (10.10)$$

$$\frac{\partial R}{\partial \alpha'} = 3a\alpha^\alpha(\alpha')^{\alpha-1}(3a + \alpha)^{3a+\alpha}(3a + \alpha')^{3a+\alpha-1}(\alpha - \alpha') \qquad (10.11)$$

over a perfect square.

From (10.11), it is clear that $\partial R/\partial \alpha'$ equals zero at $\alpha = \alpha'$ and is positive at all values of $\alpha' < \alpha$. Thus, a marginal increase (or decrease) in work ethics (a marginal **decrease/increase** in α to α') from the original equilibrium has no effect on utility as the original equilibrium is optimized already (the envelope result) but further increases in work ethics decreases utility in accordance to the intrinsic utility function. Thus, the artificial encouragement of work ethics does not benefit the society, though each individual will benefit from the increase in work ethics of the other individual.

It may appear odd that an increase in work ethics of one person benefits others yet an increase by all is not beneficial to all. This may be explained. An increase in work ethics of one person (or more persons in a model of more than two individuals) benefits others by improving the terms of trade for others through his/her attempt to sell more and buy more. An increase in work ethics of all cannot make the terms of trade better for all, hence missing the terms-of-trade effect, leaving only the distortive effect if the original situation is already efficient. Also, an increase in work ethics of a person decreases his/her utility evaluated at the original preference. The benefits to others are at the expense of the person himself/herself. When everyone increases work, the utility-decreasing effect dominates the beneficial effects.

Ng and Ng (2003, p. 349) explain their result (provided in Section 10.3) that the artificial encouragement of work ethics does not benefit the society with the statement 'as the economy of specialization has already been fully utilized at the original point ... where each individual specializes in the production of only one good'. (That paper has the number of individuals equal to the number of goods.) This explanation suggests that if the number of individuals is smaller than the number of goods and hence insufficient to allow for full specialization, the encouragement of work ethics may benefit the society by providing more scope for specialization. This is in fact misleading. In the model above, we have already made the number (three) of goods larger than the number (two) of individuals. Yet, we have shown that the artificial decrease in preference for leisure does not benefit the society, at least for the type of models where the economies of specialization is individual specific.

The reason is that, without an increase in the number of individuals, although the lower preference for leisure releases more labour time for the production of goods and hence achieve a higher productivity, the net effect on utility is negative for the following reason. The original amount of labour time allocated to the production of goods is already optimal given the price and production possibilities the individual faces. An artificial increase cannot therefore increase utility. This is not changed by considering a simultaneous increase in labour time by all individuals as such an increase does not change the relative price between goods and hence is similar to the situation faced by the optimization problem of a price-taking individual. Thus, an increase in the extent of the market through more work (a lower α increase x^s), even if leading to higher productivities in goods production through the economies of specialization, need not be utility enhancing.

Rather than increasing labour time, it is an increase in the number of individuals (which also increases the extent of the market) that can increase utility. This can be illustrated using the above model but with the number of individuals increasing to three, allowing for all three goods to be produced by specialists, with no home production needed. Using a similar method as the derivation of (10.6), we have for the symmetric case with the prices of all goods equal to one and for the person specializing in the production of X (persons specializing in producing Y and Z are symmetrical to this case as well),

$$\ell = \frac{\alpha T}{(3a + \alpha)}$$

$$l_x = \left[\frac{3aT}{(3a + \alpha)} \right]^a$$

$$x = \frac{[3aT/(3a + \alpha)]^a}{3} \tag{10.12}$$

$$y = z = k \frac{[3aT/(3a+\alpha)]^a}{3}$$

$$U_3^D = 3^{3(a-1)} k^2 a^{3a} \alpha^\alpha \left[\frac{T}{(3a+\alpha)} \right]^{3a+\alpha}$$

(10.12)

where the subscript 3 indicates that the number of individuals or traded goods is now three.
From (10.12) and (10.6), we have

$$\frac{U_3^D}{U_2^D} = 3^{(a-1)} \left(\frac{3}{2} \right)^{2(a-1)} k = \left(\frac{3}{2} \right)^{a-1} \left(\frac{9}{8} \right)^{a-1} 2^{2(a-1)} k$$

which is clearly larger than one for the case where the division of labour between two individuals dominates autarky, i.e. where $U_2^D/U^A = 2^{2(a-1)}k$ (see Eq.10.7) is larger than one. Thus, if the transaction efficiency k is large enough and/or the degree of economies of specialization (a) is large enough such that division of labour between two persons is better than autarky, division of labour between three persons is even better. In general, using a model with any number of goods, a larger population (up to the number of goods in models where this number is exogenously given) facilitates more specialization and increases per capita utility. Our results so far may be summarized as

Proposition 10.1: In our model of division of labour with economies of specialization, an artificial shift in preference from leisure to goods by all individuals decreases the utility of the representative individual evaluated at the original preference. An increase in population size increases utility by allowing more specialization if the original population size is not sufficient for full specialization.

Could we then conclude that Buchanan's hypothesis is not applicable with respect to a decrease in preference for leisure but only applicable with respect to an increase in population size? This conclusion is yet premature since a different result may be obtained in a different model. The next section examines this.

10.4.2   A model of mixed home and firm/market production

The Yang–Ng framework analyses division of labour from the level of individuals with individual-specific economies of specialization. This has the advantage of tackling the problem at the most basic level of individual choice. However, the increasing returns (due to the economies of specialization) involved do not go beyond the individual level. The majority of production in most advanced economies is undertaken by firms with increasing returns prevailing over the whole relevant range of production, but also with individual home production still taking place. Chapter 9 (based on Ng & Zhang 2007) combines the Yang–Ng analysis of economies of specialization at the individual level with the Dixit and Stiglitz's (1977) analysis of the free entry (average-cost pricing) monopolistic production by firms. (For an earlier model combining home production with market production by firms emphasizing the role of the number of intermediate goods and different stages of production, see Locay 1990. Here, the complications due to intermediate goods and stages in production are ignored.) In this section, the model in Chapter 9 is used to examine the role of work ethics.

Consider an economy with M identical consumers, each with the following decision problem for consumption which includes the set R of goods bought in the market from the firms and the set J of goods home-produced by the individual himself/herself.

$$\text{Max: } l^{1-\alpha-\beta}\left[\sum_{r \in R} x_r^{\rho_1}\right]^{\alpha/\rho_1}\left[\sum_{j \in J} x_j^{\rho_2}\right]^{\beta/\rho_2} \quad \text{(utility function)} \tag{10.13}$$

$$\text{s.t. } \sum_{r \in R} p_r x_r = 1 - l - \sum_{j \in J} l_j \quad \text{(budget constraint)}$$

$$x_j = \frac{l_j - a}{c} \quad \text{(home production function)}$$

where p_r is the price (all prices are relative to the price of labour which is used as the *numeraire*) of market good r, x_r is the amount of good r that is purchased from the market, R is the set of market goods, x_j is the amount of home good j, l_j is the amount of labour used in producing home good j, $a < 1$ is a fixed cost parameter which stands for economy of specialization in home production, c is the marginal cost in home production. (For the utility function in Eq. 10.13 to make sense, a also has to be positive. With a zero, the preference for diversity implied in the utility function will make the home number of goods m go to infinity and the amount of each home good approach zero.) J is the set of home goods, l is leisure, $(1 - l - \Sigma_{j \in J} l_j)$ is the amount of labour hired by firms, $\rho \in (0, 1)$ is the parameter of elasticity of substitution between each pair of consumption goods, α, β is a preference parameter, and u is utility level. The amount of time each individual has is normalized to unity. Each individual is a price taker and his/her decision variables are l, l_j and x_r. It is assumed that the elasticity of substitution $1/(1 - \rho) > 1$, or $1 > \rho > 0$ as usual.

Using a model similar to that in Chapter 9, we may derive as in that chapter,

$$
\begin{aligned}
u &= l^{1-\alpha-\beta} n^{\frac{\alpha}{\rho_1}} x^{\alpha} m^{\frac{\beta}{\rho_2}} x_j^{\beta} \\
&= \rho_2^{1-\alpha} \rho_1^{\alpha} \beta^{\rho_2} b^{-\alpha} M^{-\alpha} a^{\beta-\frac{\beta}{\rho_2}} c^{-\beta} A^{\alpha-\frac{\alpha}{\rho_1}} (1-\rho_2)^{\frac{\beta}{\rho_2}-\beta} \\
&\quad \times (1-\alpha-\beta)^{(1-\alpha-\beta)} [\rho_2 + \beta(1-\rho_2)]^{\alpha-\frac{\alpha}{\rho_1}+\beta-\frac{\beta}{\rho_2}-1} \\
&\quad [M\alpha\rho_2 - A(\rho_2 + \beta(1-\rho_2))]^{\alpha} \{M\alpha\rho_2(1-\rho_1) + A\rho_1[\rho_2 + \beta(1-\rho_2)]\}^{\frac{\alpha}{\rho_1}-\alpha}
\end{aligned}
\tag{10.14}
$$

where A is the fixed cost and b the constant marginal cost of firm production and u is utility level. Other variables are as explained under (10.13).

Next, we use the method similar to the derivation of R given in (10.10) above. We let the various variables be the ones that would prevail with a lower preference for leisure (noting that, in the current model, this involves a higher α and/or β, in contrast to a lower α of the model in the previous section where α is the preference-for-leisure parameter) but with the utility level (denoted as U') evaluated using the original utility function. We then see how this new utility level U' compares with the original utility level U (that from variables determined by the original preferences, as given in Eq. 10.13) and see how the ratio $R \equiv U'/U$ changes (or how $\ln R$ changes, as R always vary in the same direction as $\ln R$) with respect to a decrease in preference for leisure and an increase in preference for the market goods (from α to α') and/or an increase in preference for the home goods (from β to β'). We have

$$
\begin{aligned}
\frac{\partial \ln R}{\partial \alpha'} &= \frac{\alpha}{\alpha'\rho_1} - \frac{1-\alpha-\beta}{1-\alpha'-\beta'} + \frac{M\alpha\rho_2}{M\alpha'\rho_2 - A[\rho_2 + \beta'(1-\rho_2)]} \\
&\quad - \frac{M\alpha\rho_2}{M\alpha'\rho_2 + A\rho_1[\rho_2 + \beta'(1-\rho_2)]/(1-\rho_1)}
\end{aligned}
\tag{10.15}
$$

The right hand side of (10.15) is necessarily positive at $\alpha = \alpha'$, $\beta = \beta'$, since $1 > \rho_i > 0$ for both i, making the first term $\alpha/\alpha'\rho_1$ larger than one and hence exceeds the second term $(1 - \alpha - \beta)/(1 - \alpha' - \beta')$ which is equal to one. The positive third term and the negative fourth term have the same numerator. The first terms of their denominators are also equal. The first term of the denominator of the third term is negative and that of the fourth term is positive. This means that, as long as the whole denominator of the third term remains positive, the positive third term must be larger than the negative fourth term in absolute value, making the combined third and fourth terms positive. If we substitute the solution for n into the solution for x in the maximization problem, we have

$$x = \frac{\rho_1 A\{M\alpha\rho_2 - A[\rho_2 + \beta(1-\rho_2)]\}}{bM\{M\alpha\rho_2(1-\rho_1) + A\rho_1[\rho_2 + \beta(1-\rho_2)]\}}$$

Since the denominator is positive and $\rho_1 A$ in the numerator is also positive, the remaining part $\{M\alpha\rho_2 - A[\rho_2 + \beta(1 - \rho_2)]\}$ in the numerator must also be positive for x to be positive.[2] At $\alpha = \alpha'$, $\beta = \beta'$, this term is the same as the denominator of the third term in (10.15) which must thus also be positive. Thus, the right hand side of (10.15) must be positive at $\alpha = \alpha'$, $\beta = \beta'$. This means that, from the original position, a shift in preference from leisure to the market goods increases utility even evaluated in accordance to the original preference.

In the model of this section, given other parameters, the degree of increasing returns to scale in market production is related positively to the fixed cost parameter A. Since A occurs twice in (10.15) and in both case it is in the denominator and associated with a negative sign and with other associated terms positive, it is straightforward to see and show that

$$\frac{\partial^2 \ln R}{\partial \alpha' \partial A} > 0 \tag{10.16}$$

Thus, the higher the degree of increasing returns in the production of market goods, the larger is the utility-improving effect of a shift in preference from leisure to market goods. The discussion so far may be summarized as

Proposition 10.2: Where the market goods are produced under conditions of increasing returns and priced at average costs, a shift in preference away from leisure towards market goods increases the utility level of the representative individual even if evaluated in accordance to the original preference. The higher the degree of increasing returns, the larger is this effect.

It may be thought that the above proposition applies only in our model with both market and home goods. In fact, we may take the special case with $\beta = 0$ which signifies the absence of home goods (the number of home goods produced/consumed $m = 0$ from Eq. 10.4.13), the positivity of (10.15) and (10.16) is not affected. Thus, Proposition 10.2 applies even to a model with only market goods.

Now consider a shift in preference from leisure towards the home goods. Similar to the derivation of (10.15), we may derive

$$
\begin{aligned}
\frac{\partial \ln R}{\partial \beta'} = {} & \frac{\beta}{\beta' \rho_2} - \frac{\beta(1 - \rho_2)}{\rho_2[\rho_2 + \beta'(1 - \rho_2)]} - \frac{1 - \alpha - \beta}{1 - \alpha' - \beta'} - \frac{(1 - \alpha - \beta)(1 - \rho_2)}{\rho_2 + \beta'(1 - \rho_2)} \\
& - \frac{\alpha(1 - \rho_2)}{\rho_1[\rho_2 + \beta'(1 - \rho_2)]} - \frac{\alpha A(1 - \rho_2)}{M\alpha'\rho_2 - A[\rho_2 + \beta'(1 - \rho_2)]} \\
& - \frac{\alpha A \rho_1 (1 - \rho_2)}{M\alpha'\rho_2(1 - \rho_1) + A\rho_1[\rho_2 + \beta'(1 - \rho_2)]}
\end{aligned}
\tag{10.17}
$$

Noting that $1 - \alpha - \beta$ (being of the same sign as leisure l from Eq. 10.13), α, β, ρ_i, $1 - \rho_i$, A, M are all positive, it is easy to see that all terms in the right hand side of (10.17) except the first term are negative. (The positivity of the denominator of the second last term has already been discussed in the paragraph preceding Eq. 10.17.) From the original position with $\beta = \beta'$, this first term equals $1/\rho_2$. It can be seen that the absolute value of the negative second term must be smaller than $1/\rho_2$, as $\rho_2 + \beta'(1 - \rho_2)$ in the denominator must be larger than the term $\beta(1 - \rho_2)$ in the numerator. Thus, the first two terms combined to be positive and the signing of the right hand side of (10.17) appears to be impossible. However, if we combine these first and second terms with the fourth and fifth terms, the combined four terms can be shown to equal

$$
1 - \frac{\alpha(1 - \rho_1)}{\rho_2 + \beta'(1 - \rho_2)}
$$

where the first term of one is exactly offset by the third term in the right hand side of (10.17) which equals negative one at $\alpha = \alpha'$, $\beta = \beta'$. With the negative sign, the second term of the above displayed expression is necessarily negative. Thus, all the seven terms in the right hand side of (10.17) must add up to be negative at $\alpha = \alpha'$, $\beta = \beta'$. Hence from the original position, a shift in preference from leisure to the home goods decreases utility evaluated in accordance to the original preference.

Proposition 10.3: An artificial shift in preference from leisure towards home goods decreases utility evaluated at the original preference despite the fact that home goods are produced under conditions of increasing returns.

The contrasting results between home goods (Proposition 10.3) and market goods (Proposition 10.2) are explained intuitively in the concluding section.

We may also examine the effect of an increase in population M holding other parameters unchanged (including the conditions of increasing returns; this may not be possible for a very large M). From (10.14), we have

$$
\frac{\partial \ln u}{\partial M} = \frac{A\alpha[\rho_2 + \beta(1-\rho_2)]/M}{M\alpha\rho_2 - A[\rho_2 + \beta(1-\rho_2)]}
$$
$$
+ \frac{\alpha^2 \rho_2 (1-\rho_1)^2 / \rho_1}{M\alpha\rho_2(1-\rho_1) + A\rho_1[\rho_2 + \beta(1-\rho_2)]} > 0
$$

(10.18)

where the positivity follows from the positivity of the denominator of the first term in the right hand side as discussed in the discussion below (10.15). We have

Proposition 10.4: An increase in population, with other parameters unchanged (if feasible) increases utility by allowing the spreading of the fixed costs in market production.

The intuition of the various propositions above is discussed in the next section.

10.5 Concluding remarks

In this chapter, it has been shown that

- In a model of division of labour with economies of specialization at the level of individual/household production, a shift in preference from leisure towards goods decreases individual utility evaluated in accordance to the original preference.
- If the original population size is not large enough to allow for full specialization, an increase in population increases utility by facilitating more specialization.
- In the extended model allowing for both home and firm/market production under increasing returns and with average-cost pricing for firms, a shift (if not excessive) in preference from leisure towards market goods increases individual utility even if evaluated in accordance to the original preference.
- A shift in preference from leisure towards home goods decreases individual utility evaluated in accordance to the original preference,

even if home goods are produced under the condition of increasing returns.

- An increase in population with other parameters remaining unchanged (if feasible) increases utility by allowing the spreading of the fixed costs in market production.

The intuitive reasons for some of the above results may be mentioned. In the presence of increasing returns, the average cost of producing a good is falling with output and the marginal cost is below average cost. With average-cost pricing of firms (due to free entry), market goods are consumed until marginal valuation equals price which equals average cost. However, efficiency requires the equality of marginal valuation and marginal cost. Thus, market goods are under-consumed. A shift in preference from leisure towards market goods may thus increase efficiency. Although home goods are also produced under the condition of increasing returns in the model of Section 10.4.2, the problem does not arise. Home production is consumed by the individual/household and the decision on how much to produce/consume concerns the individual only. Hence, the individual takes the effect of increasing returns fully into account and optimizes accordingly. There is thus no under-production/consumption in home goods. An artificial shift in preference from leisure towards home goods is thus inefficient evaluated in accordance to the original preference. For market goods produced by firms, the price determined in accordance to average cost is common to all individuals consuming the good. In our model, increasing returns arise from a fixed cost component with a constant marginal cost. The fixed cost component is shared by all consumers and spread over all units of the good produced. It thus processes the essential element of publicness as in a public good. An increase in population size helps to reduce the average cost of producing such a good and hence increases the utility of an existing individual. Also, with increasing returns, higher consumption helps to reduce the average cost for other individuals. This possesses the aspect of external benefits not taken into account by the optimization decisions of individuals. This explains the beneficial effects of an increase in preference for market goods by all individuals on all individuals even in accordance to the original preferences.[3]

The above explanation, while relevant, is yet incomplete, at least in the long run. In the short run, efficiency requires the equation of marginal valuation with the short-run marginal cost and the above explanation is adequate. However, in the long run, efficiency requires the equation of marginal valuation with the long-run marginal cost. With free entry and average-cost pricing, the long-run marginal cost is determined more by the average than by the (short-run) marginal cost. In the model in Section 10.4.2, the costs (relative to the price of labour) of firms are assumed to be independent of the number of firms. A shift in preference from leisure to market goods increases the demand for the product of each firm, given the number of firms in the short run. As the cost curve/ function of the firm remains unchanged, this increases the profits of firms and induces entry. In the long-run equilibrium, profits become zero again. What is the gain? The gain consists of two parts. First, the larger number of firms/products increases utility by providing a wider range of choice. The individual utility function posited values variety and hence utility is increased this way. Second, with the larger number of firms, the demand for the product of each firm becomes more elastic and hence the demand curve is tangent to the unchanged cost curve at a lower price. Thus, despite the fact that the number of firms/products increases, the quantity produced by each firm also increases. This lowers the average cost of production due to the spreading of the fixed cost component over more units. This can be confirmed in the model of Section 10.4.2 by showing that the shift of preference from leisure to market goods will lower the price and increase the output of each market good.

While the Buchanan idea of the beneficial effect of work ethics through its facilitation of division of labour to benefit from the economies of specialization has some validity, its significance is small in the present world of global trade at relatively small transportation and other transactions costs. Nevertheless, in ancient times when the work ethics originated, the Buchanan thesis might have had more relevance. Before the development of modern mass transportation and convenient communications, most of the trade typically was confined to relatively small geographical areas with small population sizes. The opportunity for trade would thus be significantly increased through a higher level of work ethics. The gain from a higher degree of specialization may thus offset the loss of artificial encouragement of work. Of course, the work ethics might also have been fostered by factors unrelated to this factor. For example, the presence of a small proportion of people too lazy to work and preyed or relied on others might have caused sufficient external costs to generate forces promoting the work ethics.

In the contemporary world, while factors such as laziness may still be as important, there are offsetting considerations which may tilt the balance the other way round. Particularly, three factors may be mentioned here. First, beyond the biological levels of survival and comfort, higher consumption is of largely relative than absolute significance. This has been emphasized by economists from Rae (1834) and Veblen (1929) to Akerlof (1976), Ireland (1998), Frank (1999) and Layard (2005), among others. Recent studies reveal the magnitude, scope, and relative (to absolute income) importance of relative standing that are beyond the imagination of most people, myself included. For example, one may expect that the importance of relative standing is least in the area of health care where the absolute effects may be expected to dominate. However, Wilkinson (1997) shows that even in health care, relative standing is more important than absolute standards. The relatively poor, even with higher absolute incomes and health care, ended up with much lower level of healthiness than the absolutely poor but relatively well-off. Mortality is more a function of relative than absolute income and health care. The competition in relative terms, especially in income and consumption, leads to excessive amount of work from the social point of view. This at least partly explains why we need limitations in working hours rather than encouraging more work.

Second, in addition to the relative-income effect, our accumulation instinct and the omnipresent advertising in our commercial world cause a materialistic bias, making individuals placing more emphasis on making money than warranted by its real contribution to welfare, even from the individual point of view, as argued in Ng (2003). Third, the production and consumption of most goods and services, directly and indirectly (e.g. through input usage), causes significant degree of environmental disruption. The largely global public-good nature and very long-term nature of most environmental protection measures also cause them to be under-provided by national governments with relatively short time horizons. Income-earning work is related to production and consumption and leisure as such is less environmentally disruptive. (Tourist activities that are environmentally disruptive are more money-intensive than leisure-intensive.) Thus, the consideration of environmental protection also points to the discouragement rather than the encouragement of work.

Appendix 10A

In this appendix, we use a simple model of the Yang–Ng framework allowing the inframarginal comparison of different corner solutions of organizational choice (such as autarky vs. division of labour) to examine the role of different degrees of preference for leisure.

For simplicity, non-labour inputs are ignored. Each individual has T units of time which may be used for leisure or the production of either or both of the only two goods X and Y. Thus, each individual is faced with the time constraint

$$l + l_x + l_y = T \tag{10A1}$$

where l = leisure time, l_x and l_y are time used in the production of X and Y respectively. The production functions are

$$X = l_x^a; \quad Y = l_y^a \tag{10A2}$$

where a being larger than one indicates the presence of economies of specialization. Individuals are taken as ex-anti-identical and production functions are symmetrical to emphasize the point that gain from trade may arise from the economies of specialization alone.

A Cobb–Douglas utility function is used for simplicity. Since we are considering a change in preference only for leisure, we let only leisure to carry a preference variable. Those for x and y (using lower case to indicate the amount consumed) may be normalized to unity by scaling the utility function since no asymmetrical preference between the two goods has to be introduced.

$$U = xyl^\alpha \tag{10A3}$$

Consider first the case of autarky where the individual self-produces both goods. The utility function may then be written as

$$U = (T - l - l_y)^a l_y^a \, l^\alpha \tag{10A4}$$

The maximization of (10A4) with respect to the choice of l_y gives the solution

$$l_x = l_y = \frac{aT}{(2a + \alpha)}$$

$$l = \frac{aT}{(2a + \alpha)} \tag{10A5}$$

$$U = a^{2a} \alpha^\alpha \frac{[T/(2a + \alpha)]^{2a+\alpha}}{4}$$

Now consider the case of specialization where an individual produces only one of the goods and exchanges with another individual who produces the other good. Due to symmetry, we need to consider only the case where the individual produces X. From his output of X, he/she supplies x^s in exchange for y at a price of p (price of X in terms of Y). However, market transactions are supposed to incur a transactions cost of $1 - k$. Thus, while the amount of Y he/she bought is equal to px^s, the amount he/she actually consumes equals only kpx^s. His/her utility function may thus be written as

$$U = [(T - l)^a - x^s] \, kpx^s \, l^\alpha \tag{10A6}$$

The maximization of (10A6) with respect to l and x^s gives the following solution

$$\begin{aligned}
l &= \frac{\alpha T}{(2a + \alpha)}, \\
x &= x^s = \frac{[2aT/(2a + \alpha)]^a}{2} \\
y &= kp\frac{[2aT/(2a + \alpha)]^a}{2} \\
U &= 2^{2a} kpa^{2a} \alpha^\alpha \frac{[T/(2a + \alpha)]^{2a+\alpha}}{4}
\end{aligned} \tag{10A7}$$

From (10A6) and (10A7), we have

$$\frac{U^D}{U^A} = \frac{2^{2a}kp}{4} = 2^{2(a-1)}k \tag{10A8}$$

where the superscripts D and A stand for division of labour and autarky respectively. In this symmetrical model, for the case of either a large number of individuals (or price-taking behaviour), two individuals with equal bargaining ability, or with the Nash bargaining outcome, we have $p = 1$. Then, division of labour yields a higher utility if and only if $2^{2(a-1)}k > 1$, i.e. if the economies of specialization (measured by $a - 1$) is sufficiently large to offset the effect of transactions costs (measured by $1 - k$). For example, if $a = 1.1$, k has to be no smaller than 0.87055 for division of labour to dominate autarky in this simple model. It may be noted that, in this model, the relative superiority of division of labour versus autarky does not depend on the preference for leisure. However, if division of labour is chosen, then the willingness to trade decreases with higher preference for leisure; x^s is a decreasing function of α. Thus, to the extent that other people may benefit from one's willingness to trade, a higher degree of work ethics (reduced preference for leisure) may be regarded as favourable. This may be shown more formally by bringing in the other person who produces Y into the picture. His/her situation is exactly the same as the person producing X depicted above, except that his/her preference parameter for leisure is indicated by β. Then his/her supply y^s is the same as the second equation in (10A7) for x^s except that α is replaced by β. Then, from the market equilibrium requirement $px^s = y^s$ (since the price of Y in terms of X is the inverse of the price of X in terms of Y), we may solve for the equilibrium price of X in terms of Y as

$$p = \left[\frac{(2a + \alpha)}{(2a + \beta)} \right]^a \tag{10A9}$$

which clearly increases with α and decreases with β. Thus, the person producing X benefits from the higher work ethics of the person producing Y and vice versa.

Now, let us examine the effect of a higher degree of the economies of specialization (a larger a) on the benefits of the higher work ethics of others. To concentrate on the increase in work effort rather than the complication of an initial interpersonal difference in preferences for leisure, we evaluate the effect of an increase in a on the effect of a change in α (or β, the two are symmetrical) on p at an initial position when $\alpha = \beta$. (It may be noted that it is more convenient to examine the effect on others through the exchange ratio rather than on utility itself. The effect of a simultaneous change in both α and β on utility is dependent on the normalization with respect to α, β, and T. This is related to the non-arbitrariness in the choice of units discussed in Ng and Wang (1995). Moreover, with a change in preference, it also raises the question of using which preference pattern to make welfare assessment.) We then have

$$\frac{\partial^2 p}{\partial \alpha \partial a} = \left[\frac{2a + \alpha}{2a + \beta} \right]^{a-1} + \frac{a}{a - 1} > 0 \tag{10A10}$$

This means that, the higher the degree of economies of specialization, the larger is the beneficial effect of a higher work ethics on the trading partner. Thus, to this extent at least, Buchanan's conjecture has validity and is related to the economies of specialization.

11
Specialization, Trade, and Growth

*Siang Ng**

This chapter shows the emergence of trade in a model with no exogenous comparative advantage but with economies of specialization and analyses the effects of tariff protection on international trade. In the case of no retaliation, the result on the real income of the country with tariff is not definite. However, in the case of full retaliation against any tariff imposed by a country or the case of a small country, the effect of protection is unambiguously negative. Does the enrichment or growth of a sector (individual/region/country) benefit others? If the enrichment consists in a higher ability to produce goods, this tends to benefit others; if the enrichment consists in an improvement in the transaction efficiency, the result is ambiguous.

11.1 Introduction

Adam smith (1776) analysed the gains from specialization through division of labour even if all individuals are ex ante identical. The resulting concept is now referred to as endogenous comparative advantage. Pursuing an alternative line of studies of specialization and division of labour, David Ricardo (1817) emphasized exogenous comparative advantage. Based on Ricardo's concept of exogenous comparative advantage and focused on the models with constant returns to scale,

*Dr. Ng Siang (Seok Hean) is senior lecturer in the Department of Economics, Monash University. She graduated with a B.Com. from Nanyang University in Singapore and a M.Ec. from University of Sydney. She obtained her PhD in Economics from Monash University in 1996. Her research interests include economies of specialization, international trade, and Chinese economic reforms. She is the author and co-author of a number of journal papers and chapters in books, including papers in the *Journal of Economic Behavior and Organization*, *Social Choice and Welfare*.

the neoclassical trade theory explains patterns of specialization and division of labour between countries.

Dixit and Stiglitz (1977) formulate a trade-off between distortions caused by increasing returns (which give rise to economies of scale at the firm level) and pure consumers' preferences for diverse consumption to explain productivity, per capita real income, and the number of goods by the size of an economy. This line of study is further explored by Krugman (1979, 1980, 1990) and Ethier (1982). Romer (1986) formulates a model to show that growth is positively related to the human capital stock and there exists a spillover effect of knowledge and technology and further reduces the costs of production. Grossman and Helpman (1991) show that a greater degree of openness enables a country to access and absorb the advanced technological knowledge from advanced countries and thus to grow faster.

Kemp and Negishi (1970) show that gains from trade in the presence of increasing returns to scale at the firm level are positive if trade causes the expansion of the increasing-returns industries without expanding decreasing-returns industries. This result has been extended in various ways by Eaton and Panagariya (1979), Markusen and Melvin (1984), Helpman (1984), Helpman and Krugman (1985), Zhou (2007). Grinols (1991, 2006) generalizes most of these contributions.[1]

However, all of the old and new trade and growth models are featured with (static and dynamic) marginal analysis, economies of scale, and the neoclassical dichotomy between consumers and firms. None of these models has endogenized the level of specialization for individuals and for firms and hence it is still within Marshall's (1890) neoclassical framework. The dichotomy between consumers and producers makes Marshall's marginal analysis incapable of explaining the emergence of firms, business cycles, money, middlemen, and a hierarchical structure of transactions from division of labour and of explaining the evolution of the extent of the market, productivity, trade dependence, etc.

Yang (1988) and Yang and Ng (1993) formulate a general equilibrium model that endogenizes individuals' level of specialization and the level of division of labour for society as a whole by abandoning the dichotomy between pure consumers and firms. This framework is outlined in Chapter 6 and subsequent chapters discuss some issues raised. The aim of this chapter is to present a formal analysis of the emergence of trade and the effects of tariff protection on international trade within this framework. Section 11.2 begins with the basic model (subsection 11.2.1). Having explicitly modelled international trade in Subsection 11.2.2, Subsection 11.2.3 examines the effects of a tariff for the case of no retaliation (one country pursues a protectionist policy while the other pursues a *laissez-faire* policy), the case of full retaliation against any tariff imposed by a country, and the case of a small country whose tariff action is unable to affect international prices of traded goods.

11.2   The new classical trade theory

11.2.1   The basic model

It is assumed that the economy consists of M ex ante identical consumer-producers and m consumer goods. Denoting the self-provided amount of good i as x_i, the amount purchased from the market of good i as x_i^d, the amount of good i consumed is $x_i + k\,x_i^d$, where kx_i^d is the amount an individual obtains when he/she purchases x_i^d, $1 - k$ being the transaction cost coefficient and k the transaction efficiency coefficient. (The first few equations below are similar to the first few in Appendix 6A and Chapter 8. Readers already familiar with them only have to skim through and start from the next subsection.)

A Cobb–Douglas utility function is adopted to reflect the preference for diverse consumption.

$$u = \prod_{i=1}^{m}(x_i + kx_i^d) \tag{11.1}$$

Each consumer-producer also has a system of production functions

$$x_i + x_i^s = l_i^a \quad i = 1, \ldots m; \ a > 1 \tag{11.2}$$

where x_i^s is the amount of good i sold to the market and $x_i + x_i^s$ is the amount of good i produced and l_i the amount of labour used in producing good i. The assumption of $a > 1$ captures the economies of specialization, making the labour productivity in the production of each good increase with the individual's level of specialization in its production, measured by the labour time used. Apart from the per unit transaction cost $1 - k$, a fixed cost (measured by labour time) for the purchase of each good c is also assumed. With $n - 1$ goods purchased from the market, the endowment constraint of an individual is given by

$$c(n-1) + \sum_{i=1}^{m} l_i = 1; \quad 0 \le l_i, \ c(n-1) \le 1 \tag{11.3}$$

where the total amount of labour time has been normalized to unity. The budget constraint of the individual is given by

$$p_i x_i^s = \sum_{r \in R} p_r x_r^d \qquad (11.4)$$

where p_i is the price of good i, R is a set of all goods purchased. In (11.4), only one good is supplied to the market by an individual since, from $a > 1$, it can be shown that an individual sells only one good at most (see Lemma 2.1 in Yang and Ng 1993). Each individual (effectively) takes the market prices as given either because the population is large relative to the number of goods and thus the number of individuals producing each good i, M_i, is large and/or due to the coincidence with the Walrasian regime in the multilateral bargaining game of the Yang–Ng model (1993, chapter 3).

Each individual is then allowed to maximize utility by allotting his/her fixed amount of time to the production and purchase of different goods, balancing the trade-off between economies of specialization ($a > 1$) on the one hand and the costs of market transaction (c, $1 - k > 0$) on the other. Each individual is allowed not only to choose the quantities of the various goods consumed but also to choose what goods to self-provide and sell to the market. If an individual buys a good, he/she does not sell it and vice versa.

Next, market equilibrium in terms of the equality of the amount of each good supplied and demanded in the market is then imposed.

$$M_i x_i^s = \sum_{r \in R} M_r x_{ri}^d \qquad (11.5)$$

where M_i is the number of individuals selling good i, x_{ri} is the amount of traded good i purchased by individuals selling good r, it can then be shown that (Proposition 5.1 of Yang and Ng) if the transaction efficiency and/or the degree of economies of specialization are very low, the equilibrium is autarky. All individuals self-provide all goods. As the transaction efficiency improves (i.e. k increases and/or c decreases), each individual sells a good to the market and buys some other goods in exchange. The number of goods purchased from the market, division of labour and income all increase with transaction efficiency. When each person's number of goods purchased from the market is small, trade occurs within a small local community. When the number of goods purchased from the market becomes larger and larger due to the increase in transaction efficiency and endogenous increase in comparative advantage through learning by doing (Yang and Borland 1991; Yang and Ng 1993, chapter 7), trade expands to unify the national market and then to involve international trade.

11.2.2   Explicit modelling of international trade

Take the case of two countries. To avoid too many subscripts, a hat over a variable denotes its value in another country or the rest of the world. Each individual i in this country maximizes

$$u = x_i \prod_{r \in R_i} k x_r^d \prod_{s \in S_i} \bar{k} x_s^d \prod_{j \in J_i} x_j \tag{11.6}$$

where x_i is the quantity of good i retained by individual i for self-consumption, R_i is the set of goods purchased domestically (by individual selling good i) from other individuals, S_i is the set of goods purchased internationally, $1 - \bar{k}$ is the transaction costs of international trade, and J_i is the set of self-provided goods. By not making $\bar{k} = k$ necessarily, we allow for the more general case of differential transaction (including transportation) costs between domestic and international trade. Each individual i is subject to the following constraints in the above maximization problem.

$$x_i + x_i^s = l_i^a$$
$$x_j = l_j^a \qquad \forall j \in J_i \tag{11.7}$$

$$c(n-1) + l_i + \sum_{j \in J_i} l_j = 1 \tag{11.8}$$

$$P_i x_i^s + f = \sum_{r \in R_i} P_r x_r^d + \sum_{s \in S_i} \hat{P}_s x_s^d (1+t)/e \tag{11.9}$$

where e = terms of trade, t = the f.o.b. rate of uniform (across all goods) import duty, and f is the sum received by the individual from the government due to the revenue from import duty. (We have $t \geq 0$, as the case of subsidy is not being considered here.) Assuming a large number of individuals, it may be assumed that each individual takes f as given although we have, assuming negligible costs of collecting the import duty, $f = t\Sigma_{s \in S} x_s^d \hat{P}_s / e$.

Maximizing (11.6) subject to (11.7)–(11.9), we have (the detail working is available with the author)

$$
u_i = \left\{ \frac{[1 - c(n-1)]}{m - n_s t/(1+t)} \right\}^{am} (n')^{n(a-1)} e^{n_s}(1+t)^{-n_s} k^{n_r} \bar{k}^{n_s} \prod_{r \in R} P_{ir} \prod_{s \in \bar{S}} P_{i\bar{s}}
$$

$$
= u_i\left(n_s, M, t, e, a, c, k, \bar{k}, P_{ir}, \hat{P}_{is} \right)
$$

(11.10)

where m being the exogenously given numbers of goods on which no comparative statics is done and need not be explicitly listed; n_r = number of goods in R and n_s = number of goods in S. Hence the number of traded goods n equals $1 + n_r = n_s$; and $n' \equiv 1 + n_r + n_s/(1 + t)$.

Equation (11.10) gives the utility level of individuals with international trade. If we compare (such comparison is available from the author) it with the utility level with no international trade, we may show that if the transaction coefficients are low enough, international trade is better than no international trade. We have

Proposition 11.1: Even in our model with identical individuals and no comparative advantage across individuals and across countries, international trade may emerge to benefit from further specialization.

From (11.10), maximizing u_i with respect to n_s yields the optimal number of goods purchased from abroad for the individual selling good i. The optimal value n_s^* is the integer in the neighbourhood of n^{**} that is given by the first-order condition $\partial u_i/\partial n_s = 0$, giving

$$
n_s^{**} = n_s^{**}(m, t, e, a, c, k, \bar{k}, P_{ir}, \hat{P}_{is})
$$

(11.11)

Due to the symmetry of the model, the optimal number of goods purchased by an individual from abroad n_s^* (and hence also the optimal number of traded goods for an individual n^*) is the same for all individuals. The larger is n^*, the higher is the level of specialization for each individual and the higher is the level of division of labour for the economy.

The market-clearing conditions are

$$
x_i^s = \sum_{r \in R_i} x_{ri}^d + \sum_{s \in S_i} \hat{x}_{s_i}^d \quad \forall\, i
$$

(11.12)

where $x_{r_i}^d$ is the domestic demand for good i by individuals selling good r, $x_{s_i}^d$ is the foreign demand for good i by the overseas individuals selling good s, and S_i is the set of foreign individuals buying good i (from this country).

In our model with no international capital movement or lending/borrowing, we have the balance-of-trade condition.

$$\sum_{i=1}^{M}\sum_{s\in S_i} x_s^d = \sum_{i=1}^{\hat{M}}\sum_{s\in \hat{S}_i} e\hat{x}_s^d \qquad (11.13)$$

$$\sum_{s\in S_i} x_s^d = \sum_{s\in \hat{S}_i} e\hat{x}_s^d \qquad (11.13')$$

Since individuals are symmetrical, we have from (11.13), for $M = \hat{M}$.
The demand for imports by an individual in the foreign country is

$$\hat{x}_s^d = \frac{1}{e}\left\{\frac{[1-\hat{c}(\hat{n}-1)]\hat{n}'}{\hat{m}-\hat{n}_s\hat{t}/(1+\hat{t})}\right\}^{\hat{a}} /\hat{n}'(1+\hat{t})$$

where $1/e = \hat{e}$.
We also have

$$\frac{n_s e\{\bullet\}^a}{n'(1+t)} = \frac{\hat{n}_s\{\bullet\}^{\hat{a}}}{\hat{n}'(1+\hat{t})} \qquad (11.14)$$

In the symmetrical model, $a = \hat{a}$, $n_r = M - 1 = \hat{M} - 1 = \hat{n}_r$, etc. Thus, if both countries impose no duties (i.e. $t = \hat{t} = 0$) or if both countries impose the same level of duty ($t = \hat{t}$), we must have $e = 1$.

11.2.3 The effect of a tariff

11.2.3.1 The case of 'no retaliation'

Here, suppose only this country imposes the import duty with no retaliation from its trading partner. Taking $\hat{t} = 0$, we have from (11.14)

$$\frac{n_s e}{1+t}\left\{\frac{1-c(n-1)}{m-n_s t/(1+t)}\right\}^a (n')^{a-1} = \hat{n}_s\left\{\frac{1-\hat{c}(\hat{n}-1)}{\hat{m}}\right\}^{\hat{a}} \hat{n}^{\hat{a}-1} \qquad (11.14')$$

Substituting $P_{ir} = P_{is} = 1$ for all r and s into (11.10) and differentiating the resulting u_i with respect to n_s and setting the resulting expression equal to zero, we have

$$\frac{1}{u_i}\frac{\partial u_i}{\partial n_s} = \ln\frac{ek}{1+t} + (a-1)\ln n' + \frac{n(a-1)}{n'(1+t)} - \frac{cam}{1-c(n-1)}$$
$$+ \frac{amt/(1+t)}{m-n_s t/(1+t)} = 0 \qquad (11.15)$$

For the other country, the same process as described above also applies except that $\hat{t} = 0$, $\hat{n}' = \hat{n}$, $\hat{e} \equiv 1/e$. We thus have

$$\frac{1}{\hat{u}_i}\frac{\partial \hat{u}_i}{\partial \hat{n}_s} = \ln\frac{\hat{k}}{e} + (\hat{a}-1)(1+\ln\hat{n}) - \frac{\hat{c}\hat{a}\hat{m}}{1-\hat{c}(\hat{n}-1)} = 0 \tag{11.15'}$$

Taking t as exogenous, $\hat{t} = 0$ and a, etc as constant, but allowing n_s (and hence n), $\hat{n}$ and e to be endogenously determined, we may differentiate (11.14'), (11.15), (11.15') with respect to t to solve for de/dt, dn/dt, $d\hat{n}/dt$. The differentiation of (11.14'), (11.15), and (11.15') yields, after substituting in $dn_s = dn$ (from the differentiation of $n = 1 + n_r + n_s$ with $n_r = M = $ *constant*) and $dn' = dn_s/(1 + t) - n_s dt/(1 + t)^2$ from the differentiation of $n'1 + n_r + n_s/(1 + t)$, we have three equations in matrix-vector form,

$$\begin{bmatrix} 1 & A & -B \\ 1 & D & 0 \\ 1 & 0 & -F \end{bmatrix}\begin{bmatrix} de/e \\ dn/n \\ d\hat{n}/\hat{n} \end{bmatrix} = \begin{bmatrix} \dfrac{a-1}{n'}\bullet\dfrac{n_s}{(1+t)^2}\,dt \\[2mm] E\,dt/(1+t) \\[2mm] 0 \end{bmatrix} \tag{11.16}$$

where

$$A \equiv \frac{n}{n_s} - \frac{anc}{1-c(n-1)} - \frac{ant}{(1+t)\left(m - n_s\dfrac{t}{1+t}\right)} + \frac{n(a-1)}{n'(1+t)}$$

$$B \equiv \frac{(1+t)\hat{n}^{a-1}\left\{\dfrac{1-\hat{c}(\hat{n}-1)}{\hat{m}}\right\}^{\hat{a}}}{n_s e\left\{\dfrac{1-c(n-1)}{m - n_s\,t/(1+t)}\right\}^{a}(n')^{a-1}}\left[\hat{n} - \frac{\hat{a}\hat{n}_s\hat{c}\hat{n}}{1-\hat{c}(\hat{n}-1)} + (\hat{a}-1)\hat{n}_s\right]$$

$$D \equiv \frac{(a-1)n}{(1+t)n'} - \frac{c^2 amn}{\{1-c(n-1)\}^2} + \frac{amn\,t^2/(1+t)^2}{\{m - n_s\,t/(1+t)\}^2} + \frac{(a-1)n}{(1+t)n'}\left\{1 - \frac{n}{(1+t)n'}\right\}$$

$$E \equiv 1 + \frac{(a-1)n}{(1+t)n'} + \frac{am\left\{1 + \dfrac{n_s\dfrac{t}{1+t}}{m - n_s\,t/(1+t)}\right\}}{\left(m - n_s\dfrac{t}{1+t}\right)(1+t)} + \frac{(a-1)n_s}{(1+t)n'}\left\{1 - \frac{n}{(1+t)n'}\right\}$$

$$F \equiv \hat{a} - 1 - \frac{\hat{c}^2\,\hat{a}\hat{m}\hat{n}}{\{1-\hat{c}(\hat{n}-1)\}^2}$$

Solving (11.16) by Cramer's Rule, we have

$$(AF + BD - DF)\frac{de}{e} = \left(AFE - \frac{a-1}{n'} \bullet \frac{n_s}{1-t} DF \right)\frac{dt}{1+t} \tag{11.17}$$

$$(AF + BD - DF)\frac{dn}{n} = \left\{ BE + \frac{a-1}{n'} \frac{n_s}{(1+t)} F - EF \right\}\frac{dt}{1+t} \tag{11.18}$$

$$(AF + BD - DF)\frac{d\hat{n}}{\hat{n}} = \left(AE - \frac{a-1}{n'} \frac{n_s}{1+t} D \right)\frac{dt}{1+t} \tag{11.19}$$

The value of dn/dt, $d\hat{n}/dt$ and hence also du/dt and $d\hat{u}/dt$ cannot in general be signed even if $\mathring{a} = a$, $\mathring{k} = \bar{k}$ etc. Thus, we have

> *Proposition 11.2: With no retaliation from its trading partner, a tariff may make the tariff-imposing country either better off or worse off.*

The intuitive explanation is that, while the protection may be income-reducing by discouraging trade and specialization, it may be income-increasing by creating a more favourable terms of trade through the effect on the exchange rate. In the traditional model of exogenous comparative advantage, this problem is well known and is treated in the optimal-tariff literature (see, e.g., Graaff 1949; Johnson 1953; Kemp 1967; Bhagwati et al. 1969; Kemp and Negishi 1969). Here, it has been shown that in a model with no exogenous comparative advantage (with the advantage of trade being the facilitation of specialization), the problem of optimal tariff as an offsetting consideration to the case for free trade remains before considering retaliation and smallness.

11.2.3.2   The case of full retaliation

For the case of simple retaliation in the model of two symmetrical countries, $\hat{t} = t$, $e = 1$ and all variables in both countries also assume the same values (i.e. $n = \hat{n}$, $x_s^d = \hat{x}_{sl}^d$, etc.), we have from the differentiation of (11.15),

$$\frac{dn_s}{dt}|\hat{t} = t| = \frac{n}{(1+t)} \frac{E}{D} < 0 \tag{11.20}$$

Since D is negative from the second-order condition $\partial^2 u_i / \partial n_s^2 < 0$ (i.e. the differentiation of equation 11.15 with respect to n_s again) and E is necessarily positive as $a > 1$, $M > n_s$, and $(1 + t)n' > n$. Thus, we may conclude that a fully retaliated protection decreases the scope of international trade.

Substitute $e = P_{ir} = P_{is} = 1$ into (11.10) and differentiate the resulting expression for u_i with respect to t, we have

$$\frac{du_i}{dt}\big|\hat{t} = t \big| = \frac{\partial u_i}{\partial n_s}\frac{dn_s}{dt} + \frac{\partial u_i}{\partial t} \tag{11.21}$$

from the first-order condition for utility maximization with respect to ns, $\partial u_i/\partial n_s$ (i.e. Equation 11.15). Thus, $du_i/dt|t = \hat{t}| = \partial u_i/\partial t$ which is necessarily negative if $\bar{k}$ is high enough such that international trade does take place. (If not, $du_i/dt = 0$). Thus, we have

> *Proposition 11.3: A fully retaliated protection reduces real income by reducing the scope of specialization made possible by trade.*

11.2.3.3 The case of a small country

This can be taken to be the inability to affect international prices of traded goods. Then, putting $e = 1$ into (11.15) and (11.10) respectively, we may again derive

$$\frac{dn_s}{dt}\big|\text{small country}\big| = \frac{n}{1+t}\frac{E}{D} < 0 \tag{11.20'}$$

$$\frac{du_i}{dt}\big|\text{small country}\big| < 0 \tag{11.21'}$$

Thus, we have

> *Proposition 11.4: A tariff by a small country reduces its real income.*

While this result is not surprising, it is reassuring to confirm that, even where international trade is based on specialization rather than exogenous comparative advantage, the traditional case for free trade prevails for both the case of full retaliation and the case of small country.

The model of course does not include all complications in the real world (such as protection motivated by political factors, strategic trade, etc.). An integration of the Yang–Ng model emphasizing specialization and endogenous comparative advantage with the traditional model emphasizing comparative advantage as well as covering other complicating factors may provide an interesting analysis.

11.3 The enrichment of a sector benefits others: The case of trade for specialization

In our current world of globalization with the fast growing Asian economies (despite the recent financial storm, the area may be expected to grow strongly after adjustments), the effect of the enrichment/decline of a sector (including individual, region, country, area, or a group thereof) on others is an important problem with significant implications for the development planning of a country. Ng (1996) shows that the enrichment of a sector tends to benefit others as a group in its general thrust. Specifically, the improvement in the ability to produce more of some goods may benefit or harm specific trading partners. However, the proportionate expansion of the production possibility set benefits others as a group if (but not only if) the imports of the country are not mainly inferior goods. He establishes these using models of Ricardian (exogenous) comparative advantage for both the competitive and the monopolistic cases. In this section, we wish to see whether enrichment benefits others in a model with no exogenous comparative advantage, with trade gains from generalized increasing returns from division of labour and the associated economies of specialization as outlined above. The principal results are that, if the enrichment consists in a higher ability to produce goods, this tends to benefit others; if the enrichment consists in an improvement in the transaction efficiency, the result is ambiguous.

To consider the effects of enrichment, replace (11.7) above by

$$x_i + x_i^s = Al_i^a$$
$$x_j = Al_j^a \quad \forall j \in J_i \tag{11.7'}$$

where A is a productivity factor. An increase in A represents a proportionate increase in productivity across all goods. Thus, it corresponds to the proportionate enrichment of Ng (1996). Also replace (11.9) above by

$$P_i x_i^s = \sum_{r \in R_i} P_r x_r^d + \sum_{s \in S_i} \frac{\hat{P}_s x_s^d}{e} \tag{11.9'}$$

In other words, we take $t = f = 0$ as we do not consider the effects of a tariff. The other equations are similar.

Maximizing (11.6) subject to (11.7'), (11.8), and (11.9'), we have

$$u_i = \left\{ \frac{[1 - c(n-1)]}{m} \right\}^{am} (n')^{n(a-1)} e^{n_s} k^{n_i} \bar{k}^{n_s} \prod_{r \in R} P_{ir} \prod_{s \in S} P_{is}$$
$$= u_i\left(A, n_s, M, e, a, c, k, \bar{k}, P_{ir}, \hat{P}_{is}\right) \tag{11.22}$$

where m being the exogenously given numbers of goods on which no comparative statics is done and need not be explicitly listed; $n_r =$ number of goods in R and $n_s =$ number of goods in S. Hence the number of traded goods n equals $1 + n_r + n_s$.

Equation (11.22) gives the utility level of individuals with international trade. If we compare it with the utility level with no international trade, we may show that if the transaction cost coefficients are low enough, international trade results in a higher utility level than no international trade (demonstration available with the authors). From (11.22), maximizing u_i with respect to n_s yields the optimal number of goods purchased from abroad for the individual selling good i. The optimal value n_s^* is the integer in the neighbourhood of n^{**} that is given by the first-order condition $\partial u_i / \partial n_s = 0$, giving

$$n_s^{**} = n_s^{**}(m, e, a, c, k, \bar{k}, P_{ir}, \hat{P}_{is}) \tag{11.23}$$

Due to the symmetry of the model, the optimal number of goods purchased by an individual from abroad n_s^* (and hence the optimal number of traded goods for an individual n^*) is the same for all individuals. The larger is n^*, the higher is the level of specialization for each individual and the higher is the level of division of labour for the economy. For international trade to be relevant in our model, the number of goods is taken to be larger than the number of individuals in a country. Thus, in equilibrium, only one individual sells each good.

The market-clearing conditions and the balance-of-trade condition remain unchanged as (11.12) and (11.13') above. The demand for imports by an individual in this country is (derivation available with the author)

$$X_s^d = \frac{eA\{n[1 - c(n-1)]/m\}^a}{n} \quad \forall s \in S \tag{11.24}$$

and that in the other country is

$$\hat{x}_s^d = \frac{\hat{A}}{e} \left\{ \frac{\hat{n}[1 - \hat{c}(\hat{n} - 1)]}{\hat{m}} \right\}^{\hat{a}} / \hat{n}' \quad \forall s \in \hat{S} \tag{11.24'}$$

where $1/e \equiv \hat{e}$.
Substituting (11.24) and (11.24') into (11.13'), we have

$$\frac{n_s eA\{\bullet\}^a}{n'} = \frac{\hat{n}_s \hat{A}\{\bullet\}^{\hat{a}}}{\hat{n}'} \tag{11.25}$$

Substituting $P_{ir} = P_{is} = 1$ (from symmetry) for all r and s into (11.22) and differentiating the resulting u_i with respect to n_s and setting the resulting expression equal to zero, we have

$$\frac{1}{u_i}\frac{\partial u_i}{\partial n_s} = \ln e\bar{k} + (a-1)(1+\ln n) - \frac{cam}{1-c(n-1)} = 0 \tag{11.26}$$

For the other country, the same process as described above also applies except that $\hat{e} \equiv 1/e$. We thus have

$$\frac{1}{\hat{u}_i}\frac{\partial \hat{u}_i}{\partial \hat{n}_s} = \ln\frac{\hat{\bar{k}}}{e} + (\hat{a}-1)(1+\ln\hat{n}) - \frac{\hat{c}\hat{a}\hat{m}}{1-\hat{c}(\hat{n}-1)} = 0 \tag{11.26'}$$

11.3.1   The effects of enrichment

Using the model above, we may examine the effect of enrichment by letting A, $\hat{A}$, $\bar{k}$, $\hat{\bar{k}}$, c, $\hat{c}$ change exogenously. An increase in A signifies a proportionate improvement in productive capacity while an increase/decrease in $\bar{k}$ and/or c signifies an improvement in transaction efficiency. Taking a, m, etc. as constant, but allowing n_s (and hence n), $\hat{n}$ and e to be endogenously determined, we may differentiate (11.25) (11.26), and (11.26') to solve for de, dn, $d\hat{n}$. The differentiation of (11.25), (11.26), and (11.26') yields, after substituting in $dn_s = dn$ (from $n = 1 + n_r + n_s$ and the constancy of n_r as domestic trade has been exhausted), we have three equations in matrix-vector form:

$$\begin{bmatrix} X & 0 & 1 \\ 0 & \hat{X} & -1 \\ Y & -\hat{Y} & 1 \end{bmatrix} \begin{bmatrix} dn/n \\ d\hat{n}/\hat{n} \\ de/e \end{bmatrix} = \begin{bmatrix} Z(dc/c) - (d\bar{k}/\bar{k}) \\ \hat{Z}(d\hat{c}/\hat{c}) - (d\hat{\bar{k}}/\hat{\bar{k}}) \\ \dfrac{d\hat{A}}{\hat{A}} - \dfrac{dA}{A} + W\dfrac{dc}{c} - \hat{W}\dfrac{d\hat{c}}{\hat{c}} \end{bmatrix} \tag{11.26''}$$

where $X \equiv a - 1 - c^2amn/\{1 - c(n-1)\}^2$, $Y \equiv a - 1 + n/n_s - \{acn\}/\{1 - c(n-1)\}$, $Z \equiv cam/\{1 - c(n-1)\}^2 > 0$, $W \equiv ac(n-1)/\{1 - c(n-1)\} > 0$, and $\hat{X}$, $\hat{Y}$, etc. are the corresponding values for the other countries. Starting with the symmetrical case where the parameters are the same for the two countries, $X = \hat{X}$, etc. at the initial equilibrium.

Solving (11.26'') by Cramer's Rule, we have for the symmetrical case

$$\Delta\frac{dn}{n} = \hat{X}\left(\frac{dA}{A} - \frac{d\hat{A}}{\hat{A}}\right) + (\hat{Y} - \hat{X})\frac{d\bar{k}}{\bar{k}} + \hat{Y}\frac{d\hat{\bar{k}}}{\hat{\bar{k}}} + \{(\hat{X} - \hat{Y})Z - \hat{X}W\}\frac{dc}{c} \tag{11.27}$$

$$+ (\hat{X}\hat{W} - \hat{Y}\hat{Z})\frac{d\hat{c}}{\hat{c}}$$

$$\Delta \frac{d\hat{n}}{\hat{n}} = X\left(\frac{d\hat{A}}{\hat{A}} - \frac{dA}{A}\right) + (Y - X)\frac{d\hat{\bar{k}}}{\hat{\bar{k}}} + Y\frac{d\bar{k}}{\bar{k}} + \{(X - Y)\hat{Z} - X\hat{W}\}\frac{d\hat{c}}{\hat{c}}$$

$$+ (XW - YZ)\frac{dc}{c} \tag{11.28}$$

$$\Delta \frac{de}{e} = X^2\left(\frac{d\hat{A}}{\hat{A}} - \frac{dA}{A}\right) + YX\hat{}\frac{d\bar{k}}{\bar{k}} - X Y\hat{}\frac{d\hat{\bar{k}}}{\hat{\bar{k}}} + (X\hat{X}W - \hat{X}YZ)\frac{dc}{c}$$

$$- (\hat{X}XW\hat{} - XY\hat{Z})\frac{d\hat{c}}{\hat{c}} \tag{11.29}$$

where Δ is the determinant of the matrix in (11.26″) and is positive from the stability condition. Thus, an equal proportionate productive enrichment in both countries ($dA/A = d\hat{A}/\hat{A}$) leaves the exchange rate and the number of traded goods unchanged; a proportionate productive enrichment in the other country improves the exchange rate of this country. (These may be confirmed by substituting $dx = 0$ for all other exogenous variables x except $dA/A = d\hat{A}/\hat{A}$ and $d\hat{A}/\hat{A}$ respectively into the above equations.) However, a change in the transaction cost coefficients $1 - k$ or c has ambiguous effects. (This may be confirmed by substituting $dA/A = dd\hat{A}/\hat{A} \ldots = 0$ except the variable allowed to change into the above equations.) It may seem puzzling that an improvement in transaction efficiency k of a country may adversely affect the exchange rate of the other country. However, this may be explained by the fact that such an improvement means that the country has to import less to have the same effective amount of consumption of imports. At first, we also mistakenly thought that an equal proportionate productive improvement of both countries should increase the number of traded goods as it makes the fixed cost of transaction c relatively smaller. This is not true because c is specified in terms of labour, not in terms of money or goods. Substitute $P_{ir} = P_{is} = 1$ (from the symmetry of individuals and goods in each country) into (11.22) and differentiate the resulting expression for u_i with respect to $\hat{A}$, yielding

$$\frac{du_i}{d\hat{A}} = \frac{\partial u_i}{\partial n_s}\frac{dn_s}{d\hat{A}} + \frac{\partial u_i}{\partial e}\frac{\partial e}{\partial \hat{A}} + \frac{\partial u}{\partial \hat{A}} \tag{11.30}$$

Substituting (11.25), (11.27), and (11.29) at $dA = 0$, $d\bar{k} = 0$, etc. into (11.30) and evaluating (11.30) fully from (11.22), we have

$$\frac{du_i}{d\hat{A}}\frac{\hat{A}}{u_i} = n_s > 0 \tag{11.31}$$

Together with the discussion in the paragraph after (11.29), we may thus state

> *Proposition 11.5: A proportionate productive enrichment of a country benefits its trading partners (as a group) even when trade is based on the economies of specialization. However, an improvement in the transaction efficiency of a country has ambiguous effects on its trading partners.*

This proposition complements the result of Ng (1996).

It may be noted that, though the degree of economies of specialization a does not directly appear in (11.30) and (11.31), it should not be inferred that it does not affect the result, as the various numbers of traded goods are affected by a. In fact, in our present model without comparative advantage between individuals and between countries, trade is inefficient without economies of specialization ($a > 1$), as shown in Yang and Ng (1993). In real economies, trade is facilitated by both exogenous comparative advantage and economies of specialization (ignoring the relatively less important factor of the heterogeneity in preferences). For analytical clarity and to emphasize our point on trade for specialization, it is natural to abstract from the complication of exogenous comparative advantage.

12
Conceptual and Policy Implications: Concluding Discussion

The issue of increasing returns will be constantly raised because a neat general solution is lacking and many different outcomes are possible. Increasing returns are also prevalent in the real economy for a number of reasons discussed in Chapter 1. However, the introduction of increasing returns plays havoc to many basic tenets of traditional economic theory. This is probably an important reason why increasing returns have not been discussed more often, especially in the classroom. It is well known that the presence of increasing returns may no longer make the market equilibrium perfectly Pareto optimal. It is less well known that it also makes pecuniary external effects having efficiency implications and, together with the related imperfect competition, it makes money possibly non-neutral, as discussed in Chapter 2. However, productively efficient general equilibrium may exist in an economy with imperfectly competitive firms that price at average costs in equilibrium (Chapter 4). Nevertheless, encouraging the expansion of a sector with a higher degree of increasing returns is efficiency-improving (Chapter 5).

The fact that the real economy is not perfectly efficient (including due to the presence of increasing returns) means that some improvements *could* be possible. Industries or firms with marked increasing returns (hence with marginal costs much below average costs) could be taxed less than others. However, the potential advantage of doing so has to be weighed against the costs of administration, rent-seeking, mistakes, and corruption facilitation. In most economies without a highly efficient government, the policy of *laissez-faire* in this respect is probably the best. Nevertheless, this does not mean that an overall *laissez-faire* policy is best. The huge external costs of environmental disruption of most production and consumption, the prevalence of important relative-consumption effects (a form of external effects), and the existence of significant imperfect knowledge and imperfect rationality suggest substantial roles for a moderately efficient government. The presence of significant degree of increasing returns could be another factor that may call for attention.

Increasing returns at the economy level through the economies of specialization made possible by the division of labour was discussed in Chapter 6, focusing on the Yang–Ng framework. Although we need the presence of increasing returns for the Smith theorem (on the facilitation of division of labour by the extent of the market) to work and the absence of increasing returns for the Smith theory on the efficiency of the invisible hand to be proven, Chapter 7 argued that there is really no Smith's dilemma.

Our discussion of increasing returns also raises two fundamental conceptual issues. First, the presence of a significant degree of increasing returns (such as in the training of soldiers, especially if learning by doing is included as generalized increasing returns) may make freedom and fairness inherently in conflict with equity and efficiency, as discussed in Chapter 3. This *E-F conflict* may help explain the popularity of compulsory military conscription which clearly violates freedom, fairness, equity, and efficiency. As the four desiderata cannot be fully achieved, sacrificing each and every one of them may yet be the welfare-maximizing trade-off.

Analysing the welfare economic issues with the new division-of-labour framework, it is natural to focus not only on the traditional concept of allocative efficiency but also on organizational efficiency. Organizational efficiency refers to the choices between different economic structures, including different numbers of goods produced/marketed, different degrees of the division of labour, different numbers/layers of intermediate inputs, and the organization of firms. While allocative efficiency is important, organizational efficiency may be even more important in the long run. The analysis of organizational efficiency at the economy level could help answer such question as: Why should governments encourage investments in infrastructure? While this may partly be explained by the public goods nature, the presence of indirect network externalities of a higher degree of transaction efficiency (from the improved infrastructure) that results in a higher degree in the division of labour, may also be important, as analysed in Chapter 8. Another three organizational efficiency issues involving the network of division of labour, that of home versus market production, that of the desirability of encouraging work, and that of international trade, were discussed in Chapters 9, 10, and 11 respectively.

There are other efficiency issues in the presence of increasing returns not directly discussed in this book, though they may, to some extent, be covered by our rather general proposition of the desirability of encouraging sectors with higher degrees of increasing returns as discussed in Chapter 5. For example, using the imperfectly competitive representative-firm approach discussed in Section 2.1 to analyse the case of an industry, I have shown elsewhere (1986a, chapter5) that an increase in industry demand may lead to a decrease in industrial output and an increase in costs/taxes will be passed on to consumers by more than 100%. These may be briefly explained.

An increase in industrial demand may first lead to an increase in the price charged by each firm. The higher price may drive out some consumers with higher (absolute) price elasticities of demand (due either to lower incomes, lower need, or closer substitutes). This leaves remaining consumers with lower price elasticities of demand, making the demand for the product of each firm also of lower price elasticities. Firms will then find it profit-maximizing to increase the price further, leading to a lower industrial output. This adverse response of industrial output to an increase in demand is troubling, as it seems to suggest inefficiency. However, in itself, it need not necessarily be inefficient. As the demand increases for both consumers with low- and high-price elasticities, it is more important, from a pure efficiency point of view, to continue to serve those with low elasticities as they have higher consumer surpluses. The higher prices ensure that the more important demand is still served. (Actually, at the higher new equilibrium price, whoever willing to pay the higher price should be served at whatever quantities demanded irrespective of their price elasticities. However, if we compare the change from the old price to the new price, the changes in the quantities that should be served are affected by price elasticities.) The resulting lower price elasticities of remaining demand increases the price/MC (a measure of monopoly power) ratios of firms, making firms operating at points of higher degrees of increasing returns (as long-run equilibrium requires the tangency between the AC curve and the demand curve). If the industry is already one with higher degrees of increasing returns to begin with (hence under-expanded compared to other industries in accordance to the result in Chapter 5), the decrease in industry output increases the degree of under-production. This inefficiency may be traced to the two-sided coin of higher degrees of increasing returns and higher degrees of monopolistic power of firms.

Consider now an increase in costs (or taxes which have similar effects) illustrated in Figure 12.1. A representational firm of an industry under-consideration is shown at an initial long-run equilibrium point A where its AC curve is tangent to the demand curve d for its product. (Linearity in the demand curve is not needed for the analysis.) An industrial-wide increase in costs by x% shifts its AC curve vertically upward by x% to AC'. If the price is increased exactly by x%, can the point B on AC' vertically above A be an equilibrium point? No! It could be only in the virtually impossible case of a vertical, industrial demand curve. At the higher price (at the point B), the quantity demanded for each firm decreases, resulting in firms making negative profits. This forces some firms to exit, making the demand curve for the representative firm shifting rightward. A long-run equilibrium point is established when the demand curve is tangent to AC'. However, with a lower number of firms, the degree of competition is lower and the (absolute) price elasticity of demand is lower as well, making the final demand curve tangent to the unchanged AC' (assuming a small industry where the costs are not affected by the price and output levels of this industry) at a higher (compared to point B) price at the point C. Compared to the original point A, the increase in price is more than the x% increase in costs.

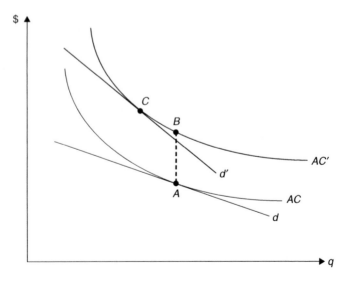

Figure 12.1   The price increases more than the increase in costs/taxes

The above analysis shows that cost and tax increases are more than fully passed on to consumers in imperfectly competitive firms with increasing returns. This explains the often-occurring complaints of consumer bodies regarding the excessive passing on of increases in costs/taxes. The excessive price increase may again be troubling but may be explained by the two-sided coin of higher degrees of increasing returns and higher degrees of monopolistic power of firms resulting from the cost/tax increase. This again is consistent with the general result of Chapter 5. As industries with high degrees of increasing returns are already under-expanded, they should not be taxed more unless justified on some separate efficiency consideration like external costs.

For another example, consider the request often for governmental promotion of demand for goods and services provided by certain industries/firms. For imperfectly competitive firms facing downward-sloping demand curves, the long-run free entry/exit equilibrium is at the tangency of the demand curve with the (also downward-sloping) average-cost curve (hence with increasing returns), as illustrated in Figure 12.1. Each firm has a strong desire to have an increase in the demand for its product (the demand curve for its product shifting to the right), as this will increase the amount of (supernormal) profits from zero to a big positive amount. This desire is particularly strong when the industry is in recession, with the demand curves of most firms failing to reach the AC curves. That is, firms are making losses. If the situation persists, some firms have to leave the industry for the remaining firms to be able to break even. The reluctance to exit is particularly strong if the fixed costs (especially if the component of sunk costs is high) of production are high. In such a situation, a sufficiently large increase in industrial demand will turn a loss-making situation into a breaking-even one or even a profit-making one.

As illustrated in Figure 12.2, a representative firm in a certain industry in recession is loss-minimizing at the initial equilibrium point A (with the no-shutdown condition met), with loss equalling the rectangle ABCD. If the demand curve shifts rightward to d' with unchanged cost curves (as may be true for a 'small' industry), the new profit-maximizing point F involves a huge profit of rectangle FGHD. Thus, the increasing-returns industry, especially when in recession, has a huge incentive in promoting industrial demand. We thus often have pressures to have the government lending a helping hand. For example, in many countries, we have the tourist promotion boards; tourist demand travel, accommodation, eating-out meals, sightseeing tours, souvenirs shopping, etc. Most of these industries are imperfectly competitive with

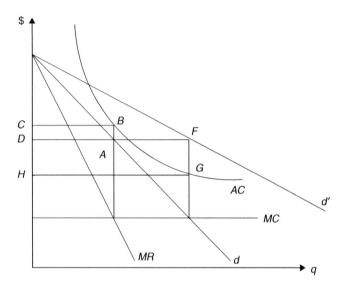

Figure 12.2 The big incentive for demand promotion

downward-sloping average-cost curves. All such firms see an increase in demand as conducive to big increases in profits. Tourism promotion is popular also because the increase in demand may come mainly from overseas and not at a substantial expense of a decrease in demand for some other domestic industries.

However, most of the tourism-related industries are also characterized by free entry/exit. Thus, the situation of a huge amount of profit at the point F illustrated in Figure 12.2 is not sustainable in the long run. If the situation of supernormal profits is expected to persist, more firms will enter the industry, shifting the demand curve faced by each firm leftward until supernormal profits are eliminated. Sometime further, a decrease in industrial demand may then cause another recession in the industry, leading to another round of calls for assistance in promoting demand. If the costs of demand promotion are substantial as likely so, the long-run inefficiency involved could be very large. This is so if the industries concerned do not have real factors like external benefits justifying encouragement. If they have higher degrees of increasing returns than other industries, the analysis in Chapter 5 suggests that some efficiency gains may be involved. Though the AC curve is unchanged (for the case of a small industry), the higher industrial demand allows more firms to operate. This higher degree of competition makes the demand curve for each firm more elastic, hence achieving a long-run tangency with the AC curve at a lower point and at a higher output per firm (than the case with no demand promotion). Although there is no gain in the production side as firms are just breaking even in the long run, consumers gain by having a lower price and a larger number of firms to choose from.

For yet another example, around half a century or so ago, many development economists and policy-makers were keen on the idea/ practice of encouraging manufacturing industries, on grounds such as the need for a 'big push' (Rosenstein-Rodan 1943), the evidence from developed countries (Hirschman 1958; Chenery 1960), the excess of industrial wages over agricultural marginal productivities (Hagen 1958; Bhagwati & Ramaswami 1963). The subsequent failure of many cases of unjustified and excessive protection, import substitution, and encouragement of manufacturing industries, coupled with inherent inefficiencies in government intervention, not to mention the fostering of corruption, made the case for visible hand disreputable. The subsequent success of the opposite policy of relying on existing comparative advantage and the international markets of trade and investment by the Asian dragons (Hong Kong, Korea, Singapore, and Taiwan) further made the policy of encouraging manufacturing through protection and import substitution unpopular.

However, with the possible exception of Hong Kong, the success of the Asian dragons was carefully nurtured with the visible hands of export promotion and foreign investment promotion by the relevant governments, not to mention the provision of necessary infrastructures and the specific promotion of certain sectors or certain areas, such as the Jurong Industrial Estate in Singapore. If we live in the traditional world satisfying the first theorem in welfare economics, such visible hands by the government can only harm but cannot help the development process. However, we live in a world with the prevalence of increasing returns and imperfectly competitive firms. This possibly makes certain government interventions desirable. In particular, if certain manufacturing goods do have higher degrees of increasing returns, especially in the long run with the effects of learning by doing incorporated, their encouragement now may be consistent with long-term comparative advantage, even if it may be opposite to the short-term comparative advantage.

Nevertheless, as already discussed in Chapter 5, since the required information to effect optimal intervention is costly if not impossible to acquire and since the policy of visible hands is likely to encourage wasteful rent-seeking activities, corruption, and the like, it may be optimal to follow the invisible hand in most cases. However, we cannot rule out completely the possible existence of some cases where intervention may be desirable. For example, the Chinese government recently mentioned the strategy of developing the great northwest. So, why can't the geographical location choice of firms be all left to the market? It is true that the strategy of developing the great northwest of China is partly a distributional one. However, if it is efficient not to develop the northwest, it will be more efficient to fulfil the distributional objective to transfer incomes to the poor in the northwest and for people in the northwest to migrate to the southeast. Thus, it is likely that increasing returns (including those of economies of conglomeration) led to the concentration of development in China in the southeast. However, after a certain point, higher congestion may make it desirable to disperse development to other less-developed areas. However, the importance of increasing returns may mean that no one wants to take the first step. It is only after a sizable concentration of firms and consumers in a city that it begins to attract more people to join. This may then explain the need for a strategy for the development of a certain area. Nevertheless, many such strategies may yet prove to be white elephants. How to estimate the significance of increasing returns involved to help judge whether such strategies are desirable is a challenge to empirical economics that is beyond the scope of this book and the competence of its author.

Notes

1 Introduction

1. On the empirical evidence for increasing returns, see Ades and Glaeser (1999), Allen and Liu (2007), Antweiler and Trefler (2002), Athreye and Keeble (2002), Davis and Weinstein (1999), Benarroch (1997), Christoffersen et al. (2007), Duggal et al. (2007), Fingleton (2003), Garicano and Hubbard (2007), Jin et al. (2005), Kangasharju et al. (2005), Kwack and Sun (2005), Latruffe et al. (2005), McCombie et al. (2003), Oliveira et al. (2006), Truett and Truett (2006), Walker (1998). See also McCombie and Roberts (2007) on the argument that estimates of returns to scale obtained using the static approach are subject to a spatial aggregation bias, which biases the estimates towards constant returns, while the dynamic approach yields estimates of substantial increasing returns. On the role of increasing returns in affecting the economic and social welfare at the country level, see Rose (2006).

2. Increasing returns at the world level may also be observed from both the economies of specialization of division of labour and from economies of scale at the firm level if the range of increasing returns is large relative to demand.

3. Houthakker (1956, p. 182) believed that 'there is hardly any part of economics that would not be advanced by a further analysis of specialization'. Stigler (1976, pp. 1029–210) also deplored that 'almost no one used or now uses theory of division of labor, for the excellent reason that there is scarcely such a theory. ... there is no standard, operable theory to describe what Smith argued to be the mainspring of economic progress. Smith gave the division of labor an immensely convincing presentation – it seems to me as persuasive a case for the power of specialization today as it appeared to Smith. Yet there is no evidence, so far as I know, of any serious advance in theory of the subject since his time'.

4. Similarly, Chandra and Sandilands (2005) argue that 'Endogenous growth theory ... which took off with Romer and Lucas, often makes Allyn Young's concept of increasing returns and Marshall's distinction between internal and external economies its starting point ... this is not the case as these theorists actually misrepresent Young in important ways.'

2 Devastating Implications of Increasing Returns on Some Traditional Conclusions

1. Many economists (see Dixon and Rankin 1994 for a survey) still regard additional distortions or frictions, such as menu costs, as necessary, in combination with non-perfect competition, to make money non-neutral. Really, instead of showing the neutrality of money under non-perfect competition, it has only been shown that a real equilibrium can still be an equilibrium

even if money supply changes. However, a change in money supply may also shift the economy from one equilibrium to another, making money possibly not really neutral (Ng 1998).

2. On the role of increasing returns and imperfection in competition in the persistence of business cycles, see also Zhang (2007).

3. Subsequent analyses of multiple equilibria abound, e.g. Krugman (1991a) relates multiple equilibria to technological increasing returns, Wirl and Feichtinger (2006) relate them to the social multiplier of Glaeser et al. (2003), and Julien and Sanz (2005) relate them to increasing returns in transaction technology. See also the large literature on sunspot.

4. The introduction of such factors as time lags may mean that the *MC* curve may not move up fully immediately, making the output level possibly increasing somewhat in the short term. However, unless there are other sustaining factors, such output levels are not sustainable.

5. This dichotomy and the neutrality of money need not be exactly equivalent in more complicated models.

6. Including cases where only the (set of) price(s) of one (set of) good(s) change (proportionately), with the (relative) prices of all other goods remaining unchanged when the composite commodity theorem may be strictly used and where the possible changes in the prices of other goods are not focused upon when the use of the theorem is similar to the assumption of *ceteris paribus*. The fact that other things do not usually remain unchanged does not prevent us from using *ceteris paribus*. We focus on: if other things remained unchanged, what would be the case. Similarly, if other prices do not changed, what would be the case.

7. They show that, for the case of a constant elasticity of substitution between different goods, the market equilibrium under free entry/exit coincides with the (non-negative profit) constrained optimum but no general conclusion is possible with non-constant elasticity.

8. The issue of equality is also ignored. This issue is less relevant if we accept the argument for treating a dollar as a dollar on specific issues, leaving equality to be pursued by the general tax/transfer policy (Ng 1979, 1984). On some special interaction of equity and efficiency issues in the presence of increasing returns, see Brown and Heal (1979) and Vohra (1992).

3   Equity and Efficiency versus Freedom and Fairness: An Inherent Conflict

1. The pursuit of equality by the use of preferential treatment between the rich and the poor (in addition to the progressive income tax system) such as the use of differential weights in cost-benefit analysis, and other distortions to the free function of the market economy are however inefficient methods to achieve equality as they have additional distortion effects apart from their disincentive effects (usually for-gotten). See Ng (1984) for the argument (which takes account of second and third best considerations) that a dollar should be treated as a dollar to whomsoever it goes.

2. If the number of urban residents is not equal to that of rural residents, this amount of income is not defined until the desired distribution between

urban and rural per capita income is determined. The simultaneous attainment of efficiency, distribution, and the urban-rural division is discussed in Section 3.3.

3. To speak in terms of marginal utilities we are using a cardinal utility framework. It is true that the efficiency conditions (Eqs 3.5–3.7 in Section 3.3) can be expressed in the form of MRS, but the equity condition (Eq. 3.4) for a welfare maximum has to be expressed in the form of the welfare weighted marginal utilities. As the existence of an individualistic Bergson-Samuelson *SWF* (Eq. I in Section III) presupposes interpersonal comparison of cardinal utilities (Kemp & Ng 1976, 1977; Parks 1976; Pollak 1979 and in particular Ng 1985), we lose no generality but gain in pedagogic simplicity in using a cardinal utility approach. On the cardinal measurability of utilities in principle and in practice, see Ng (1975, 1996, 1997). Those who do not like the marginal utility approach may use Figure 3.3 instead.

4. Cf. Buchanan (1965), Ng (1974), Hillman and Swan (1979, 1983) and Sandler and Tschirhart (1980). Ng (1973) deals with general Pareto efficiency as such, not with a specific maximum maximorum, and hence his condition need not include the difference in the private good allocation $x_u^m - x_r^{m'}$. The difference in the general Pareto efficiency approach and the specific welfare maximum approach is explained in Ng (1978).

4   Existence of Average-Cost Pricing Equilibria with Increasing Returns

1. That some of each good is needed may also be included to ensure an interior solution and the use of the conventional first-order conditions. Also, points like the no explicit treatment of joint production are also implicit.

6   Division of Labour: Increasing Returns at the Economy Level

1. Chu (1997), Wen (1997), and Wen and King (2004) also use the Yang–Ng framework to analyse the role of infrastructure in economic growth. However, they concentrate the positive aspects (such as the role of population density, resource endowment, and the time path of growth) without discussing the possible rationale for encouragement.

2. In the Yang–Ng framework, leisure has been considered by Lio (1996, 2003) who addresses the question of productivity but not the question of welfare or the desirability of encouraging work.

3. If animal welfare (on which see Ng 1995) is considered, again ideal morality dictates the maximization of total welfare inclusive of animal welfare but may be partial towards our own welfare.

4. This appendix is based on Yang and Ng (1993) and S. Ng (1998).

5. I wrote this appendix after discussion with Yang Chow who explored the overcoming of the coordination problem in response to my emphasis of this problem in a number of occasions. He has discussed his analysis in a chapter in his PhD thesis to be submitted to Monash University (Chow 2009).

7   The Smith Dilemma and Its Resolution

1. While there are different senses in Smith's usage of the invisible hand (e.g. see Ahmad 1990; Rothschild 1994), the commonly used interpretation is clear.

8   Why Should Governments Encourage Improvements on Infrastructure? Indirect Network Externality of Transaction Efficiency

1. However, where there is competition between jurisdictions/regions to attract mobile factors, there may be an excessive number of regions engaging in competition, leading to waste (see Bucovetsky 2005 and Taylor 1992). On the other hand, Cohen and Paul (2004) find positive spillover effects in inter-state public infrastructure investment for the U.S.
2. The network effects discussed here through the division of labour are thus different from those analysed by other researchers such as Economides (1996) and Nagurney (2003), though some similar aspects are present.
3. Chu (1997) and Wen (1997) also use the Yang–Ng framework to analyse the role of infrastructure in economic growth. However, they concentrate on the positive aspects (such as the role of population density and the time path of growth) without discussing the possible rationale for encouragement.
4. For simplicity, the model here concentrates on the division of labour between individuals with respect to the final goods produced, ignoring the division of labour or specialization within a production unit including with respect to different intermediate goods or processes. However, Yang and Ng (1993) also analysed the use of intermediate goods.
5. The same index *i* is used to denote both the good and the individual who specializes in producing that good. This is convenient and is used throughout the whole literature using this framework.

9   Average-Cost Pricing, Increasing Returns, and Optimal Output: Comparing Home and Market Production

1. Economically, the size of the fixed cost of market production A must not be too large in relation to the population size M. Otherwise the economy may not be viable if the labour of all people combined is insufficient to provide for the fixed cost of production, allowing for the necessity of producing some home goods and having some leisure.

10   Do the Economies of Specialization Justify the Work Ethics? An Examination of Buchanan's Hypothesis

1. It is not difficult to check that the second-order condition is satisfied; the demonstration is available from the author. For the more general question on the existence of equilibrium for this types of models, see Yang and Ng (1993), Sun et al. (2004).

2. Economically, the size of the fixed cost of market production A must not be too large in relation to the population size M. Otherwise the economy may not be viable if the labour of all people combined is insufficient to provide for the fixed cost of production, allowing for the necessity of producing some home goods and having some leisure.
3. Further welfare implications of increasing returns are examined in Ng and Zhang (2005).

11 Specialization, Trade, and Growth

1. See also Ethier and Ruffin (2008) who show that increasing returns external to the firm may enable a country to export a good with a comparative cost disadvantage due to the scale effect.

References

ADES, ALBERTO F. and GLAESER, Edward L. (1999). Evidence on growth, increasing returns, and the extent of the market, *Quarterly Journal of Economics*, 114(3): 1025-45.

AHMAD, Syed (1990). Adam Smith's four invisible hands, *History of Political Economy*, 22(1): 137-44.

AKERLOF, George (1976). The economics of caste and of the rat race and other woeful tales, *Quarterly Journal of Economics*, 90(4): 599-617.

ALLEN, Jason and LIU, Ying (2007). Efficiency and economies of scale of large Canadian banks, *Canadian Journal of Economics*, 40(1): 225-44.

American Economic Association (1952). *Readings in Price Theory*. Chicago: Irwin.

ANDERBERG, D. and BALESTRINO, A. (2000). Household production and the design of the tax structure, *International Tax and Public Finance*, 7: 563-84.

ANTWEILER, Werner and TREFLER, Daniel (2002). Increasing returns and all that: A view from trade, *American Economic Review*, 92: 93-119.

ARROW, Kenneth J. (1951/1963). *Social Choice and Individual Values*. New York: Wiley.

ARROW, Kenneth J. (1987). Technical information, returns to scale, and the existence of competitive equilibrium, in GROVES, Theodore, RADNER, Roy, and REITER, Stanley, eds. *Information, Incentives, and Economic Mechanisms: Essays in Honor of Leonid Hurwicz*, Minneapolis: University of Minnesota Press, pp. 243-55.

ARROW, Kenneth J. (1995). Returns to scale, information and economic growth, in KOO, Bon H. and PERKINS, Dwight H. (eds) *Social Capability and Long-Term Economic Growth*. London: Macmillan.

ARROW, Kenneth J. (2000). Increasing returns: Historiographic issues and path dependence, *European Journal of the History of Economics Thought*, 7(2): 171-80.

ARROW, Kenneth J., NG, Yew-Kwang, and YANG, Xiaokai (1998). *Increasing Returns and Economic Analysis*. London: Macmillan.

ARTHUR, W. B. (1994). *Increasing Returns and Path Dependence in the Economy*. Ann Arbor: University of Michigan Press.

ASCHAUER, David A. (1989). Is public expenditure productive? *Journal of Monetary Economics*, 23: 177-200.

ASCHAUER, David A. (2001). Output and employment effects of public capital, *Public Finance and Management*, 1(2): 135-60.

ATHREYE, Suma S. and KEEBLE, David (2002). Sources of increasing returns and regional innovation in the UK, *Regional Studies*, 36(4): 345-57.

ATKINSON, Anthony B. and STIGLITZ, Joseph E. (1976). The design of tax structure: Direct versus indirect taxation, *Journal of Public Economics*, 6: 55-75.

ATKINSON, Anthony B. and STIGLITZ, Joseph E. (1980). *Lectures on Public Economics*. New York: McGraw-Hill.

BALCER, Yves and SADKA, Efraim (1982). Horizontal equity, income taxation and self-selection with an application to income tax credits, *Journal of Public Economics*, 19: 291-309.

BALDWIN, Richard, FORSLID, R., MARTIN, Philippe, OTTAVIANO, Gianmarco, and ROBERT-NICOUD, Frederic (2003). *Economic Geography and Public Policy*. Princeton University Press.

BATINA, Raymond G. (2001). The effects of public capital on the economy, *Public Finance and Management*, 1(2): 113–34.

BECKER, G. S. (1965). A theory of the allocation of time, *Economic Journal*, 75: 493–517.

BEINHOCKER, Eric D. (2006). *The Origin of Wealth: Evolution, Complexity, and the Radical Remaking of Economics*. Boston: Harvard Business School Press.

BENARROCH, Michael (1997). Returns to scale in Canadian manufacturing: An interprovincial comparison, *Canadian Journal of Economics*, 30(4): 1083–103.

BENHABIB, J., ROGERASON, R., and WRIGHT, R. (1991). Homework in macroeconomics: Household production and aggregate fluctuations, *Journal of Political Economy*, 99: 1166–87.

BERG, Sanford V., POLLITT, Michael G. and TSUJI, Masatsugu (eds) (2002). *Private Initiatives in Infrastructure: Priorities, Incentives, and Performance*. Tokyo: Institute of Developing Economies [and] Japan External Trade Organization, 2000.

BERGSTROM, Theodore (1986). Soldiers of fortune? Essays in *Honor of Kenneth J. Arrow. Volume 2. Equilibrium Analysis*, edited by Heller, Walter P., Starr, Ross M. and Starrett, D. A., Cambridge, New York, and Sydney: Cambridge University Press, pp. 57–80.

BESLEY, T. (1989). Commodity taxation and imperfect competition: A note on the effects of entry, *Journal of Public Economics*, 40(3): 359–67.

BHAGWATI, J. and RAMASWAMI, V. K. (1963). Domestic distortions, tariffs and the theory of the optimum subsidy, *Journal of Political Economy*, 71: 44–50.

BHAGWATI, J., RAMASWAMI, V. K., and SRINIVASAN, T. N. (1969). Domestic distortions, tariffs, and the theory of optimum subsidy: Some further results, *Journal of Political Economy*, 77(6): 1005–10.

BONNISSEAU, Jean-Marc and MEDDEB, Moncef (1999). Existence of equilibria in economies with increasing returns and infinitely many commodities, *Journal of Mathematical Economics*, 31(3): 287–307.

BOOTH, Alison L. and COLES, Melvyn (2007). A microfoundation for increasing returns in human capital accumulation and the under-participation trap, *European Economic Review*, 51(7): 1661–81.

BORGHANS, Lex and GROOT, L. (1998). Superstardom and monopolistic power: Why media stars earn more than their marginal contribution to welfare, *Journal of Institutional and Theoretical Economics*, 154(3): 546–71.

BOSERUP, Ester (1981). *Population and Technological Change*. Chicago: University of Chicago Press.

BOUGHEAS, Spiros, DEMETRIADES, Panicos O., and MAMUNEAS, Theofanis P. (2000). Infrastructure, specialization, and economic growth, *Canadian Journal of Economics*, 33: 506–22.

BROWN, Donald J. and HEAL, Geoffrey, M. (1979). Equity, efficiency, and increasing returns, *Review of Economic Studies*, 46(4): 571–85.

BROWN, Donald J. and HEAL, Geoffrey M. (1983). Marginal vs. average cost pricing in the presence of a public monopoly, *American Economic Review*, 73(2): 189–93.

BROWN, Donald J., HEAL, Geoffrey, M., KHAN, Ali, and VOHRA, R. (1986). On a general existence theorem for marginal cost pricing equilibria, *Journal of Economic Theory*, 38(2): 371–79.

BROX, James A. and FADER, Christina A. (2005). Infrastructure investment and Canadian manufacturing productivity, *Applied Economics*, 37(11): 1247–56.

BUCHANAN, James M. (1965). An economic theory of clubs, *Economica*, 32: 211–2.

BUCHANAN, James M. (1991). Economic interdependence and the work ethics, in *The Economics and the Ethics of Constitutional Order*. Ann Arbor: University of Michigan Press, 159–78.

BUCHANAN, James M. (1994). The supply of labor and the extent of the market, in Buchanan, J. M. and Yoon, Y. J. (eds) *The Returns to Increasing Returns*. Ann Arbor: University of Michigan Press, 331–42.

BUCHANAN, James M. and YOON, Y. J. (1994a). Increasing returns, parametric work-supply adjustment, and the work ethic, in Buchanan and Yoon (1994b), pp. 343–56.

BUCHANAN, James M. and YOON, Y. J. (1994b). *The Returns to Increasing Returns*. Ann Arbor: University of Michigan Press.

BUCHANAN, James M. and YOON, Y. J. (1999). Generalized increasing returns, Euler's theorem, and competitive equilibrium, *History of Political Economy*, 31(3): 511–23.

BUCHANAN, James M. and YOON, Y. J. (2002). Globalization as framed by the two logics of trade, *Independent R*, 6(3): 399–405.

BUCOVETSKY, S. (2005). Public Input competition, *Journal of Public Economics*, 89(9–10): 1763–87.

CHAKRABORTY, B. S. (2003). Trade in intermediate goods in a model with monopolistic competition, *Economica*, 70(279): 551–66.

CHANDLER, Alfred D. (1990). *Scale and Scope: The Dynamics of Industrial Capitalism*. Cambridge, MA: Belknap Press of Harvard University Press.

CHANDRA, V., FRANCK, D., and NAQVI, N. (2002). World increasing returns and production subsidies, *Economica*, 69: 223–7.

CHANDRA, Ramesh and SANDILANDS, Roger J. (2005). Does modern endogenous growth theory adequately represent Allyn Young? *Cambridge Journal of Economics*, 29(3): 463–73.

CHENERY, Hollis B. (1960). Patterns of industrial growth, *American Economic Review*, 50: 624–54.

CHENG, Wenli and YANG, Xiaokai (2004). Inframarginal analysis of network division of labour: A survey, *Journal of Economic Behavior & Organization*, 55: 137–74.

CHIPMAN, John S. (1965). The nature and meaning of equilibrium in economic theory, in Martindale, D. (ed.) *Functionalism in Social Sciences*, reprinted in Townsend.

CHIPMAN, John S. (1970). External economies of scale and competitive equilibrium, *Quarterly Journal of Economics*, 84: 347–85.

CHOW, Yang (2009). 'Skill-Based Portfolio Choices: Portfolio Decision Making under Agent-Specific Uncertainty'. PhD thesis to be submitted to Monash University.

CHRISTOFFERSEN, Henrik, PALDAM, Martin and WURTZ, Allan H. (2007). Public versus private production and economies of scale, *Public Choice*, 130(3–4): 311–28.

CHU, C. Y. Cyrus (1997). Population density and infrastructure development, *Review of Development Economics*, 1(3): 294–304.

COHEN, Jeffrey P. and PAUL, Catherine J. M. (2004). Public infrastructure investment, interstate spatial spillovers, and manufacturing costs, *Review of Economics and Statistics*, 86(2): 551–60.

DAVIS, Donald R. and WEINSTEIN, David E. (1999). Find more like this economic geography and regional production structure: An empirical investigation, *European Economic Review*, 43(2): 379–407.

DELIPALLA, S. and KEEN, M. (1992). The comparison between ad valorem and specific taxation under imperfect competition, *Journal of Public Economics*, 49: 351–67.

DEMETRIADES, Panicos O. and MAMUNEAS, Theofanis P. (2000). Intertemporal output and employment effects of public infrastructure capital: Evidence from 12 OECD countries, *Economic Journal*, 110: 687–712.

DIAMANTARAS, Dimitrios and GILLES, Robert P. (2004). On the microeconomics of specialization, *Journal of Economic Behavior & Organization*, 55: 223–36.

DIXIT, Avinash K. and STIGLITZ, Joseph E. (1977). Monopolistic competition and optimum product diversity, *American Economic Review*, 67(3): 297–308.

DIXON, Huw and RANKIN, Neil (1994). Imperfect competition and macroeconomics: A survey, *Oxford Economic Chapters*, 46: 171–99.

DOI, J. and FUTAGAMI, K. (2004). Commodity taxation and the effects of entry: A case of variety preference, *Journal of Economics*, 83: 267–79.

DUGGAL, Vijaya G., SALTZMAN, Cynthia, KLEIN, and Lawrence, R. (2007). Infrastructure and productivity: An extension to private infrastructure and it productivity, *Journal of Econometrics*, 140(2): 485–502.

EATON, Jonathan and PANAGARIYA, Arvind (1979). Gains from trade under variable returns to scale, commodity taxation, tariffs and factor market distortions, *Journal of International Economics*, 9: 481–501.

ECONOMIDES, Nicholas (1996). The economics of networks, *International Journal of Industrial Organization*, 14(6): 673–99.

EINARSSON, T. and MARQUIS, M. H. (1997). Home production with endogenous growth, *Journal of Monetary Economics*, 39: 551–69.

ELLIS, Howard S. and FELLNER, William (1943). External economies and diseconomies, *American Economic Review*, 33: 493–511.

EPIFANI, Paolo and GANCIA, Gino (2006). Increasing returns, imperfect competition, and factor prices, *Review of Economics and Statistics*, 88(4): 583–98.

ESFAHANI, Hadi S. and RAMIREZ, Maria T. (2003). Institutions, infrastructure, and economic growth, *Journal of Development Economics*, 70: 443–77.

ETHIER, Wilfred J. (1979). Internationally decreasing costs and world trade, *Journal of International Economics*, 9: 1–24.

ETHIER, Wilfred J. (1982). National and international returns to scale in the modern theory of international trade, *American Economic Review*, 72: 389–405.

ETHIER, Wilfred J. and RUFFIN, Roy (2008). External economies of scale and comparative advantage, *PIER Working Paper*, No. 08–008.

EVANS, Paul and KARRAS, George (1994). Are government activities productive? Evidence from a panel of US States, *Review of Economics and Statistics*, 76: 1–11.

FAFCHAMPS, M. and QUISUMBING, A. R. (2003). Social roles, human capital, and the intrahousehold division of labour: Evidence from Pakistan, *Oxford Economic Chapters*, 55(1): 36–80.

FERNAND, John G. (1999). Roads to prosperity? Assessing the link between public capital and productivity, *American Economic Review*, 89: 619–38.

FINGLETON, Bernard (2003). Increasing returns: Evidence from local wage rates in Great Britain, *Oxford Economic Chapters*, 55(4): 716–39.

FRANCOIS, Joseph F. and NELSON, Douglas (2002). A geometry of specialization, *Economic Journal*, 112: 649–78.

FRANK, Robert H. (1999). *Luxury Fever: Why Money Fails to Satisfy in an Era of Excess*. New York: The Free Press.

FRANK, Robert H. and COOK, Philip J. (1995). *The Winner-Take-All Society: How More and More Americans Compete for Ever Fewer and Bigger Prizes, Encouraging Economic Waste, Income Inequality, and an Impoverished Cultural life*. New York, London, and Toronto: Simon and Schuster, Free Press, Martin Kessler Books.

FUJITA, Masahisa, KRUGMAN, Paul, and VENABLES, Anthony J. (1999). *The Spatial Economy: Cities, Regions and International Trade*. Cambridge, MA: MIT Press.

GABSZEWICZ, Jean J. and LAUSSEL, Didier (2007). Increasing returns, entrepreneurship and imperfect competition, *Economic Theory*, 30(1): 1–19.

GALLO, Fredrik (2006). Increasing returns, input-output linkages, and technological leapfrogging, *Topics in Economic Analysis and Policy*, 6(1): 1–27.

GARICANO, Luis and HUBBARD, Thomas N. (2007). Managerial leverage is limited by the extent of the market: Hierarchies, specialization, and the utilization of lawyers' human capital, *Journal of Law and Economics*, 50(1): 1–43.

GAUTHIER, David (1986). *Morals by Agreement*. Oxford: Clarendon Press.

GINTIS, Herbert (2007). Review of Beinhocker (2006), *Journal of Economic Literature*, XLIV(4): 1018–31.

GLAESER, E. L., SACERDOTE, B. I., and SCHEINKMAN, J. A. (2003). The social multiplier, *Journal of the European Economic Association*, MIT Press, 1(2–3): 345–53.

GRAAFF, J. (1949). On optimum tariff structures, *Review of Economic Studies*, 17: 47–59.

GRAMLICH, Edward M. (1994). Infrastructure investment: A review essay, *Journal of Economic Literature*, 32: 1176–96.

GREENWOOD, Jeremy and HERCOWITZ, Zvi (1991). The allocation of capital and time over the business cycle, *Journal of Political Economy*, 99(6): 1188–214.

GREPPERUD, Sverre and PEDERSEN, Pål Andreas (2001). The crowding-out of work ethics, *Studies in Economics 0102*, Department of Economics, University of Kent. http://econchapters.repec.org/chapter/ukcukcedp/0102.htm

GRINOLS, Earl L. (1991). Increasing returns and the gains from trade, *International Economic Review*, 32(4): 973–84.

GRINOLS, Earl L. (2006). The intervention principle, *Review of International Economics*, 14(2): 226–47.

GROSSMAN, G. and HELPMAN, E. (1991). Quality ladders and product cycles, *Quarterly Journal of Economics*, 106: 557–86.

GUESNERIE, Roger (1975). Pareto optimality in non-convex economies, *Econometrica*, 43: 1–29.

HAGEN, E. E. (1958). An economic justification for protection, *Quarterly Journal of Economics*, 72(4): 496–514.

HARSANYI, John C. (1953). Cardinal utility in welfare economics and in the theory of risk-taking, *Journal of Political Economy*, 61: 434–5.

HARSANYI, John C. (1955). Cardinal welfare, individualistic ethics, and inter-personal comparison of utility, *Journal of Political Economy*, 63: 309–21.

HART, Oliver D. (1985). Monopolistic competition in the spirit of Chamberlin: Special results, *Economic Journal*, 95(380): 889–908.

HAUGHWOUT, Andrew F. (2002). Public infrastructure investments, product-ivity and welfare in fixed geographic areas, *Journal of Public Economics*, 83(3): 405–28.

HEAL, Geoffrey (1980). Spatial structure in the retail trade: A study in prod-uct differentiation with increasing returns, *Bell Journal of Economics*, 11(2): 545–83.

HEAL, Geoffrey (ed.) (1999). *The Economics of Increasing Returns*. Cheltenham, UK: Edward Elgar.

HELPMAN, Elhanan (1984). Increasing returns, imperfect market, and trade the-ory, in Jones, R. W. and Kenen, P. B. (eds) *Handbook of International Economics, Vol. 1, International Trade*. Amsterdam, North-Holland.

HELPMAN, Elhanan and KRUGMAN, Paul R. (1985). *Market Structure and Foreign Trade: Increasing Returns, Imperfect Competition, and the International Economy*. Cambridge, MA: MIT Press.

HENDERSON, J. Vernon (ed.) (2005). *New Economic Geography*, Elgar Reference Collection. International Library of Critical Writings in Economics, vol. 184. Cheltenham, UK and Northampton, MA.: Elgar.

HICKS, John R. (1939). Foundations of welfare economics, *Economic Journal*, 49: 696–712.

HILLMAN, Arye L. and SWAN Peter L. (1979). Club participation under uncer-tainty, *Economic Letters*, 4: 307–12.

HILLMAN, Arye L. and SWAN Peter L. (1983). Participation rules for Pareto-optimal clubs, *Journal of Public Economics*, 20: 55–76.

HIRSCHMAN, A. O. (1958). *The Strategy of Economic Development*. New Haven: Yale University Press.

HOLTZ-EAKIN, D. (1994). Public sector capital and the productivity puzzle, *Review of Economics and Statistics*, 76: 12–21.

HOUTHAKKER, M. (1956). Economics and biology: Specialization and speci-ation, *Kyklos*, 9: 181–9.

IRELAND, Norman J. (1985). Product diversity and monopolistic competition under uncertainty, *Journal of Industrial Economics*, 33(4): 501–13.

IRELAND, Norman J. (1998). Status-seeking, income taxation and efficiency, *Journal of Public Economics*, 70: 99–113.

JIN, Songqing, ROZELLE, Scott, ALSTON, Julian, and HUANG, Jikun (2005). Economies of scale and scope and the economic efficiency of China's agricul-tural research system, *International Economic Review*, 46(3): 1033–57.

JOHNSON, H. G. (1953). Optimum tariff and retaliation, *Review of Economic Studies*, 21: 152–3.

JULIEN, Ludovic A. and SANZ, Nicolas (2005). Monopolistic competition, trans-action costs and multiple equilibria, *Economics Letters*, 87(1): 21–6.

KANGASHARJU, Aki, PEHKONEN, Jaakko, and PEKKALA, Sari (2005). Returns to scale in a matching model: Evidence from disaggregated panel data, *Applied Economics*, 37(1): 115–8.

KEEN, M. (1998). The balance between specific and ad valorem taxation, *Fiscal Studies*, 19(1): 1–37.

KEMP, Murray C. (1964). *The Pure Theory of International Trade*. Englewood Cliffs, NJ: Prentice-Hall.

KEMP, Murray C. (1967). Notes on the theory of optimum tariff, *Economic Record*, 43: 395–403.

KEMP, Murray C. and NEGISHI, T. (1969). Domestic distortions, tariffs and the theory of optimum subsidy, *Journal of Political Economy*, 77: 1011–3.

KEMP, Murray C. and NEGISHI, T. (1970). Variable returns to scale, commodity taxes, factor market distortions and their implications for trade gains, *Swedish Journal of Economics*, 72: 1–11.

KEMP, Murray C. and NG, Yew-Kwang (1976). On the existence of social welfare functions, social orderings, and social decision functions, *Economica*, 43: 59–66.

KEMP, Murray C. and NG, Yew-Kwang (1977). More on social welfare functions: The incompatibility of individualism and ordinalism, *Economica*, 44: 89–90.

KIRZNER, Israel M. (1997). Entrepreneurial discovery and the competitive market process: An Austrian approach, *Journal of Economic Literature*, 35(1): 60–85.

KNIGHT, F. H. (1924). Some fallacies in the interpretation of social cost, *Quarterly Journal of Economics*, 38: 582–606.

KRUGMAN, P. R. (1979). Increasing returns, monopolistic competition, and international trade, *Journal of International Economics*, 9: 469–79.

KRUGMAN, P. R. (1980). Scale economies, product differentiation, and the pattern of trade, *American Economic Review*, 70: 950–9.

KRUGMAN, P. R. (1982). Trade in differentiated products and the political economy of trade liberalization, in Bhagwati, J. (ed.), *Import Competition and Response*. National Bureau of Economic Research Conference Report.

KRUGMAN, P. R. (1990). *Rethinking International Trade*. Cambridge, MA: MIT Press.

KRUGMAN, P. R. (1991a). History versus expectations, *Quarterly Journal of Economics*, 106: 651–67.

KRUGMAN, P. R. (1991b). Increasing returns and economic geography, *Journal of Political Economy*, 199(1): 483–99.

KWACK, Sung Yeung and SUN, Lee Young (2005). Economies of scale, technological progress, and the sources of economic growth: Case of Korea, 1969–2000, *Journal of Policy Modeling*, 27(3): 265–83.

LA FERRARA, Eliana (2001). TFP, costs, and public infrastructure: An equivocal relationship, No 176, Working Papers from IGIER (Innocenzo Gasparini Institute for Economic Research), Bocconi University.

LANCASTER, Kelvin (1979). *Variety, Equity, and Efficiency*. New York: Columbia University Press.

LANCASTER, Kelvin (1990). The economics of product variety, *Management Science*, 9(3): 189–206.

LATRUFFE, Laure, BALCOMBE, Kelvin, DAVIDOVA, Sophia, and ZAWALINSKA, Katarzyna (2005). Technical and scale efficiency of crop and livestock farms in Poland: Does specialization matter? *Agricultural Economics*, 32(3): 281–96.

LAYARD, Richard (2005). *Happiness: Lessons from a New Science*. New York and London: Penguin.

LIO, Monchi (1996). 'Three essays on increasing returns and specialization: A contribution to new classical microeconomic approach'. PhD dissertation, Department of Economics, National Taiwan University.

LIO, Monchi (2003). The division of labor and the allocation of time, in Ng, Yew-Kwang, Heling Shi and Guangzhen Sun, (eds), *The Economics of e-Commerce and Networking Decisions: Applications and Extensions of Inframarginal Analysis*, London: Palgrave/Macmillan.

LOCAY, L. (1990). Economic development and the division of production between households and markets, *Journal of Political Economy*, 98: 965–82.

MARKUSEN, James R. and MELVIN, James R. (1984). The gains-from-trade theorem with increasing returns to scale, in Kierzkowski, Henryk (ed.) *Monopolistic Competition and International Trade*, Oxford: Clarendon Press.

MARSHALL, Alfred (1920). *Principles of Economics*, 8th edn London: Macmillan.

MCCOMBIE, John, PUGNO, Maurizio, and SORO, Bruno (2003). *Productivity Growth and Economic Performance: Essays on Verdoorn's Law*. Basingstoke: Palgrave/Macmillan.

MCCOMBIE, John S. L. and ROBERTS, Mark (2007). Returns to scale and regional growth: The static-dynamic Verdoorn law paradox revisited, *Journal of Regional Science*, 47(2): 179–208.

MCELROY, M. B. (1997). The policy implications of family bargaining and marriage markets, in Lawrence Haddad, John Hoddinott, and Harold Alderman (eds), *Intrahousehold Resource Allocation in Developing Countries*, Baltimore: Johns Hopkins University Press, c1997.

MCMILLAN, John and WOODRUFF, Christopher (2002). The central role of entrepreneurs in transition economies, *Journal of Economic Perspectives*, 16(3): 153–170.

MOSSAY, Pascal (2006). The core-periphery model: A note on the existence and uniqueness of short-run equilibrium, *Journal of Urban Economics*, 59(3): 389–93.

MYLES, G. D. (1987). Tax design in the presence of imperfect competition, *Journal of Public Economics*, 34: 367–78.

MYLES, G. D. (1989). Ramsey tax rules for economies with imperfect competition, *Journal of Public Economics*, 38(1): 95–115.

MYLES, G. D. (1995). *Public Economics*. Cambridge, U.K. and New York: Cambridge University Press.

NAGURNEY, Anna (2003). Financial and economic networks: An overview, in Nagurney, Anna (ed.), *Innovations in Financial and Economic Networks*, Cheltenham, UK and Northampton, MA.: Elgar, pp. 1–25.

NG, Siang (1998). Economies of specialization and trade, in Arrow, Ng and Yang (eds).

NG, Yew-Kwang (1965). Why do people buy lottery tickets? Choices involving risk and the indivisibility of expenditure, *Journal of Political Economy*, 73: 530–5.

NG, Yew-Kwang (1973). The economic theory of clubs: Pareto optimality conditions, *Economica*, 40: 291–8.

NG, Yew-Kwang (1974). The economic theory of clubs: Optimal tax/subsidy, *Economica*, 41: 308–21.

NG, Yew-Kwang (1975). Bentham or Bergson? Finite sensibility, utility functions and social welfare functions, *Review of Economic Studies*, 42: 545–69.

NG, Yew-Kwang (1977). Aggregate demand, business expectation, and economic recovery without aggravating inflation, *Australian Economic Chapters*: 130–40.

NG, Yew-Kwang (1978). Optimal club size: A reply, *Economica*, 45: 407–10.

NG, Yew-Kwang (1979/1983). *Welfare Economics: Introduction and Development of Basic Concepts*. London: Macmillan.

NG, Yew-Kwang (1980). Macroeconomics with non-perfect competition, *Economic Journal*, 598–610.

NG, Yew-Kwang (1981). Welfarism: A defence against Sen's attack, *Economic Journal*, 91: 527–30.

NG, Yew-Kwang (1982). The necessity of interpersonal cardinal utilities in distributional judgments and social choice, *Zeitschrift fur National ökonomie* (J of E), 42: 207–33.

NG, Yew-Kwang (1984). Quasi Pareto social improvements, *American Economic Review*, 74: 1033–50.

NG, Yew-Kwang (1985). Some fundamental issues in social welfare, in George, Feiwel (ed.), *Issues in Contemporary Microeconomics and Welfare*. London: Macmillan.

NG, Yew-Kwang (1986a). *Mesoeconomics: A Micro-Macro Analysis*. London: Harvester.

NG, Yew-Kwang (1986b). On the welfare economics of population control, *Population and Development R*, 12: 247–66.

NG, Yew-Kwang (1989). Individual irrationality and social welfare, *Social Choice and Welfare*, 6: 87–101.

NG, Yew-Kwang (1992). Business confidence and depression prevention: A mesoeconomic perspective, *American Economic Review*, 82(2): 365–71.

NG, Yew-Kwang (1995). Towards welfare biology: Evolutionary economics of animal consciousness and suffering, *Biology and Philosophy*, 10: 255–85.

NG, Yew-Kwang (1996). The enrichment of a sector (individual, region, or country) benefits others: The third welfare theorem? *Pacific Economic Review*, 1: 93–115.

NG, Yew-Kwang (1997). A case for happiness, cardinal utility, and interpersonal comparability, *Economic Journal*, 107(445): 1848–58.

NG, Yew-Kwang (1998). Non-neutrality of money under non-perfect competition: Why do economists fail to see the possibility? in Arrow, K. J., Ng, and Yang (eds), *Increasing Returns and Economic Analysis*, London: Macmillan, pp. 232–52.

NG, Yew-Kwang (1999). On estimating the effects of events like the Asian financial crisis: A mesoeconomic approach, *Taiwan Economic Review*, 27(4): 393–412.

NG, Yew-Kwang (2002). The welfare economics of encouraging more births, in A. E. Woodland *ed.E Theory and International Trade: Essays in Honour of Murray C. Kemp*, ed., Elgar.

NG, Yew-Kwang (2003). From preference to happiness: Towards a more complete welfare economics, *Social Choice and Welfare*, 20: 307–50.

NG, Yew-Kwang (2004). *Welfare Economics: Towards a More Complete Analysis*. London: Palgrave/Macmillan.

NG, Yew-Kwang (2005). Division of labour & transaction costs: An introduction, *Division of Labour & Transaction Costs*, 1(1): 1–13.

NG, Yew-Kwang (2008). Why is the military draft common? Conscription and increasing returns, *Annals of Economics and Finance*, November.

NG, Yew-Kwang and NG, Siang (2003). Do the economies of specialization justify the work ethics? An examination of Buchanan's hypothesis, *Journal of Economic Behavior & Organization*, 50: 339–53.

NG, Yew-Kwang and NG, Siang (2007). Why should governments encourage improvements in infrastructure? Indirect network externality of transaction efficiency, *Public Finance and Management*, 7(4): 340–62.

NG, Yew-Kwang, SHI, Heling, and SUN, Guang-Zhen (ed.) (2003). *The Economics of E-Commerce and Networking Decisions: Applications and Extensions of Inframarginal Analysis*. London: Palgrave/Macmillan.

NG, Yew-Kwang and WANG, Jianguo (1995). A case for cardinal utility and non-arbitrary choice of commodity units, *Social Choice & Welfare*, 12: 255–66.

NG, Yew-Kwang and ZHANG, Dingsheng (2005). Increasing returns and the Smith dilemma, *Singapore Economic Review*, 50: 407–16.

NG, Yew-Kwang and ZHANG, Dingsheng (2007). Average-cost pricing, increasing returns, and optimal output in a model with home and market production, *Journal of Economics*, 90(2): 167–92.

OLIVEIRA, Francisco H. P., JAYME, Frederico G. Jr, and LEMOS, Mauro B. (2006). Increasing returns to scale and international diffusion of technology: An empirical study for Brazil (1976–2000), *World Development*, 34(1): 75–88.

PANAGARIYA, Arvind (2002). Cost of protection: where do we stand? *American Economic Review*, May 2002, 92(2): 175–79.

PARISH, Ross M. and Weisser, Mendel (1970). Paying the soldier his hire: The economics of abolishing conscription, *Current Affairs Bulletin*, 46, July 27.

PARKS, Robert P. (1976). An impossibility theorem for fixed preferences: A dictatorial Bergson-Samuelson welfare function, *Review of Economic Studies*, 43: 447–50.

PAUL, Satya, SAHNI, Balbir S., and BISWAL, Bagala P. (2004). Public infrastructure and the productive performance of Canadian manufacturing industries, *Southern Economic Journal*, 70(4): 998–1011.

PEREIRA, Alfredo M. (2001). Public investment and private sector performance–international evidence, *Public Finance and Management*, 1(2): 261–77.

PERLI, R. (1998). Indeterminacy, home production, and the business cycle: A calibrated analysis, *Journal of Monetary Economics*, 41: 105–25.

PIGOU, Arthur C. (1912/1920/1932). *Wealth and Welfare*. Later editions (1920, 1924, 1929, 1932) assume the title *The Economics of Welfare*, London: Macmillan.

POLLAK, Robert A. (1979). Bergson-Samuelson social welfare functions and the theory of social choice, *Quarterly Journal of Economics*, 93: 73–90.

POMINI, Mario and TONDINI, Giovanni (2006). The idea of increasing returns in neoclassical growth models, *European Journal of the History of Economic Thought*, 13(3): 365–86.

QUINZII, Martine (1992a). An existence theorem for the core of a productive economy with increasing returns, *Journal of Economic Theory*, 28(1): 32–50.

QUINZII, Martine (1992b). *Increasing Returns and Efficiency*. New York & Oxford: Oxford University Press.

RADNER, R. and STIGLITZ, J. (1984). A non-concavity in the value of information, in Boyer and Kihlstrom (ed.), *Bayesian Models of Economic Theory*, Amsterdam: Elsevier.

RAE, John (1834). *New Principles of Political Economy*. Reprinted as *The Sociological Theory of Capital*, edited by Mixter, Charles W. (1990), New York: Macmillan.

RICARDO, D. (1817). *The Principle of Political Economy and Taxation*. London: Gaernney Press, 1973.

RÖLLER, Lars-Hendrik and WAVERMAN, Leonard (2001). Telecommunications infrastructure and economic development: A simultaneous approach, *American Economic Review*, 91: 909–23.

ROMER, Paul M. (1986). Increasing returns and long-run growth, *Journal of Political Economy*, 94(5): 1002–37.

ROMER, Paul M. (1987). Growth based on increasing returns due to specialization, *American Economic Review, Chapters and Proceedings*, 77: 56–62.

ROSE, Andrew K. (2006). Well-being in the small and in the large, *Monetary and Economic Studies*, 24(2): 55–72.

ROSENSTEIN-RODAN, Paul N. (1943). Problems of industrialization of Eastern and South-Eastern Europe, *Economic Journal*, 53(210/211): 202–11.

ROTHSCHILD, E. (1994). Adam Smith and the invisible hand, *American Economic Review*, 84(2): 319–22.

SALCHOW, Hans-Jurgen (2006). An essay on the state of economic science, *Journal of Mathematical Economics*, 42(6): 653–60.

SANDLER, Todd and TSCHIRHART, John (1980). The economic theory of clubs: An evaluative essay, *Journal of Economic Literature*, 18: 1481–521.

SANDMO, A. (1990). Tax distortions and household production, *Oxford Economic Chapters*, 42: 78–90.

SEMMLER, Willi and MARVIN, Ofori (2007). On poverty traps, thresholds and take-offs, *Structural Change and Economic Dynamics*, 18(1): 1–26.

SEN, Amartya K. (1979). Personal utilities and public judgements; or what's wrong with welfare economics?, *Economic Journal*, 89: 537–58.

SI-MA, Qian (104 BC). Huo zhi lie zhuan, in *A Cronicle of History*, in Chinese; for English readers, see Si-ma, Qian & Watson, Burton (1993), *Records of the Great Historian*, Columbra University Press, 3rd Edition.

SMITH, Adam (1776). *An Inquiry into the Nature and Causes of the Wealth of Nations*. Reprint, edited by Cannan, E. Chicago: University of Chicago Press.

SMITH, Adam (1776/1976). *The Wealth of Nations*. Reprint, edited by Cannan, E. Chicago: University of Chicago Press.

SMYTHE, Donald (1994). Book review of Yang & Ng (1993), *Journal of Economic Literature*, 32: 691–92.

SPENCE, Michael (1976). Product selection, fixed costs and monopolistic competition, *Review of Economic Studies*, 43(2): 217–35.

STIGLER, George (1951). The division of labor is limited by the extent of the market, *Journal of Political Economy*, 59(3): 185–93.

STIGLER, George (1976). The successes and failures of professor smith, *Journal of Political Economy*, 84: 1199–213.

STIGLITZ, Joseph E. (2002). Information and the change in the paradigm in economics, *American Economics Review*, 92(3): 460–501.

SUN, Guangzhen (2005). *Reading in Economics of the Division of Labor*. Singapore: World Scientific.

SUN, Guangzhen, YANG Xiaokai, and ZHOU Lin (2004). General equilibrium in large economies with endogenous structure of the division of labor, *Journal of Economic Behavior & Organization*, 55(2): 237–56.

SUZUKI, Takashi (1996). Intertemporal general equilibrium model with external increasing returns, *Journal of Economics Theory*, 69: 117–33.

TAYLOR, Leon (1992). Infrastructural competition among jurisdictions, *Journal of Public Economics*, 49(2): 241–59.

TOMBAZOS, Christis and YANG, Xiaokai (eds) (2006). *Inframarginal Contributions to Development Economics,* Increasing Returns and Inframarginal Economics, vol. 3. Hackensack, N.J. and Singapore: World Scientific.

TOWNSEND, H. (ed.) (1971/1980). *Price Theory*, Harmondsworth, UK: Penguin.
TRUETT, Lila J. and TRUETT, Dale B. (2006). Production and costs in the South African motor vehicle industry, *Applied Economics*, 38(20): 2381–92.
VAUGHN, Karen I. (1994). *Austrian Economics in America*. Cambridge: Cambridge University Press.
VEBLEN, Thorstein (1929). *The Theory of the Leisure Class*. Reprinted in 1970 by London: Unwin.
VILLAR, Antonio (1996). *General Equilibrium with Increasing Returns*. Berlin: Springer.
VOHRA, Rajiv (1992). Equity and efficiency in non-convex economies, *Social Choice and Welfare*, 9(3): 185–202.
VOHRA, Rajiv (1994). Efficient resource allocation under increasing returns, in Dutta, B. (ed.), *Welfare Economics and India*, Oxford University Press.
WALKER, Greg (1998). Economies of scale in Australian banks 1978–1990, *Australian Economic Chapters*, 37(1): 71–87.
WANG, Eric C. (2002). Public infrastructure and economic growth: A new approach applied to East Asian economies, *Journal of Policy Modelling*, 24(5): 411–35.
WEN, Mei (1997). Infrastructure and evolution in division of labor, *Review of Development Economics*, 1(2): 191–206.
WEN, Mei (1998). An analytical framework of consumer-producers, economies of specialization and transaction costs, in Arrow, Kenneth J., Ng, Yew-Kwang, and Yang, Xiaokai, (ed.), *Increasing Returns and Economic Analysis*, New York, NY: St. Martin's Press.
WEN, Mei and KING, Stephen P. (2004). Push or pull? The relationship between development, trade and primary resource endowment, *Journal of Economic Behavior and Organization*, 53(4): 569–91.
WILKINSON, Richard G. (1997). Health inequalities: Relative or absolute material standards? *British Medical Journal*, 314(22): 591–5.
WILSON, Robert (1975). Informational economies of scale, *Bell Journal of Economics and Management Science*, 6(1): 184–95.
WINCH, Donald (1997). Adam Smith's problems and ours, *Scottish Journal of Political Economy*, 44 (4): 384–402.
WIRL, Franz and FEICHTINGER, Gustav (2006). History versus expectations: Increasing returns or social influence? *Journal of Socio-Economics*, 35(5): 877–88.
World Bank (1994). *World Development Report: Infrastructure for Development*. Oxford: Oxford University Press.
YANG, Xiaokai (1988). A microeconomic approach to modelling the division of labor based on increasing returns to specialization, PhD Dissertation, Dept. of Economics, Princeton University, University Microfilms International Order # 8816042, Ann Arbor.
YANG, Xiaokai (2001). *Economics: New Classical Versus Neoclassical Frameworks*. Cambridge, MA: Blackwell.
YANG, Xiaokai (2003). *Economic Development and the Division of Labor*. Cambridge, MA: Blackwell.
YANG, Xiaokai and BORLAND, J. (1991). A microeconomic mechanism for economic growth, *Journal of Political Economy*, 99: 460–82.
YANG, Xiaokai and HEIJDRA, B. (1993). Monopolistic competition and optimum product diversity: Comment, *American Economic Review*, 83: 295–301.

YANG, Xiaokai and NG, Siang (1998). Specialization and division of labor: A survey, in Arrow, Ng & Yang (ed.) (1998).

YANG, Xiaokai and NG, Yew-Kwang (1993). *Specialization and Economic Organization, a New Classical Microeconomic Framework.* Amsterdam: North-Holland.

YANG, Xiaokai and SHI, Heling (1992). Specialization and product diversity, *American Economic Review,* 82: 392–8.

YAO, Shuntian (2002). Walrasian equilibrium computation, network formation, and the Wen theorem, *Review of Development Economics,* 6: 415–27.

YOUNG, Allyn (1913). Pigou's wealth and welfare, *Quarterly Journal of Economics,* 27(4): 672–86.

YOUNG, Allyn (1928). Increasing returns and economic progress, *Economic Journal,* 38: 527–42.

ZHANG, Junxi (2007). Endogenous markups, intensity of competition, and persistence of business cycles, *Southern Economic Journal,* 74(2): 546–65.

ZHOU, Haiwen (2007). Increasing returns, the choice of technology, and the gains from trade, *Southern Economic Journal,* 74(2): 581–600.

Author Index

Ades, Alberto F., 177
Ahmad, Syed, 180
Akerlof, George, 150
Allen, Jason, 177
Anderberg, D., 103
Antweiler, Werner, 177
Arrow, Kenneth J., 2, 4, 18, 59, 78, 87
Arthur, W. B., 2, 4, 79, 87, 127, 128, 130, 131, 132, 133
Aschauer, David A., 63, 89
Athreye, Suma S., 177
Atkinson, Anthony B., 22, 23

Balcer, Yves, 22
Baldwin, Richard, 8
Balestrino, A., 103
Batina, Raymond G., 89
Becker, G. S., 103
Beinhocker, Eric D., 79
Benarroch, Michael, 177
Benhabib, J., 103
Berg, Sanford V., 91
Bergstrom, Theodore, 32
Besley, T., 103
Bhagwati, J., 162, 175
Bonnisseau, Jean-Marc, 40
Booth, Alison L., 120
Borghans, Lex, 8
Borland, J., 72, 158
Boserup, Ester, 62, 88
Bougheas, Spiros, 63, 89, 91
Brown, Donald J., 40, 42, 59, 60, 178
Brox, James A., 89
Buchanan, James M., 4, 5, 65, 66, 67, 68, 77, 78, 102, 122, 123, 124, 125, 127, 129, 131, 133, 134, 135, 136, 137, 139, 141, 142, 143, 145, 147, 149, 151, 153, 179, 180
Bucovetsky, S., 180

Chakraborty, B. S., 102
Chandler, Alfred D., 62, 88
Chandra, V., 68, 177

Chenery, Hollis B., 175
Cheng, Wenli, 5, 7, 72, 76
Chipman, John S., 3, 59, 77
Chow, Yang, 179
Christoffersen, Henrik, 177
Chu, C. Y. Cyrus., 179, 180
Cohen, Jeffrey P., 180
Cook, Philip J., 8

Davis, Donald R., 177
Delipalla, S., 103
Demetriades, Panicos O., 64, 91
Diamantaras, Dimitrios, 93
Dixit, Avinash K., 7, 19, 42, 65, 66, 76, 77, 80, 81, 87, 101, 102, 120, 122, 143, 155
Dixon, Huw, 4, 177
Doi, J., 120
Duggal, Vijaya G., 62, 177

Eaton, Jonathan, 155
Economides, Nicholas, 180
Einarsson, T., 103
Ellis, Howard S., 19
Epifani, Paolo, 8
Esfahani, Hadi S., 89
Ethier, Wilfred J., 58, 65, 66, 68, 91, 102, 124, 155, 181
Evans, Paul, 89

Fafchamps, M., 103
Feichtinger, Gustav, 178
Fellner, William, 19
Fernand, John G., 89
Fingleton, Bernard, 177
Francois, Joseph F., 58
Frank, Robert H., 8, 150
Fujita, Masahisa, 8
Futagami, K., 120

Gabszewicz, Jean J., 61
Gallo, Fredrik, 79
Gancia, Gino, 8

Garicano, Luis, 177
Gauthier, David, 135
Gilles, Robert P., 93
Gintis, Herbert, 79
Glaeser, E. L., 177, 178
Graaff, J., 162
Gramlich, Edward M., 63, 89
Greenwood, Jeremy, 103
Grepperud, Sverre, 135
Grinols, Earl L., 155
Groot, L., 8
Grossman, G., 155
Guesnerie, Roger, 4, 18

Hagen, E. E., 175
Harsanyi, John C., 29, 36
Hart, Oliver D., 80
Haughwout, Andrew F., 89
Heal, Geoffrey, 1, 4, 18, 19, 20, 40,
    42, 77, 78, 86, 119, 178
Heijdra, B., 105, 120
Helpman, Elhanan, 20, 68, 155
Henderson, J. Vernon, 8
Hercowitz, Zvi, 103
Hicks, John R., 6, 16
Hillman, Arye L., 30, 179
Hirschman, A. O., 175
Holtz-eakin, D., 89
Houthakker, M., 5, 177
Hubbard, Thomas N., 177

Ireland, Norman J., 80, 150

Jin, Songqing, 177
Johnson, H. G., 162
Julien, Ludovic A., 178

Kangasharju, Aki, 177
Karras, George, 89
Keeble, David, 177
Keen, M., 102, 103
Kemp, Murray C., 20, 155, 162, 179
King, Stephen P., 179
Kirzner, Israel M., 70
Knight, F. H., 19
Krugman, P. R., 8, 20, 68, 104,
    155, 178
Kwack, Sung Yeung, 177

La ferrara, Eliana, 63
Lancaster, Kelvin, 19, 80
Latruffe, Laure, 177
Laussel, Didier, 61
Layard, Richard, 150
Lio, Monchi, 128, 130, 179
Liu, Ying, 177
Locay, L., 5, 102, 103, 143

Mamuneas, Theofanis P., 64, 91
Markusen, James R., 155
Marquis, M. H., 103
Marshall, Alfred, 3, 17, 56, 77,
    155, 177
Marvin, Ofori, 8
Mccombie, John, 177
Mcelroy, M. B., 103
Mcmillan, John, 61
Melvin, James R., 155
Mossay, Pascal, 8
Myles, G. D., 103, 119, 120

Nagurney, Anna, 180
Negishi, T., 155, 162
Nelson, Douglas, 58
Ng, Siang, 56, 154, 179
Ng, Yew-Kwang, 4, 5, 6, 7, 8, 10, 11,
    13, 15, 17, 23, 30, 32, 34, 55, 56,
    57, 58, 59, 62, 64, 66, 67, 68, 69,
    70, 71, 72, 86, 88, 91, 92, 93, 94,
    102, 122, 123, 124, 128, 132,
    134, 135, 136, 139, 140, 142, 143,
    150, 153, 155, 157, 158, 161, 164,
    168, 170, 178, 179, 180, 181

Oliveira, Francisco H. P., 177

Panagariya, Arvind, 9, 155
Parish, Ross M., 24
Parks, Robert P., 179
Paul, Catherine J.M., 180
Paul, Satya, 89
Pedersen, Pål Andreas, 135
Pereira, Alfredo M., 89
Perli, R., 103
Pigou, Arthur C., 18, 19, 20
Pollak, Robert A., 179
Pomini, Mario, 8

Quinzii, Martine, 4, 18, 40
Quisumbing, A. R., 103

Radner, R., 2
Rae, John, 150
Ramaswami, V. K., 175
Ramirez, Maria T., 89
Rankin, Neil, 4, 177
Ricardo, D., 154
Roberts, Mark, 177
Röller, Lars-Hendrik, 89
Romer, Paul M., 77, 91, 102, 124, 155, 177
Rose, Andrew K., 177
Rosenstein-rodan, Paul N., 175
Rothschild, E., 180
Ruffin, Roy, 181

Sadka, Efraim, 22
Salchow, Hans-Jurgen, 40
Sandilands, Roger J., 177
Sandler, Todd, 179
Sandmo, A., 103
Sanz, Nicolas, 178
Semmler, A., 8
Sen, Amartya K., 34
Shi, Heling, 102
Si-ma, Qian, 76
Smith, Adam, 5, 62, 63, 67, 76, 77, 78, 79, 81, 83, 85, 86, 87, 89, 154, 170, 177, 180
Smythe, Donald, 56
Spence, Michael, 19, 80, 101
Stigler, George, 77, 177
Stiglitz, Joseph E., 2, 7, 19, 22, 23, 42, 65, 66, 70, 76, 77, 78, 80, 81, 87, 101, 102, 120, 123, 143, 155
Sun, Guangzhen, 5, 58, 92, 180
Sun, Lee young, 177
Suzuki, Takashi, 77
Swan, Peter L., 30, 179

Taylor, Leon, 180
Tombazos, Christis, 5
Tondini, Giovanni, 8
Townsend, H., 59
Trefler, Daniel, 177
Truett, Lila J., 177
Tschirhart, John, 179

Vaughn, Karen I., 70
Veblen, Thorstein, 150
Villar, Antonio, 4, 18
Vohra, Rajiv, 79, 103, 178

Walker, Greg, 177
Wang, Eric C., 89
Waverman, Leonard, 89
Weinstein, David E., 177
Weisser, Mendel, 24
Wen, Mei, 93, 179, 180
Wilkinson, Richard G., 150
Wilson, Robert, 2
Winch, Donald, 77
Wirl, Franz, 178
Woodruff, Christopher, 61
World bank, 62, 88

Yang, Xiaokai, 5, 6, 7, 55, 56, 57, 58, 59, 60, 64, 66, 67, 68, 70, 71, 72, 76, 86, 88, 91, 92, 93, 94, 102, 105, 120, 122, 123, 124, 128, 136, 142, 143, 150, 155, 157, 158, 163, 168, 170, 179, 180
Yao, Shuntian, 93
Yoon, Y. J., 4, 66, 67, 77, 102, 124, 135
Young, Allyn, 5, 19, 31, 32, 177

Zhang, Dingsheng, 7, 122, 124, 135, 143, 178, 181
Zhang, Junxi, 178
Zhou, Haiwen, 155
Zhou, Lin, 58

Subject Index

average-cost pricing equilibrium, 40–5, 101–21

big push, 175
Buchanan's hypothesis, 65–6, 122–53

conscription, 23–31, 38
constant returns, 2–3
continuum of equilibria, 13–16
coordination, 60, 61, 62, 71, 72–5, 79, 86, 87, 135, 179

demand promotion, inefficiency of, 174–5
distributional, 8, 67
division of labour, 55–75
welfare economic issues of, 62–6, 88–100, 122–53
Dixit-Stiglitz's model, 7, 65, 80–6, 101–21, 123

economies of specialization, 5–7, 18, 55–75
and consumption constraints, 124–9
and home vs. market production, 88–100
and infrastructure, 88–100
and international trade, 154–68
and the Smith's dilemma, 76–87
and work ethics, 122–53
E-F conflict, 22–39
entrepreneur/entrepreneurship, 59–62, 67, 70, 72–5, 95
equity and efficiency vs. freedom and fairness, 22–39
excessive price changes/increases following cost/tax changes/ increases, 172–3

fixed costs, 2, 3, 5, 65, 71, 81, 83, 91, 93, 101, 103, 105–7, 111, 112, 118, 119, 123, 135, 143, 144–9, 156, 167, 173, 180, 181

generalized increasing returns, 5–7, 78, 87, 164, 170

home vs. market production, 101–21

imperfect competition, 9–16
increasing returns
degree of, 49
devastating implications, 9–21
and division of labour, 55–75
and equilibrium existence, 40–5
sources of, 1–8
and stock keeping, 3
indirect network externalities, 62–5, 88–100
indivisibility, 2–3, 30
inframarginal analysis/economics, 5, 6, 55–75, 91–8, 122–53, 154–68
infrastructure improvements, 62–5, 88–100
international trade, 154–68

learning, 2–3, 25, 31, 72, 78, 101, 158, 170, 175

market equilibrium, 18–21

non-neutrality of money, 9–16
non-perfect competition, 9–16

organizational efficiency, 7, 67, 73, 95, 150, 170

Pareto efficiency/optimality, 4, 6, 18–21, 49–54, 59–62, 77–80, 111, 132, 169, 179
and conflict with freedom and fairness, 22–39
pecuniary external effects, 16–18
perfect competition, 9–16

perverse response to demand
    changes/increases, 171–2
public capital, *see* infrastructure

Smith's dilemma, 76–87
specialization, economies of, *see*
    economies of specialization
tariff, effects of, 160–3
total conditions, 6
trade, 154–68
transaction costs/efficiency, 6, 7, 14,
    55–75, 88–168, 170

urban-rural segregation, 22–39

welfare economic issues, 62–6,
    88–100, 122–53
work ethics, 65–6, 122–53

Yang's framework, *see* Yang-Ng's
    framework
Yang-Ng's framework, 6–7, 55–75
    and infrastructure, 91–8
    and international trade,
        154–68
    and work ethics, 122–53